Process-based Strategic Planning

Rudolf Grünig
Richard Kühn

Process-based
Strategic Planning

Translated by Anthony Clark

Third Edition
with 137 Figures

 Springer

Professor Dr. Rudolf Grünig
University of Fribourg
Chair of Management
Avenue de l'Europe 20
1700 Fribourg
Switzerland
E-mail: rudolf.gruenig@unifr.ch

Professor Dr. Richard Kühn
University of Bern
Engehaldenstrasse 4
3012 Bern
Switzerland
E-mail: kuehn@imu.unibe.ch

Cataloging-in-Publication Data applied for
Library of Congress Control Number: 2004114270
A catalog record for this book is available from the Library of Congress.

Bibliographic information published by Die Deutsche Bibliothek
Die Deutsche Bibliothek lists this publication in the Deutsche Nationalbibliografie;
detailed bibliographic data available in the internet at *http://dnb.ddb.de*

ISBN 3-540-23571-X Springer Berlin Heidelberg New York
ISBN 3-540-43502-6 2nd Edition Springer Berlin Heidelberg New York

Springer is a part of Springer Science+Business Media
springeronline.com

© Springer-Verlag Berlin Heidelberg 2002, 2005
Printed in Germany

Hardcover-Design: Erich Kirchner
Production: Helmut Petri
Printing: betz-druck

SPIN 11337829   Printed on acid-free paper – 42/2202 – 5 4 3 2 1 0

Preface for the third edition

In the third edition, Part II has been enlarged with a new chapter about the strategic analysis and planning toolbox. In addition, some revisions have been made to the text and figures and the visibility of the text has been improved with a new font format.

The authors would like to express their thanks to Tu Le for her substantial and excellent work in revising the manuscript and the figures for this third edition.

October 2004
Rudolf Grünig, Richard Kühn

Preface for the second edition

As a result of valuable feedback on the first edition of this book, some revisions have been made to the text and the figures for this second edition. In addition, the section in Chapter 12 which deals with strategic options at the corporate level has been improved and new findings about diversification have been added.

The authors would like to express their thanks to Wira Tandjung for his expert assistance with this second edition.

March 2002
Rudolf Grünig, Richard Kühn

Preface

The strategies of a company define its future way of doing business: they determine for years to come the target markets and the competitive advantages it must construct and maintain. It is the development of successful strategies, an essential and a complex task, which forms the focus of this book. The book begins with a brief introduction to strategic planning. This is followed by the presentation of a method for determining future strategies. Here seven stages in planning are proposed. They are afterwards described in detail and procedures are provided for dealing with each stage. The recommended procedures are sometimes rather complex: we have done our best, while avoiding oversimplification, to make our methodological suggestions accessible by using clear terminology, charts where appropriate, and a large number of examples and case studies as illustrations.

The authors would like to express their gratitude to all those who have helped in the writing of this book. Many of the ideas and examples came from practice. We are therefore especially indebted to the many managers who have allowed us to share their strategic work. The authors would also like to thank all those former and present students, doctoral candidates and assistants, who contributed to the book. In addition we would like to address our special thanks to three people. This book could not have been produced without the considerable talents of Anthony Clark who translated large sections of the book from German into English and improved the language of the parts we wrote in English. Kiruba Levi and Barbara Roos merit special thanks for their efficient and excellent work in typing the text, designing the figures and producing the lists, the index and the bibliography.

March 2001
Rudolf Grünig, Richard Kühn

Brief contents

Contents

List of figures

List of insets

Introduction

Strategic management has the central objective of providing for long term company success. The task of strategic management can be broken down into strategic planning, the implementation of strategies, and strategic control. Strategic planning forms the basis for the other two tasks and so it is the production of successful strategies which is of central importance in strategic management.

Deregulation and internationalization have increased competitive intensity. Together with accelerated technological change, shortening market life cycles and increasingly dynamic markets, the risk of committing strategic errors has increased considerably. Companies which neglect conscious strategic planning can expect to drift into a hopeless position. A systematic approach to strategic planning, which is firmly grounded in reality, is seen by many company leaders and management researchers as an essential requirement for long-term corporate success. Empirical studies confirm this view (see for example Raffée, Effenberger & Fritz, 1994, 383 ff.).

Many companies today view strategic planning as the task of top management, the CEO and other members of the top executive team. Unfortunately, despite the best efforts of those responsible, results are often unsatisfactory. Strategies are often not sufficiently well based on realities to survive in the face of competitive pressures. Or they may be too vague to provide genuine guidance for corporate action. For example, there may be a lack of concrete strategic programs to compel the attention of managers overloaded with day to day operational tasks. Another common mistake is that companies have too many strategic documents: typically these are not properly coordinated and may even contradict one another. This happens because in practice, especially in larger corporations, strategic documents are initiated at different times by managers of different organizational units and at different levels.

To find such mistakes in companies may seem surprising in the light of the considerable amount of literature on strategic management. We might expect the many specialized books and articles to aid strategic planning and lead in practice to the development of effective strategic plans. However, it would seem that the literature on corporate strategy does not altogether provide what companies need:

- A number of publications on strategic management are not aimed at aiding practice: they contribute primarily to the basic scientific concern with the explanation of difference in company success in terms of chosen markets, competitive strategies, and resource positions (Rühli, 1994, 33 ff.). They report research results which are relevant to companies. But given the objectives of the publications, they do not present comprehensive procedural suggestions for strategic planning.
- Unfortunately, even those works which propose frameworks of analysis and planning, and therefore meet the direct needs of companies planning strategies, often do not offer the necessary support to executives in charge of strategic planning. One basic reason for this is that, in practice, what is required is the combined application of more than one method of analysis and planning in order to answer a number of different and complex questions. However, a large proportion of the methods-oriented literature is devoted to the presentation of a single method (see for example The Boston Consulting Group, 1970; Porter, 1980; Porter, 1985; Prahalad & Hamel, 1990).
- There are, of course, also strategy textbooks presenting in one book the various methods of strategic analysis and planning (see for example Hill & Jones, 1992; Johnson & Scholes, 2002). However, these books only partly address the problem of appropriate selection and combination of methods. Furthermore, in describing the different techniques, these works mostly retain the original terminology and do not therefore offer a comprehensive system of strategic thinking with uniform terminology.

It is the principal objective of the authors of this book to present an integrated system of analysis and planning tools. The book is intended to offer a complete view of strategic planning, using a uniform system of terms and combining the most important methodological approaches within a single recommended planning procedure.

There are six parts to the book. Part I presents an introduction to strategic planning. Part II gives an account of strategic documents and how to produce them. The remaining four parts of the book deal with approaches and methods to the solution of problems arising out of the different phases of the recommended analysis and planning procedure. In Part III, the planning of a strategic project and the strategic analysis are examined. Parts IV and V are concerned with the two central problems in strategic planning: the development of corporate strategies and of business strategies. To conclude, Part VI addresses the problems of implementation, and the final assessment and approval of strategies.

The book is addressed primarily to practitioners: it aims to give them the knowledge they need to solve strategic planning problems. The book can also be used for executive courses in strategic planning and is a suitable text for introductory courses in strategic planning at universities and business schools. It will give students of Business Administration an overview of the complex area of strategic planning and show them ways of proceeding to solve problems in strategic planning. The book will also provide students with a framework within which they can more easily situate the extensive specialist literature.

The authors have tried to confront the problems of developing and assessing strategies in all their real complexity and not to hide difficulty through inappropriate simplifications. The book will repay careful reading rather than superficial skimming.

In order to facilitate study of the text, a number of didactic means have been used:

- Each part is introduced by a short text explaining the content and, where necessary, the reasons for the structure. This should enable the reader to skip topics which deal with familiar matters or which are not a current point of interest and to concentrate on the parts and chapters which seem most important in the light of existing knowledge and needs.
- Whenever possible, basic ideas are presented in visual form.
- Insets into the main text are used frequently, sometimes to carry the discussion of theory and method further, sometimes to give examples. In this way the insets allow a deeper view of the material, but reading them is not absolutely essential to following and understanding the main text.

- A subject index is provided to enable rapid access to themes of special interest.
- We also provide a glossary of the most important terms in strategic planning.

We very much hope that, despite the complexity of the subject, the book remains understandable and helpful. And in particular, we hope that this information will prove useful in practice.

Part I

The idea of strategic planning

Part I provides a short introduction to strategic planning, based mainly on Kühn & Grünig (2000, p. 25 ff).

Part I has three chapters. The opening chapter deals with what is meant by strategy and strategic planning and states the purpose of strategic thinking. The second chapter sketches the development of strategic planning and goes on to discuss the place of strategic planning within the overall field of strategic management. The third chapter in Part I addresses one of the central methodological problems in strategic planning: the evaluation of strategies. An assessment model is described on which the process of strategic planning, introduced in part II and described in parts III to VI, can build.

1 Strategies, strategic planning and success potentials

1.1 Strategies

As the term strategy can refer both to strategic plans and to actually realized strategies, we therefore first need to distinguish between intended strategies and realized strategies. In practice it is rarely possible to realize intended strategies completely, and so the realized strategies normally diverge to a greater or lesser extent from the intended strategies. Additionally, in some cases companies do not have any specified intended strategy: the realized strategy is thus the product of many different decisions taken individually. This case is referred to as an emerged strategy (Mintzberg, 1994, p. 23 ff.). **Figure 1-1** displays these different cases.

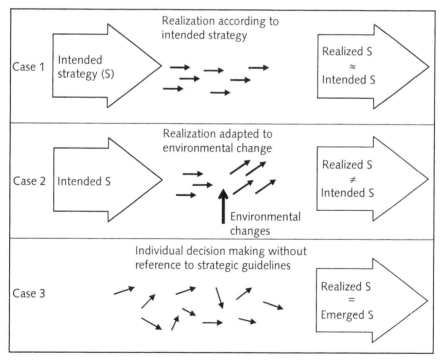

Figure 1-1: Intended and realized strategies
(adapted from Mintzberg, 1994, p. 24)

Where the term strategy is used in this book, it always means intended strategies.

An (intended) strategy has the following characteristics:

- It presents long-term guidelines
- It is relevant for the company as a whole or for important parts of the company
- It is normally determined by the management
- It should guarantee the permanent accomplishment of the company's overriding goals and objectives.

Intended strategies can therefore be defined as managerial guidelines or statements which serve decision-making and subsequent action by providing points of reference. They are intended to ensure coordination in a situation where a number of managers are acting at different places and times.

1.2   Strategic planning

The process by which strategies are produced can be called strategic planning:

- Strategic planning is a systematic process; strategy formulation through internal power struggles or simply by muddling through is not strategic planning.
- The analysis and the guidelines developed by strategic planning are long-term oriented.
- The planning process looks at the company as a whole or at important parts of the company.
- Competencies and responsibilities for strategic planning should be concentrated at the level of the management.
- The objective of the planning process is to guarantee the long-term accomplishment of the company's overriding goals and objectives.

Figure 1-2 shows the relationship between strategic planning and strategies.

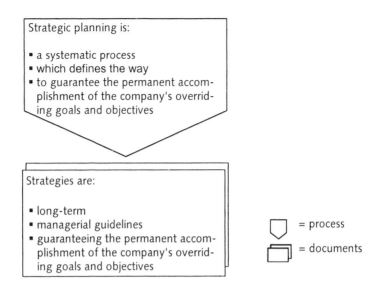

Strategic planning is:

- a systematic process
- which defines the way
- to guarantee the permanent accomplishment of the company's overriding goals and objectives

Strategies are:

- long-term
- managerial guidelines
- guaranteeing the permanent accomplishment of the company's overriding goals and objectives

= process

= documents

Figure 1-2: Strategic planning and strategies

1.3 Building success potentials as the main purpose of strategic planning

The long-term accomplishment of a company's overriding goals and objectives is enabled through the construction and careful maintenance of success potentials (Gälweiler 1987, p. 26 ff.). As **Figure 1-3** shows, strategic planning is not primarily concerned with optimizing success during the planning period itself. What the strategic planning process does, is focus on the investments which will be required to ensure the preservation of existing success potentials and to build new ones. This guarantees future success both during and beyond the planning period.

There are three types of success potential:
- Strong positions in attractive markets. Strong positions mean substantial market shares in the served markets or market niches. The attractiveness of markets depends on their size, growth rate and intensity of competition.

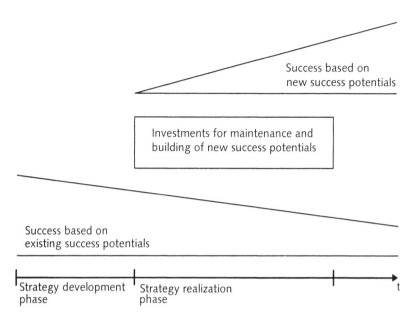

Success based on
new success potentials

Investments for maintenance and
building of new success potentials

Success based on
existing success potentials

Strategy development   Strategy realization   t
phase   phase

Figure 1-3: Building success potentials as the main purpose of strategic planning

- Long-term competitive advantages in market offers. Strong market positions can be gained in different ways. These include better product quality, recognizably better customer services, more effective or intensive advertising, long-term price advantages etc.
- Long-term competitive advantages in resources. 'Resources' is meant here in a very wide sense: Not only superior technological means, human resources, information systems and financial resources, but also soft factors such as company culture and brand image, as well as complex capabilities such as innovation capabilities, cooperation capabilities, the ability to change and so on.

From **Figure 1-4** we see that success potentials do not operate independently, but interact with each other. As the chart shows, the different categories of success potential can also be fairly clearly attributed to the two most important categories of strategy: The target market positions are normally defined in the corporate strategy; the competitive advantages necessary to achieve these positions at the level of the market offer and at the level of resources are usually determined in the business strategies.

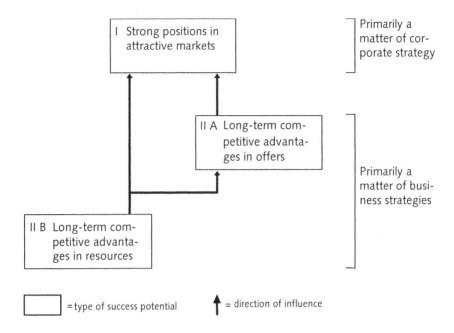

Figure 1-4: Types of success potential

Inset 1-1 illustrates the practical importance of the three different types of success potential with the strategic problems of a coffee roasting business.

Inset 1-1: The interdependencies of the different types of success potential for a coffee producer

Espresso is a well established Swiss firm which imports and roasts coffee beans, a medium sized family company currently with 80 employees and achieving a turnover of around 40 million dollars. The firm was founded in the post-war period by the father of its present owner. He had been a buyer for coffee and tea in a large food company and had thus gained precise knowledge of the market and was able to build up excellent relationships with coffee and tea suppliers around the world. Within a short time he had built up a flourishing wholesale business with food products, tea and coffee for the Swiss market. Coffee quickly became the main contributor to turnover and produced the strongest contribution margins.

At the beginning of the eighties the firm earned about two thirds of its turnover through retail trade and the rest through direct sales to customers like hotels, restaurants, canteens and hospitals. The success on the retail side, with a relatively strong market share of 10-15%, was attributed principally to the fact that the company had been able to establish its brand with a high degree of recognition and an excellent quality image (= attractive competitive position). This success in building the brand was in turn attributed to creative advertising, blends which met customer requirements and good product quality (= competitive advantages in the market offer). These in turn depended on above average marketing ability and the motivation and creativity of the marketing team as well as the specific talents of the management in buying and product development (= competitive advantages at the level of resources) .

In the middle of the eighties the management decided to review their strategy. There were three main factors which contributed to this decision: (1) The company found itself obliged to pay higher and higher prices for its coffee imports, while its larger competitors could take advantage of their greater bargaining power to obtain favorable terms. The company's buying expertise was thus no longer able to compensate for the competitive disadvantage of the company's small size. (2) The budgets required for advertising and sales promotion needed to maintain the competitive position had now grown so large that the firm was no longer able to fund them. (3) The limited resources for investment in advertising and promotions were already having an effect: The statistics for the last few years had been showing reductions in market share despite continued attractive advertising.

Analysis showed that both the company's lack of bargaining power in comparison with their competitors and also its limited financial resources (= competitive disadvantages at the level of resources) had led to insufficient advertising impact (= competitive disadvantages in the market offer), which in turn adversely affected the market share (= competitive position). Because the owners were unwilling to go public, the competitive disadvantage in resources would remain as a permanent feature of the company's situation. The management therefore took the logical decision to gradually reduce their activity in the retail sector and to use the money saved to extend their activity with the customer group of hotels, restaurants, canteens and hospitals, where the disadvantages in resources would have less impact.

2   The development of strategic planning

2.1   Four phases in the development of strategic planning

Before the end of the sixties there was no form of planning which focused on the building and maintenance of success potentials and which could therefore be properly called strategic planning. The quantitative long-term planning available to companies was a form of analysis which proceeded by extrapolating trends and attempting to project past developments into the future. One example of a long-term oriented method of analysis which is based on the extrapolation of trends is gap analysis. This form of analysis looks at products already in existence and at products in development and predicts the rate of turnover or contribution margin they will achieve. Because of the product life cycle, turnover or contribution margin tend to reduce over time. By comparing projected future figures with what would be necessary to ensure the survival of the company, a crucial gap can be identified. **Figure 2-1** shows how this is done.

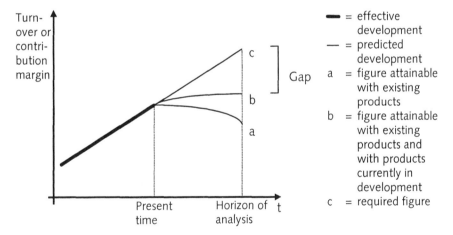

Figure 2-1: Gap analysis

While gap analysis identifies the gap which needs to be bridged, it offers no clues as to how this can be done. If we consider the Ansoff matrix shown below in **Figure 2-2** we see that the gap in turnover or contribution margin can be closed with an improved market penetration, with new customers for existing products, with new products for existing customers, or with new products for new customers. But the Ansoff matrix cannot help a company to decide which of these alternatives is to be preferred and to be attempted (Ansoff, 1979, p. 98 f).

	Existing products	New products
Existing markets	Improved market penetration	Product diversification
New markets	Market diversification	Lateral diversification

Figure 2-2: Ansoff matrix

At the beginning of the seventies suggestions from management consultants led to the development of portfolio methods of strategic analysis and planning. Unlike trend analysis, portfolio methods afford a strategic view of the company. The development of portfolio methods is the first step in the development of strategic planning. The methods are still used today to determine the strategic objectives of the businesses as a key element of developing a corporate strategy. They are therefore explained in detail in part IV "Developing corporate strategies".

At the end of the seventies, strategic planning at the corporate level with the help of portfolio methods began to be complemented by strategic planning for individual businesses. The crucial problem in developing strategies for businesses is how to win the battle against competitors. A prime mover in this second phase of the development of strategic planning was Porter, whose "Competitive Strategy" (1980) presented three generic competitive strategies which can serve as the basis for the competitive strategy of a business. Porter's ideas are presented in detail in part V "Developing business strategies".

After the publication of "From Strategic Planning to Strategic Management" (Ansoff, Declerck & Hayes, 1976) the term "strategic management" gained in currency. Since the mid-eighties, it has increasingly been preferred to "strategic planning", not only in the research literature but also in business practice. The term strategic management implies a broader view. Strategic management goes beyond planning, including the realization of strategies as well as strategic control. The reason for this widening of view is that in practice the introduction of strategic planning frequently did not lead to improved performance in the company concerned: "The outcome of strategic planning is only a set of plans and intentions. By itself, strategic planning produces no actions, no visible changes in the firm. To effect the changes, the firm needs appropriate capabilities: trained and motivated managers, strategic information, fluid and responsive systems and structures. Lacking these, the firm will appear to resist implementation of the plans. The resistance will be real enough, but it will not be due to some inner perversities, but rather due to a lack of requisite capabilities and motivations, reluctance of people to abandon tried and familiar activities in favor of unknown and risky ones" (Ansoff, Declerck & Hayes 1976, p. 47 f.).

A company's resources have always been considered implicitly within the process of strategic analysis and planning. However, from the mid-nineties on, companies have been able to use the findings of Barney (1991), who developed criteria for the identification of strategically valuable resources. These are presented in detail in chapter 15 of this book.

Figure 2-3 displays the different stages of the development of strategic management and gives a visual summary of section 2.1.

2.2   The role of strategic planning within strategic management

As we have seen, the change in terminology from strategic planning to strategic management went together with an enlargement of the view. Strategic planning was complemented by the aspects of implementation and control. This means that strategic management comprises: (1) strategic planning, (2) the implementation of strategies,

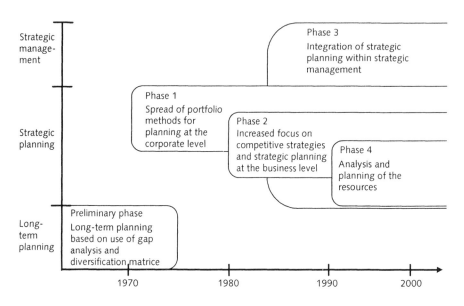

Figure 2-3: The development of strategic planning

(3) strategic control.

These three tasks can be understood as forming three stages of a single process. The first phase, strategic planning, sets out long - term goals and provides a rough guide to what is necessary in terms of actions and resources. This provides a clear direction and basis for the second stage: implementation. The final stage, strategic control, has a dual function: First it provides feedback on how strategies are realized. Secondly it checks whether the assumptions or premises underlying the strategic plans correspond to reality. If there is too much divergence from the strategic plans and their implementation, or if the premises behind the strategies do not correspond to reality, then planning must begin again.

Although the three stages form a single process, they do not take place consecutively; there is considerable temporal overlapping. For example, stages two and three, implementation and strategic control, will obviously take place simultaneously. This overlapping in time means that there is an interplay between the three separate tasks, with each influencing the other two.

It is also difficult to distinguish sharply between strategic management and management of daily business. While strategic planning has its own specific methods and can be distinguished clearly from medium and short term planning, the distinction cannot be made so clearly in the other two stages. Apart from early warning systems, there are no specific methods for the tasks of strategy implementation and control.

Figure 2-4 summarizes this view of strategic management.

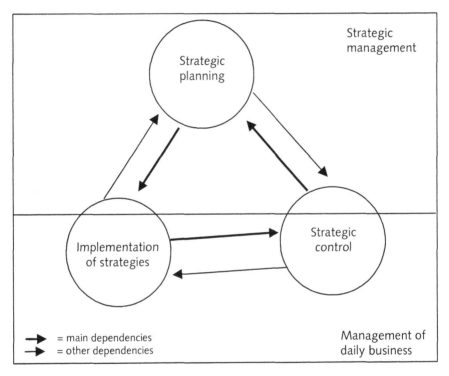

Figure 2-4: The three sub-systems of strategic management

As the chart shows, strategic planning plays a key role within strategic management. Strategic planning is perceived as a process which is run independently of daily business but which determines it, while the other two tasks, strategy implementation and control, are part of the ongoing day-to-day management process. Strategic management is thus to a great extent the product of strategic planning.

Strategy implementation refers to the realization of strategies at the material level of market offers and hard resources, but it also includes complementary measures concerning personnel. Unsatisfactory implementation at the personnel level is the most frequent cause of failure in achieving success with strategies. This is not surprising. The most important realization measures, such as the development of new products, the reduction in the number of production facilities, the outsourcing of production, the building up of foreign markets and so on, will be clearly stated in the strategies. This is not the case for the measures which concern the personnel. In strategic plans they are mentioned either in passing or not at all. This is because those participating in a strategy development process tend to concentrate on visible intended competitive advantages. But without realization measures at the personnel level the best strategies will fail hopelessly.

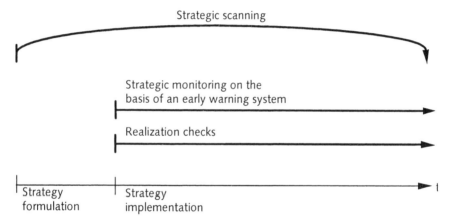

Figure 2-5: Elements of strategic control
(Steinmann & Schreyögg, 1993, P. 221)

Strategic control comprises three elements: strategic realization checking, strategic monitoring and strategic scanning. Realization checking serves to guarantee that strategic measures are realized. After the strategy is formulated, strategic monitoring begins. For this reason an early warning system is built up and maintained. It observes indicators for key premises. But as it is impossible to look at all premises, the risk remains that one may be surprised by unexpected developments. The role of the third element, strategic scanning, is to minimize this risk. Strategic scanning involves the global intuitive observation of the environment and therefore implicitly includes all premises. **Figure 2-5** shows the relationship between the three types of checking (Steinmann & Schreyögg 1993, p. 221 ff.).

---

(1) Number of study places in the German-speaking universities
- for biology as main branch
- for biology as secondary branch
- for medicine

(2) Percentage of English textbooks used in 10 universities selected randomly
- for the study of biology
- for the study of medicine

(3) Percentage of the 50 most well-known scientists publishing their textbooks mainly or exclusively at Bigler Ltd in comparison with the percentages of the competitors
- for the German-speaking biologists
- for the German-speaking medical doctors

(4) Number of innovations compared to the whole of deliverable books for Bigler Ltd in comparison with the number of the competitors
- for the books of biology in German
- for the books of medicine in German

(5) Average number of copies over all editions of Bigler Ltd in comparison with the average number of the competitors
- for the books of biology in German
- for the books of medicine in German

Figure 2-6: Indicators for a publisher of German university textbooks of medicine and biology

The methods used for checking the realization of strategic programs are the same as those for checking medium-term projects, milestone setting and control being the principal tool.

A number of methods have been suggested for the determination of early warning systems. Although procedures recommended for the construction of early warning systems vary considerably, they all have one central focus: the determination of indicators for observing key premises. The quality of an early warning system essentially depends on the quality of these indicators. **Figure 2-6** gives the example of the indicators of a publisher of German university textbooks for students of medicine and of biology.

Global strategic scanning should be carried out on an intuitive basis by top management. It would not be appropriate for it to be delegated and carried out using fixed procedures.

3   Assessment of strategies

3.1   Basic reflections on the assessment of strategies

As we have seen, the purpose of strategic planning is to construct or maintain success potentials. Accordingly, the development of strategies means the definition of possible success potentials and the evaluation of these in terms of their importance for success. Following our classification in section 1.3 above, we distinguish three types of success potential:

- existing or targeted competitive positions in specific markets
- existing or targeted competitive advantages in the market offer
- existing or targeted competitive advantages in resources

Evaluation of strategies thus focuses mainly on success potentials: either already existing success potentials or those which need to be built up within the planning period. We must now consider what methods are available for the systematic assessment of the importance of success potentials.

As the construction and maintenance of success potentials is linked to investments, the first approach to assessing strategic options is by financial evaluation. We can, for instance, try to calculate the net present value resulting from the investments required for a strategic option. This will indicate the increase in the value of the company produced by a strategic option. Where companies are listed on the stock market, this net present value should, in the long-term, lead to a corresponding increase in the share price (Kühn & Grünig, 2000, p.78 ff.). Evaluation of strategies by determining their net present value is fundamentally correct from the point of view of management science. It is recommended by many writers as the theoretically best method of assessment (see for example Grant, 2002, p.38 ff.). Recently the use of option analysis for assessing strategic alternatives as "real options" has been advocated to complement discounted cash-flow analysis (see for example Luehrmann, 1998, p.51 ff.).

The assessment of strategies and their associated success potentials through financial evaluation seems an obvious choice. However it fails in many cases because of the impossibility of making realistic forecasts of the long-term financial outcomes of specific strategic options. While it is usually possible to make good estimates of the investment amounts required to secure or build particular success potentials, to predict their effect on revenues and payments in years to follow is often not possible. It seems especially problematic when the success potentials under discussion involve the construction of new competitive positions in developing markets, or innovative products and services, or 'soft' factors. But even the prediction of the effects of investments to protect existing success potentials is often fraught with considerable uncertainty, given the problems posed by long-term forecasting (Kühn & Grünig, 2000, p. 80 ff.).

If the theoretically desirable assessment of strategies and success potentials proves impossible to achieve, because of the impossibility of obtaining reliable data, then another method must be chosen. This consists of evaluating success potentials with the help of substitute assessment criteria. These must fulfill two requirements:

- On the one hand it must be possible to obtain the data required for the assessment of success potentials using the substitute criteria.
- On the other hand there should be a high probability that assessment of the success potentials using substitute criteria will in practice select the strategic option whose positive effect on long-term success is greatest. So there needs to be a well founded link between substitute criteria and company success.

In section 3.2 we present a model for the assessment of strategic options which is based on the use of substitute assessment criteria.

3.2   Model for the assessment of strategies

Figure 3-1 provides an overview of the proposed assessment model.

As the illustration shows, the assessment of success potentials is a four stage procedure. In Stage One the target market positions are assessed. Stage Two assesses the market offers. Stage Three assesses

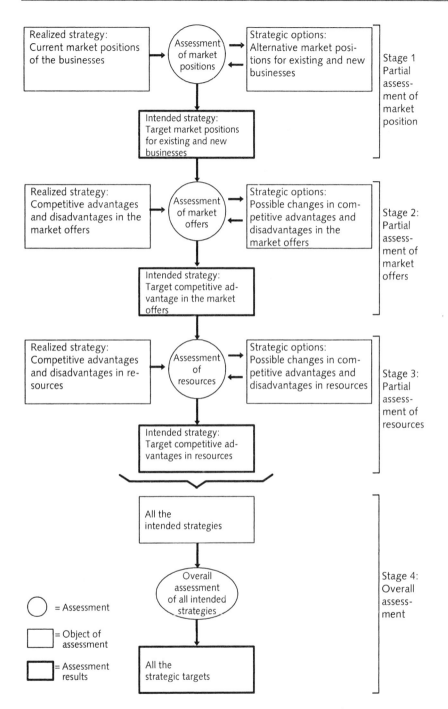

Figure 3-1: Overview of the model for the assessment of strategies

	Assessment of market and industry aspects	Assessment of competitive strength
Stage 1: **Assessment of** **market positions**	Assessment of market attractiveness especially of competitive intensity	Assessment of market share or other indicators of competitive strength
Stage 2: **Assessment of** **market offers**	Assessment of the relevance of the competitive advantages, based on the industry specific success factors	Assessment of the relative strength and weaknesses of product, price and other dimensions of the market offer
Stage 3: **Assessment of** **resources**	Assessment of the ability of resources to produce market offers which meet customer needs	Assessment of the sustainability of competitive advantages of resources, using indicators like rarity, imitability and substitutability

Figure 3-2: Assessment criteria for Stages 1 to 3

the resources and the final stage is an overall assessment.

Stage Four is necessary, because in stages Two and Three, which are partial assessments related to different businesses, overall corporate aspects might be neglected. This can be a particular problem if the assessments in Stages Two and Three are carried out by different individuals. The final overall assessment is also required to make sure that there is no danger of failing to recognize potential synergies between different businesses. In addition, the final stage will need to evaluate not only the success potentials, but also the probability of succeeding in getting the strategies implemented, the possibilities of financing the realization and the risks of the planned strategies.

Every change in strategy involves risks and a successful strategy should not be changed without reason. Accordingly, in each of the first three stages the existing strategy is assessed first. Another advantage of this is that after the existing strategy has been assessed and found to be deficient, a solid basis of knowledge will then exist, which can guide the search for a new and better strategic option. This knowledge base guarantees that more realistic strategic options will be developed. The strategy development and assessment process continues until a strategy is identified which corresponds to the company's objectives.

Figure 3-2 gives an overview of the substitute criteria to be used in Stages One, Two and Three. As you can see, in all three stages the assessment of success potentials includes both criteria focused on the market and industry aspects and criteria focused on competitive strength (Ohmae, 1982).

The model of assessment outlined here will be incorporated into the process of strategic planning and will be described in more detail later when we consider the individual steps in this process, but to provide an immediate indication, **Inset 3-1** gives a short description of the assessment of the businesses of a playing card producer.

Inset 3-1: Assessment of strategies for a producer of playing cards

Ludens is a small company based in the centre of Europe. Despite having a turnover of only 30 million dollars, over the years the firm has been able to develop into a diversified company with the following product groups:
- Accessories for textile manufacturers, especially Jacquard cards
- Games and playing cards for children and adults
- Tarot cards and esoteric literature for a small but growing customer group

With the exception of certain games and the books, the products are produced at the company's own facilities.

The company is now part of a larger group which acquired 100% of the shares from the previous owners a few years back. In the first few years after this takeover the company increased its turnover and produced handsome profits. However in the middle of the nineties things began to change. For a time the company showed a loss, attributable to stagnating turnover in two of the three product groups and rising costs in production and marketing. The managers of the group became alarmed and whereas the management of the subsidiary had previously enjoyed a good deal of freedom, the group board now began to intervene, deciding, among other things, to review the company's strategy.

Detailed strategic analysis revealed the need for a reorientation, both in the overall strategy of the company and for the different product groups. The strategy assessment problems which had to be tackled were as follows:

- For Level One (competitive position) the question was this: in which of the three product groups or businesses should the company aim for growth and which should be merely consolidated at existing levels of activity or even run down. To make this judgment it was necessary to assess how attractive the markets were. It was also necessary to evaluate how far the company's products would be able to-build and maintain adequate market share.
- Level Two (competitive advantages in the market offer) an assessment had to be made for each product group of the competitive advantages and disadvantages for products, prices, communication and distribution. On the basis of this evaluation of existing success potentials ways to construct competitive advantages and eliminate competitive disadvantages had to be examined.
- Closely linked to the analysis at Level Two was Level Three (competitive advantages in resources) in which the capacities, capabilities and other resources of the firm were examined, again separately for each business. Of interest here was, first of all, the question of how suitable existing or constructable resources were for the safeguarding of planned competitive advantages in the market offer. Secondly, resource strengths had to be assessed in terms of how they could be defended in the

long term against competitors. For strategically relevant weaknesses, the question was, whether these could be overcome, given the limited financial means of the company.

- Level Four (overall evaluation) finally focussed on how to coordinate the business strategies, the feasibility of the financial investment required and the risks of implementation of the strategic guidelines which had been provisionally determined in Levels One, Two and Three. At this stage insurmountable financial problems were revealed. The consequence was that some of the strategic options that had been fixed on, had to be readjusted. In particular it was decided to sell one of the three businesses, leading to a management buy-out.

Part II

The process of strategic planning and the resulting documents

Having introduced the fundamental idea of strategic planning in Part I, we now turn to methods and procedures. Part II presents the overall procedure for strategic planning, which we will then specify in Parts III to VI by providing detailed recommendations for methods concerning the different stages of the process.

Part II comprises three chapters:

- Before dealing with the procedure for strategic planning itself, Chapter Four describes the most important strategic documents and shows the constellations in which these may apply in different types of company. By beginning with the results of the strategic process we may find it easier to understand what follows: Experience shows that the sequence of steps we propose can be followed more easily if the resulting systems of documents are already familiar.
- Chapter Five then presents the strategic planning process. After explaining the need of systematic procedure, the recommended process of strategic planning is introduced. It is geared towards companies with a number of product groups in a single geographical market or companies with a single product group in a number of different geographical markets. It also assumes a classical strategy project aimed at producing both a corporate strategy and a set of business strategies. Where these conditions are not met, the procedure will require modification. The last section therefore discusses adaptations of the planning process for different conditions.
- Chapter Six finally gives an overview about the various methods of strategic analysis and planning. The different tools are briefly explained and linked with the process of strategic analysis and planning introduced in Chapter Five.

4 Strategic documents as the result of strategic planning

4.1 Basic types of strategic document

In Chapter One of this book intended strategies were defined as long-term guidelines for a company as a whole or for significant sections of it. They aim at ensuring the permanent achievement of the company's overriding goals. These strategic guidelines can only produce the desired effects if they are communicated effectively. In addition to oral communication they must be communicated through written documents.

In business practice, strategic aims and measures are normally set out in a variety of types of strategic plan. There can be considerable differences, both in the names given to these plans and in what they typically contain. The literature on strategic planning, however, generally accepts the terminology developed by Hofer & Schendel (1978, p. 27 ff.): The most important strategic documents are identified as

- corporate strategies and
- business strategies.

Other important documents for Hofer & Schendel are

- mission statements and
- functional area strategies.

Figure 4-1 displays the essential content of the four basic types of strategic document.

We have not included functional area strategies here, such as production or marketing strategies. The main purpose of these documents is not to build and maintain success potentials relevant for the company as a whole and they therefore do not fall into the class of strategies in our sense. In the context of functional or sub-functional areas the word 'strategy' often indicates no more than the fixing of priorities for the areas concerned, typically providing guidelines for the next one to three years. It would be preferable to find another term for these documents, such as 'plan' or 'agenda'.

Basic types / Content	Mission statement	Corporate strategy	Business strategy	Strategic program
Overriding objectives and values	***			
Success potentials • target market positions	*	***	*	*
• competitive advantages in the market offers		*	***	*
• competitive advantages in resources		*	***	*
Implementation measures				***

*** = main content focus
* = possible complementary content

Figure 4-1: Essential content of the basic types of strategic document

We have however, added implementation programs as a fourth category of strategic document. The implementation of strategic intentions will be based, principally, on these plans, which are thus of considerable importance from a practical point of view.

As it is apparent from Figure 4-1, the mission statement is not a central strategic document, as its main purpose is not to ensure the maintenance or construction of strategic success potentials. It serves to communicate explicitly the overriding aims and values of the company. These take precedence over the other strategic documents and influence the process of strategy development, particularly the assessment of strategic success potentials. However, their effect on decisions and actions in the company is very often quite superficial. Mission statements usually confine themselves to a small number of rather abstract principles which do not fundamentally constrain the possibilities for action. Sometimes mission statements specify the served markets and the target market positions, but their strategic content is generally negligible. Usually, the mission statement gives only a broad indication of the field of activity of the company.

The main content of corporate strategy indicates the strategically relevant businesses together with target competitive positions for each of them. This means that it is not just a matter of identifying the product categories and the geographical markets in which the company will compete, but corporate strategy also requires the fixing of target competitive positions, generally in terms of absolute or relative market share. In practice such a target is often vaguely described, i.e. 'considerably improved market share', but it can be expressed more precisely. It is also a good idea to include investment priorities or investment targets. Specifying the size and type of investments that need to be undertaken for each business strengthens the steering impact of corporate strategy and increases the likelihood of successful implementation.

Where one of the classical portfolio methods is used for planning, target market positions and investment targets can be represented visually in a target portfolio. **Figure 4-2** shows the target portfolio for a producer and distributor of food products for hotels, restaurants and canteens. This portfolio plan is based on the Boston Consulting Group method (see p. 168 ff.). In practice sometimes companies simply adopt a matrix of this type in order to define or communicate the corporate strategy. We would like to stress that this is not an adequate solution: the most important strategic decisions need to be stated clearly and with a certain level of detail and the matrix cannot do this on its own.

As Figure 4-1 shows, the corporate strategy can also include guidelines for competitive strategy and indicate the competitive advantages considered most important. This is only useful when there are important shared elements between the businesses, such as common customer groups or shared resources like brands, patents or production facilities.

Corporate strategies are required to plan strategically for companies, or divisions within companies, which have a medium to high degree of heterogeneity. This means they have a number of different product

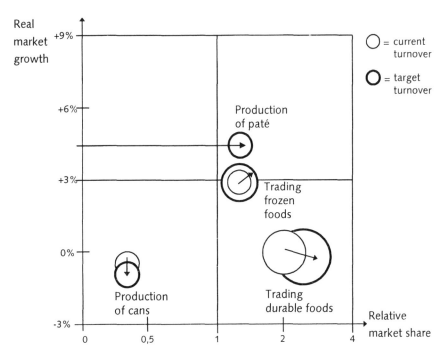

Figure 4-2: Portfolio plan using the Boston Consulting Group method

groups and/or are active in a number of different national markets.

Typically even small and medium-sized companies have more than one business and therefore require more than one business strategy. Figure 4-1 shows that a business strategy specifies success potentials for the market offer and success potentials in resources. In practice it seems best to make first a broad specification of the type of target competitive advantage (price or differentiation) and the scope of the market to be served (whole market or niche). Broad specifications of this kind are called generic competitive strategies. But defining the generic competitive strategy is not enough to ensure the maintenance and construction of strategic success potentials. It is of great importance to specify in detail the target features of the market offer, because it is through these concrete competitive advantages that we reach the target market positions. In addition we must establish what the crucial competitive advantages in resources are, on which the value and sustainability of the advantages in the offer depend. Thus the content of business strategy must consist principally of many concrete statements about the development or maintenance of success potentials. The business strategy can therefore serve as a starting point for the formulation of implementation measures.

Figure 4-1 indicates that business strategies can also include statements about target competitive positions. This occurs in those cases where the business strategy concerns a rather heterogeneous complex business with, for example, a number of different products or geographical markets varying in attractiveness. In such a case the company may have different target competitive positions for each product or market.

In practice business strategies are developed either for a product group (in all its markets), or for a national market (with all the product groups offered), or indeed for a single product group in a single national market.

Once the corporate and business strategies have been developed, their implementation is detailed in a limited number of strategic programs. Each of these determines the scope and the objectives of the program, includes a decision as to whether to hire a consultant, prescribes the project organisation, fixes the milestones, and sets out the budget.

Figure 4-3 offers an overview of the usual content and possible additional content of the four basic types of strategic document.

4.2   Combinations of strategic documents for specific companies

The type and number of strategic plans to be adopted as management instruments must be selected according to the specific situation of the company concerned. Small companies with a simple structure which are active in only one business can usually set out their strategic guidelines in a single document. Multinational corporations with a complex structure will require a whole set of documents to provide strategic guidance for the different divisions, products, countries, subsidiaries and so on. It seems best if a list of required documents

Document	Scope of content
Mission statement	• Broad characterization of company activities (market positions aspired to) • Overriding objectives and values (expressing attitudes to its principal stakeholders)
Corporate strategy	• Definition of businesses (combinations of products and/or services offered and served markets or niches) • Market position aspirations (usually in terms of market share objectives for the businesses) • Investment objectives (priorities given to the investments in the different businesses) (it can also include a broad definition of company-wide competitive advantages)
Business strategy (for each business)	• Generic competitive strategy (cost leadership or differentiation) • Competitive advantages on the level of offers (USPs or UAPs) • Competitive advantages on the level of resources (resources which satisfy Barney's four conditions) (it can also include statements relating to the division of the business into sections and corresponding differentiated market share objectives)
Strategic program (for each group of implementation measures)	• Program objectives and boundary conditions (Intended effects of the program, important restrictions) • Program organization (Organizational structure, persons involved) • Process and milestones (Program steps, timetable) • Budget (Internal and external program cost)

Figure 4-3: Content of the basic types of strategic document

is drawn up right at the beginning of the planning process. The project organization can then be adjusted to the required documents. This facilitates the integration of the line managers concerned into the process of strategy development for their areas of responsibility, which is vital for realistic planning and motivation.

Although the set of documents required by a company to implement strategies depends on its particular situation, it is possible to describe a number of standard systems of strategic plans, based on the most frequent kinds of company situation. These will be useful as a starting point in working out a solution for a specific company. In selecting the appropriate system and adapting it to a specific situation it is necessary to take account of the different businesses and of the management structure of the company in question. In addition, sometimes it is preferable to use local in-house names for the documents, rather than those proposed by Hofer & Schendel.

Figure 4-4 presents the six standard systems of strategic documents.

Standard system I is the simplest strategic planning system. Corporate strategy and business strategy are summarized in a single document. This will usually contain only a short characterization of target market positions and will address itself primarily to questions of business strategy. This system recommends itself principally to small and medium-sized regionally or nationally-based companies.

Standard systems II & III differ from the first in so far as there is a greater complexity of products and services offered, either concentrated in a single industry market (standard system II) or in a number of different industry markets (standard system III). In comparison with standard system I, the variety of products and services means that more weight is given to corporate strategy, defining realistic target market positions and investment priorities. These two standard systems will be used mainly by medium-sized nationally-based companies.

Standard system IV will appeal to highly specialized internationally

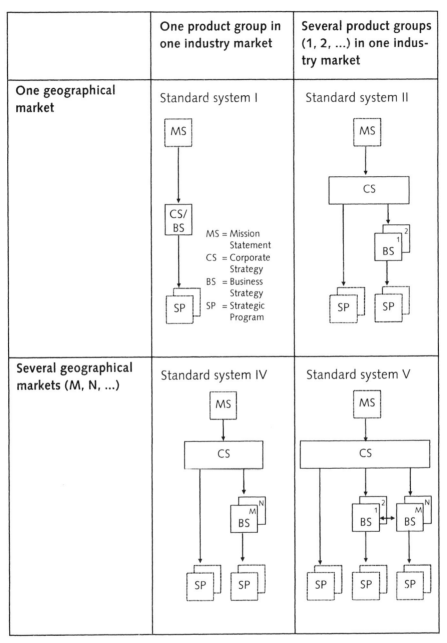

Figure 4-4: Standard systems of strategic documents

Several product groups (1, 2, ...) in
several industry markets (A, B, ...)

Standard system III

Standard system VI

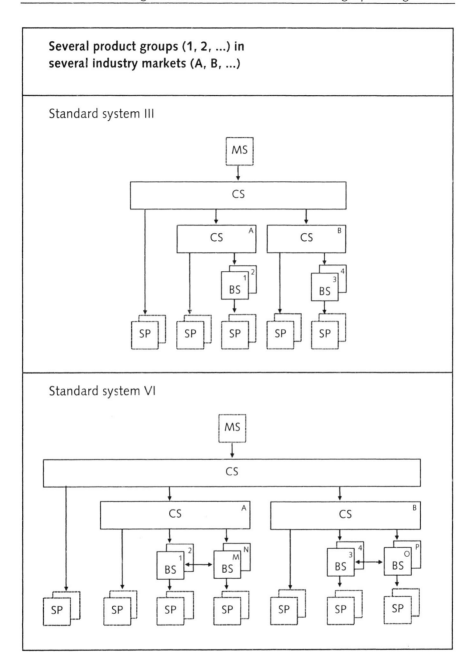

oriented companies operating in niche markets. As this type of company will be active in many different national markets it is worth developing separate business strategies for important economic regions or national markets.

Standard system V will be suitable for many medium-sized internationally oriented manufacturing and service companies. The double arrow linking product and country-based businesses is intended to show that more than one procedure is possible. One possibility is that product oriented and market oriented business strategies are produced at the same time. Another solution is that product oriented strategies take precedence over the country strategies and are produced first. Only in very special circumstances would one wish to do it the other way round, producing the country strategies first.

Standard system VI is the most complex and is a logical combination of III and V. It would be relevant for large, internationally active, corporations.

Inset 4-1 describes two examples of specific systems of strategic documents which illustrate the need to adapt the basic schemes to the specific situation of a company.

Inset 4-1: Two examples of strategic plan systems

Figure 4-4 presents six standard systems of strategic plans. As we have noted, these do not represent ready-made solutions which can be directly used by companies. But they do make it easier and faster to produce a solution adapted to an individual case.

Companies wishing to establish their strategic plan system on the basis of the standard systems should proceed as follows: First select the system which comes closest to the company's needs, and then adapt it to the specifics of the situation. In this inset we look at this process and present two illustrations of how it might work.

Our first example is a national company which markets honey,

nuts and dried fruit. The basic products are imported and processed on two separate production lines. For honey it is a matter of
mixing and filling only, while the other products demand a greater
variety of processes in production, including cleaning, deshelling,
destoning, grinding and mixing, as well as packing in bags. The
products are sold both under the firm's own brand and under different private labels of wholesalers.

Because this firm operates in two different markets at the national
level, standard system III could be selected. However, as **Figure 4-
5** reveals, its strategic plan system follows standard system II. This
is not a large company and one strategic plan for each of the two
markets is adequate. Information concerning the different products
and customer groups for each division can be in sections within
these plans without requiring separate documents.

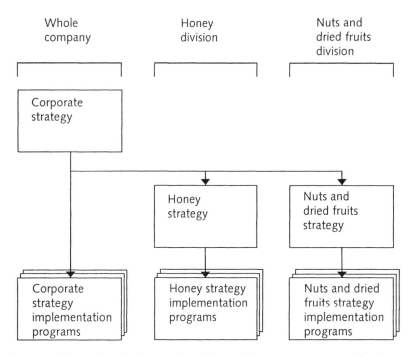

**Figure 4-5: Strategic plan system for a national company producing
honey, nuts and dried fruits**

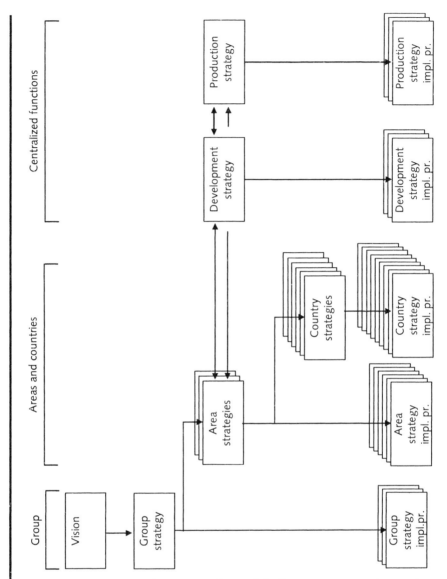

Figure 4-6: Strategic plan system for a globally operating producer of Elevators

Our second example is a producer of elevators. This company has grown rapidly in the post-war period by acquiring other elevator manufacturing companies. By the beginning of the eighties the company was globally active and it decided to start to coordinate and rationalize production. Production is now carried out in decentralized component factories which are large enough to take full advantage of economies of scale. The various acquisitions were transformed into sales, assembly and service firms. The group was able to reduce costs considerably and to survive in an increasingly competitive environment.

With its internationally marketed comprehensive range of elevators this company would select standard system V. As a comparison of **Figure 4-6** with standard system V shows, the company's strategic plan system follows this standard system but there are differences:

- In accordance with its structure, the company has a set of area strategies as well as strategies for each national market. The area strategies fix priorities and define measures area-wide. This is especially important in those areas where the company distributes through agents, rather than through its own subsidiaries.

- The company does not have a set of strategies for each product group as in standard system V. Instead there is one development strategy and one production strategy, both applying to the whole range. The reason for this lies in the high degree of centralization of product range planning, product development and production. Although these two documents are functional plans, they are indeed strategic in our sense, because they include essential guidelines for building up and maintaining success potentials.

5 The process of strategic planning

5.1 The need for a systematic process of strategic planning

The case for systematic development of planned strategies has been challenged, both by managers and by certain researchers:

- On the one hand it is claimed that the difficulties of long-term prediction make any systematic process of analysis and planning impossible (Mintzberg, 1994, p. 227 ff).
- On the other hand the strategies, it is claimed, do not contribute to the achievement of company goals, because rapidly changing market conditions and fierce competition mean that the systematic construction of long-term success potentials is impossible.

Recent experience has shown - this is not at issue - that both the development of long-term predictions and the ongoing construction of success potentials over a period of several years has grown considerably more difficult. But to draw the conclusion that systematic strategic planning has become impossible or pointless is, in our view, throwing out the baby with the bathwater.

- One does not deal with increased turbulence, which makes prediction more difficult, by simply abandoning planning. On the contrary, the increased difficulty of long-term forecasting should lead us to intensify planning efforts. This conclusion is inescapable because, no matter whether there is a planned strategy or not, investment in resources will take place and this will determine the long-term competitive position of the company. If there is no intended strategy, these investments produce an emergent strategy, and this will contain considerable risks and can threaten the existence of the firm.
- There is no opposition between strategic thinking and rapid and flexible decision-making. On the contrary, correctly understood and unbureaucratically applied strategies will generally increase the quality of daily operational decision-making. Strategies used as management tools can help to prevent companies from slipping into competitive positions and markets which offer little hope of success. Clear strategies mean that companies do not fragment their limited resources by pursuing too many new ideas. Dynamic

market development and tough competitive conditions do not change the fact that a company always needs clear ideas in order to achieve and to defend competitive advantages in attractive markets.

Prahalad & Hamel seem to get it about right: "While much of the criticism of the field may be valid, critics often miss the point. We believe that the need for strategic thinking, during this turbulent decade, is greater than ever" (Prahalad & Hamel, 1994 p. 6).

5.2   Overview of the process of strategic planning

Figure 5-1 shows the suggested process of strategic planning.

The suggested process of strategic planning is founded on four elements:
- The model for the assessment of strategic success potentials presented in Chapter Three.
- Published processes of strategic planning.
- Heuristic principles, which simplify the identification and evaluation of options. **Inset 5-1** describes the most important of these principles.
- Practical experience of the authors as strategic management consultants, which serves as a basis to evaluate the applicability of particular problem solving tools in business reality. Following the action research approach (see for example Clark, 1972; Stringer, 1996) a considerable number of consulting projects have been systematically assessed and thus made available for the development and improvement of the method.

Figure 5-2 displays the elements on which the strategic planning process is based.

In the next section, we will briefly describe the content of each step in the process. We restrict the explanations at this stage as a more detailed account follows in parts III to VI where each step will be analyzed in detail and where practical recommendations will be made.

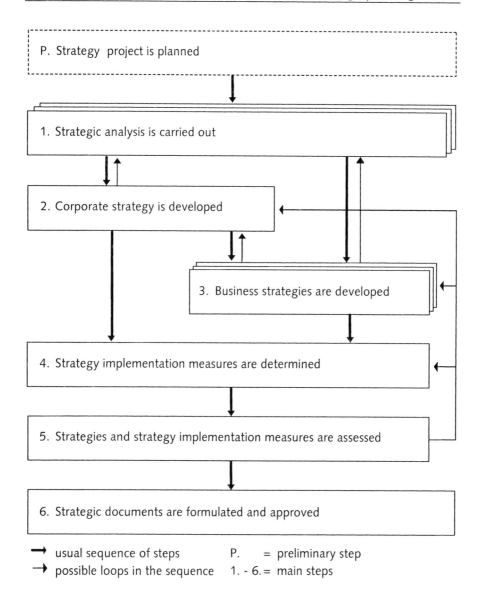

P. Strategy project is planned

1. Strategic analysis is carried out

2. Corporate strategy is developed

3. Business strategies are developed

4. Strategy implementation measures are determined

5. Strategies and strategy implementation measures are assessed

6. Strategic documents are formulated and approved

→ usual sequence of steps   P.   = preliminary step
→ possible loops in the sequence   1. - 6. = main steps

Figure 5-1: The process of strategic planning

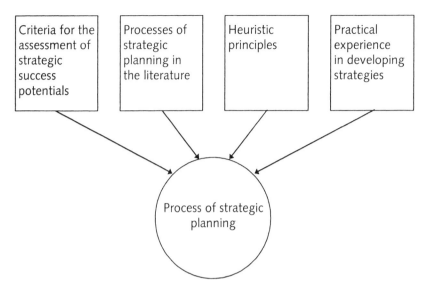

Figure 5-2: Elements underpinning the process of strategic planning

Inset 5-1: The most important heuristic principles and how they are used in strategic planning
(Kühn, 1978, p. 176 ff.)

Difficult decision-making problems, like developing strategies, are often characterized by the following features:

- There are a large number of decision variables, each of them having many possible values. This leads to a large number of possibilities.
- These possibilities have to be evaluated on the basis of a number of different criteria.
- An additional difficulty is that decisions must be taken against the background of an environment which may develop in a number of different ways.
- The decision variables, criteria and environmental factors include variables which can be quantified only approximately, if at all.

Problems like this are ill-defined and ill-structured (Minsky, 1963, p. 408). For this reason it is not possible to develop a decision-making process which will produce the optimal solution. For complex problems like these, only heuristic processes can be used.

They provide practical help by reducing complexity, although they cannot guarantee an optimal solution (Feigenbaum & Feldmann, 1963, p. 6).

Developing a future strategy is an extremely complex problem. In order to successfully cope with this task, we recommend a decision-making procedure based on heuristic principles. The most important ones are summarized in the following paragraphs.

One of the most important heuristic rules concerns the factorization of problems. This requires that the original complex problem should be broken down into a set of manageable sub-problems. Our recommended procedure for strategic planning applies this rule by breaking down the task into seven steps.

Another heuristic principle is that of setting up sub-problems in such a way that proven problem solving tools can be applied to them. This principle is applied especially in the definition of the problem-solving Steps Two and Three of the suggested strategic planning process, which have been structured in a way which facilitates the use of known methods.

A third important principle is sub-goal reduction. This principle suggests we can "...make progress by substituting for the achievement of a goal the achievement of a set of easier goals" (Newell, Shaw & Simon, 1965, p. 259). The principle is applied in the definition of the various criteria for the assessment of success potentials (see Chapter Three).

In Step Five of the suggested planning process, the strategies and implementation programs are subjected to a global assessment. If the result of this process is unsatisfactory, strategies and programs have to be revised. This recommendation follows the heuristic principle of generate-and-test. For problems comprising many dimensions, it suggests developing one solution at a time, testing it and proceeding to the development of another solution only if the test leads to unsatisfactory results.

Another important heuristic principle which is applied in the suggested strategic planning process is bounded rationality (Simon, 1966, p. 19). This rule is based on the idea that in ill-defined and ill-structured problem situations, the optimal solution cannot be determined and therefore the problem solver should content himself with a satisfactory solution. The principle of bounded rationality is applied in Steps Two, Three and Four, in determining the corporate strategy, developing the business strategies and drawing up the implementation programs, as well as in the final global assessment in Step Five.

The final principle is that of proximity. This demands the prior development and testing of variants which are close to the existing arrangement. Variants of this type are easier to evaluate and often less risky. Of course they should not restrain the strategic planner from looking for more distant alternatives, which, although riskier, may offer greater opportunities. The assessment process described in Chapter Three first tests the realized strategy, at each of the three assessment levels. It goes on to consider new options if the existing strategy is found to be unsatisfactory. In this case the new options which are closest to the existing situation are examined first.

5.3   A brief note on the steps of the process

The development of strategies is a complex task requiring competence in a number of different functional areas within the firm. For this reason, it is useful to see strategy planning as a project. Because of the complexity involved, and the considerable amount of work required, a preliminary step is necessary to plan the management of the project.

The planning of a strategy project (step P in our standard procedure) involves tackling a large number of practical tasks. The scope of the project must be clearly defined with precise objectives and conditions. The project organization and schedule are of great importance. They must be able to deliver efficient and competent work and involve as many of the line managers as possible in order to increase the likelihood of effective strategy realization. The question of whether to bring in outside consultants can also be difficult, but must be resolved before strategic planning starts. Finally the project costs must be budgeted. To budget project costs precisely, some idea of the number of businesses which will require separate analysis and planning is required, along with a preliminary assessment of the desirability of obtaining external data.

As most researchers and consultants agree, the planning of corporate strategy and business strategies must be preceded by a phase of strategic analysis. Step One in our standard system follows this idea. The main emphasis is on data collection in three fields:

- Global environment.
- Specific task environments or industries.
- The company itself.

In practice, it is often difficult to determine the scope of strategic analysis; at this stage in strategy development we do not yet have a clear view about the target market positions and competitive advantages. Therefore we do not know what information we will need. For this reason there is the danger that a large amount of data will be gathered which will later turn out to be irrelevant to decisions being taken. This must be avoided, because strategic analysis is a particularly expensive undertaking. Costs will depend on the number of different industries analyzed, on the complexities of the industries involved and on the complexities of the sections of the company which deal with them. It is of critical importance for cost to decide whether to proceed on the basis of data already available within the company or to plan additional data collection. Of course, the quality and quantity of data produced in strategic analysis will affect both the cost and the quality of strategic decisions.

Strategic analysis ends with problem diagnosis. This is restricted to an approximate evaluation of strategic opportunities and threats, because detailed assessment of current strategies is provided for in Steps Two and Three. The reason for the coupling of detailed evaluation with the planning of new strategic options is that many strategic planning methods generate strategic options on the basis of the assessment of the current realized strategy. This is, for instance, the case for all portfolio methods, in which the evaluation of the current portfolio forms the basis for the development of ideas about the target portfolio.

Step Two is the development of corporate strategy. This involves first of all the definition of strategic businesses. It is generally accepted that this is a difficult task. There are two reasons for this. Firstly, there are many different principles according to which one can divide the activity of a company into businesses. Secondly it is important to distinguish between

- business fields, parts of the company which can be run independently because they share no markets and hardly any resources with other businesses, and
- business units, parts of the company which are strategically dependent because they have common markets and/ or resources with other businesses.

Through the definition of strategic businesses a structure is set up which can guide the following steps. In particular, the definition of businesses determines which areas will require business strategies.

Step Two also requires the assessment of the company's current market positions and the corresponding strategic options. This is evaluated according to the criteria of industry attractiveness and competitive strength. Step Two further includes the definition of the target positions for the businesses. These positions can only be provisionally defined within the framework of corporate strategy and will be revaluated in Step Three. Finally, it is important to define approximate investment budgets for each business along with market position objectives.

The assessment of the current market positions of the businesses and of the strategic options, as well as the determining of target positions for the businesses is normally carried out with reference to a portfolio method.

Step Three, developing the business strategies, first involves evaluating the competitive strategy of each business. After this, the intended business strategies must be defined. A business strategy consists first in the choice of the target market (whole market or niche) and of competitive positioning (cost leadership or differentiation). We are thinking here in terms of Porter's generic competitive strategies. Business strategy also requires the concrete specification of competitive advantages, both for the market offer and in terms of resources.

In practice, business strategies often suffer from the fact that competitive advantages are only expressed in general terms. For example, the expression "leader in quality" as the main competitive advantage at the level of the market offer allows a great deal of interpretation and does not contain any indication as to how it can be realized. What is necessary here is a specific understanding of quality which can be the basis for the planning of concrete strategic programs. Experience shows that the formulation of business strategies tends to become particularly vague and abstract when the strategic analysis is only done in a superficial way. In this case, planners do not know enough to be able to formulate specific aims and measures.

Step Four involves the planning of the implementation measures, especially the creation of the strategic programs. This step is missing in many approaches to the process of strategic planning. It is proposed here because it seems very important to make the link between planning and realization.

There are five different types of strategic programs:

- Programs to realize the corporate strategy.
- Programs to realize the business strategies.
- Programs to utilize synergies.
- Programs to improve the management system.
- Programs to motivate and qualify people.

Step Five is the global assessment of both strategies and programs. Normally the business strategies and the strategic programs are developed in parallel. It is therefore essential to get a global view before strategies and programs are approved and realized. Step Five might, for example, uncover an accumulation of too many high risks in the different business strategies or the impossibility of financing all the programs. In this case, strategies and programs must be re-examined. Such loops are an essential feature of the proposed heuristic planning process.

Step Six involves the formulation and approval of strategic documents and is therefore mostly a straightforward affair. It has been included here as a part of the planning process sequence, because in practice it often happens that realization of strategies fails because strategies are not clearly formulated.

It is important to produce strategic documents which are effective as guidelines for managers during the phase of strategy implementation. To fulfil this purpose, the strategies and the program plans must be formulated both concisely and very precisely. As well as setting out strategies and program plans in a clear way, it is also useful to provide the detailed results of strategic analysis, normally in the form of an appendix. Well-documented analysis makes strategic control a simpler matter as well as facilitating strategy review, which will at some time become necessary. It also offers to those not involved in strategy development the information they need in order to properly understand strategic decisions.

5.4   The strategic planning process of an electricity provider

Inset 5-2 illustrates the suggested process of strategic planning with a description of a strategy project for an electricity provider.

Inset 5-2: How a strategy project is developed in an electricity company

It is in the character of a heuristic process that it is hardly ever usable without adaptation to the specific context. The special situation of a company and its specific strategic questions always demand greater or smaller adjustments to the strategy process. In our example the departures are relatively small, making it a typical case.

Figure 5-3 shows the structure of the company at the beginning of the project. As you can see, the company's activity goes beyond the production and distribution of electricity: it also provides electrical installation services, engineering services, constructs electrical lines and stations, and runs specialized shops.

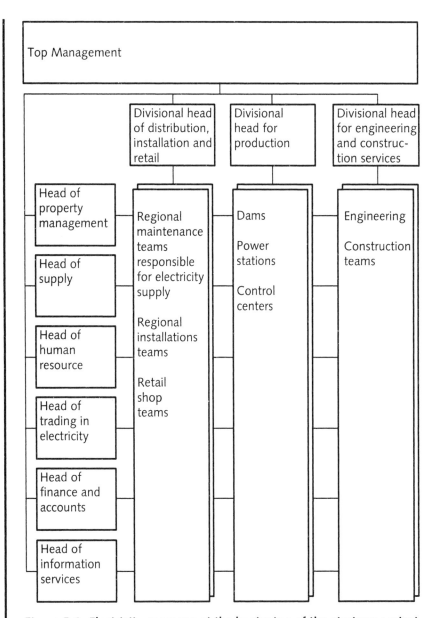

Figure 5-3: Electricity company at the beginning of the strategy project

In October 1995, the management decided to carry out strategic analysis and planning. There were three main reasons:

- Deregulation of the industry in the country of operation was due

in 2000: if the company examined the issues in 1995, it could act rather than react.
- The company's activity in providing electrical installation services was showing a loss and this demanded a long-term reorientation.
- The company structure seemed cumbersome and in need of review. But before reorganizing, the company wanted to define its strategic direction, following Chandler's well-known dictum "structure follows strategy" (Chandler, 1962, p.14)

Following the procedure in Figure 5-1, the strategy project was planned in detail before starting.

The strategic analysis phase took longer than planned, lasting four months. Three working groups examined the areas of activity:
- Production, purchase and distribution of electricity
- Electrical installation services and electrical goods shops
- Engineering and construction services

On the one hand, it was necessary to analyze the markets: the customer needs, the trends in demand, the competing suppliers and their market shares were investigated. On the other hand, the company's own resources and their strengths and weaknesses were examined. The analysis produced catalogues of threats and opportunities for the different activities.

At the same time, a fourth working group analyzed the likely impact of the planned deregulation of the served market in the year 2000. The strategic analysis phase ended with half a day of presentations of the results to the whole of the management.

After this, the steering committee defined the future strategic business fields as the first element of the future corporate strategy. **Figure 5-4** shows the business fields and their position in the market.

After the identification of the business fields, it was necessary to change the project organization. The working groups used in the strategic analysis phase were dissolved and replaced by seven teams which would work on the business strategies. At the same time a working group on corporate strategy was formed which was composed of the top management. As the project was already behind schedule, the timing was revised. To help to catch up on lost time, the corporate strategy and the business strategies would now be developed simultaneously, in a revision of the earlier plan.

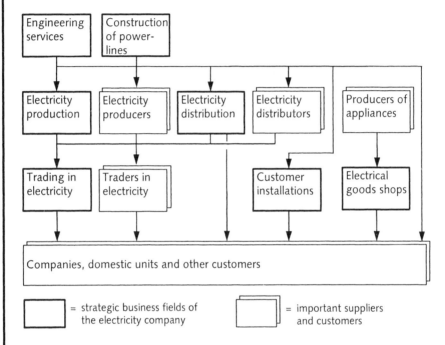

Figure 5-4: Strategic business fields for the electricity company

The corporate strategy group began by defining more closely the boundaries of the seven business fields. As these were rather unlike the existing structure of the firm, the allocation of resources to these fields presented a problem. Next the group turned to portfolio analysis and planning in which they used the General Electrics and McKinsey method. Finally they conducted a preliminary analysis of how to structure the company for the future. With business strategies being worked on at the same time, the group passed its results on to the business strategy teams as soon as possible.

All of the business strategies had to be defined within a single framework, which had been drawn up by the steering committee. According to this framework, first the business field had to be divided into business units. Then a generic competitive strategy for the business field had to be set. Next the target competitive advantages at the level of the market offers had to be determined, both for business fields and business units. Finally key resources had to be identified, which had to be maintained.

The corporate strategy and the business strategies were presented in a workshop session and necessary fine-tuning took place to dovetail them together. Next came a short and intensive period of work in which implementation programs were developed, both for corporate and business strategies. **Figure 5-5** presents the new organisational structure of the company which was developed and introduced in the context of an implementation program for the corporate strategy.

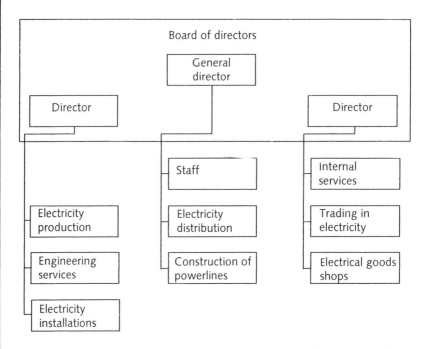

Figure 5-5: New organisational structure following Chandler's dictum "structure follows strategy"

The final phase saw a presentation of the corporate strategy and the business strategies to the board, which approved the corporate strategy and noted the business strategies. The business strategies were then approved by the top management.

Figure 5-6 gives an overview of the whole project, which took eighteen months. The reason that it took such a long time can be

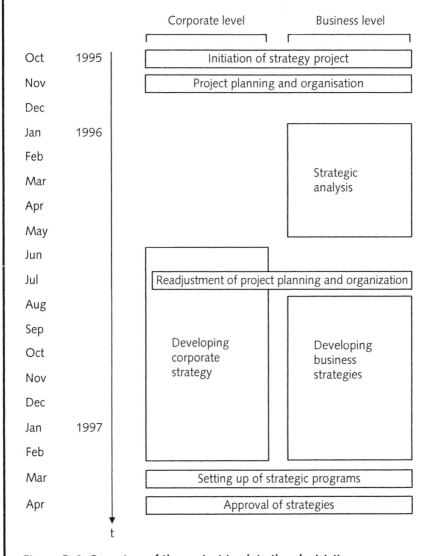

Figure 5-6: Overview of the project track in the electricity company

attributed to the fact that it was the first time that the company had carried out strategic analysis and planning. This meant that a lot of information gathering took place which was new to the company, and experience shows that this takes much longer than updating existing information. Methodological problems were also a major contributory factor to the length of time taken. However, on the positive side, a considerable amount of valuable learning took place, not only in terms of strategy methodology, but also in regard to the company's strategic situation and options.

5.5   Adapting the process of strategic planning

5.5.1   Reasons for adapting the process

Section 5.2 presented our basic design for a strategic planning project. This is a standardized process, which must be adapted by companies to the specifics of their own particular situation. In section 5.5, we look at the question of when adaptations are required and describe the most important types of adapted processes.

The basic process we described in section 5.2 can be used without major modifications for medium-sized companies which have either (1) a number of product groups in a single industry or (2) one product group in a number of geographical markets. In practice, these two types occur very frequently and account for a large proportion of small and medium-sized companies. The strategic documents required by these types of firm are given by standard systems II and IV as described in Chapter Four above.

The process proposed thus far also assumes that we are dealing with classical strategy projects, where the aim is to examine strategies pursued up to the present and, building on existing strategies, to formulate strategies for the future. While this is the most common form of project, other types of strategy project exist.

It is possible to adapt the basic procedure for strategic planning so that it will be appropriate to cases where strategy must be developed for a company with reduced complexity or greater complexity and for cases, where the strategy project has to address a specific question. The first kind of adaptation is treated in section 5.5.2. and the second case is discussed in section 5.5.3.

5.5.2   Adapting the process to companies with reduced or greater complexity of structure

For a company which is offering a single product group in a specific geographical market, the process can be simplified. In terms of the documents required, the company corresponds to standard system I as described in Chapter Four.

The process of planning is simplified as follows:

- Steps Two and Three are not separated as a single strategy is developed which contains both target market position and target competitive advantages in offer and resources.
- The remaining steps can be resolved more easily, especially steps Three and Four. With only one strategy, joint programs are not required. The final evaluation is also straightforward, requiring the assessment only of a single strategy and the programs for its implementation.

In contrast, where a company has a number of product groups in different industries and/or geographical markets, the planning process can require much more time and money. There are three typical cases:

- The basically national company, active in a number of industry markets, in each of which it has a number of different product groups.
- A company active internationally in a single industry market but with a number of product groups. Many manufacturers of machinery fall into this category, as do international insurance companies, if they focus on insuring and have not diversified into financial services.

- Diversified companies, which are usually globally active, such as Novartis or Nestlé.

Figure 5-7, 5-8 and **5-9** give the recommended planning process for these three types of company with a complex strategic structure. As the sequence of numbered steps shows, there are no basically new problems, compared with the standard process presented in Section 5.2. However, a number of steps have to be subdivided in view of the complex structure of the company.

The resulting steps can be carried out in parallel (at the same time) or in sequence (one after the other).

Inset 5-3 shows the course of a strategy project for a manufacturer of elevators. This is an example of the planning process for an internationally active company with a number of product groups in a single industry market.

Inset 5-3: The Africa strategy review by an elevator manufacturer

At the end of the eighties, an internationally active elevator manufacturer marketed its products in African countries through agents, who were independent importers and dealers in capital goods or subsidiaries of international technology companies. They identified building projects which required elevators and made initial contacts with customers. They also looked after maintenance and repairs.

Once an agent had brought a builder to the point where an offer could be made, he contacted the elevator manufacturer's area manager for Africa, who then decided which company in the group would make the offer and, if the offer was accepted, install the product. Subsidiaries who had already fulfilled orders in the country concerned usually got the new projects, because of their market knowledge and existing relationship with the general agent.

At the end of the eighties, the area manager decided to review the

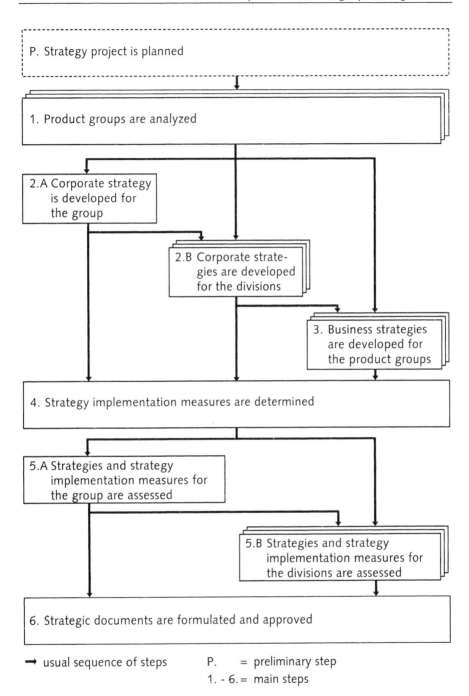

Figure 5-7: The process of strategic planning for a diversified company operating at a national level

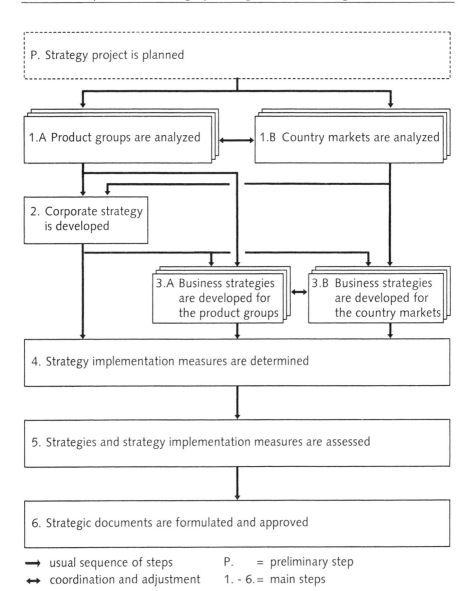

Figure 5-8: The process of strategic planning for a company operating internationally with different product groups in a single industry market

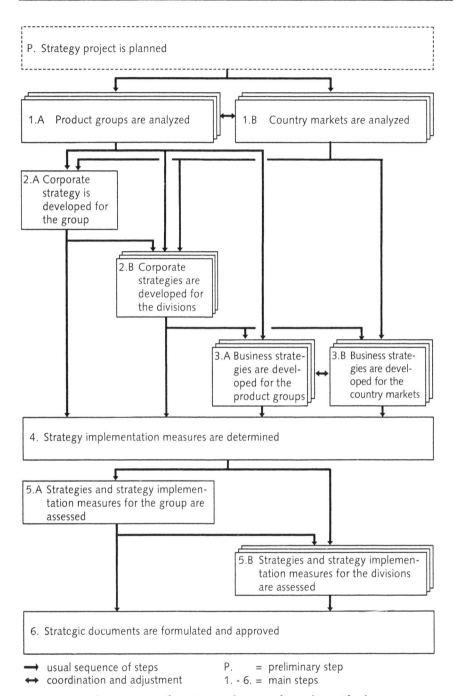

Figure 5-9: The process of strategic planning for a diversified company operating internationally

strategies for Africa, which were relatively rudimentary and had been based on market information which was now out of date. The main aim of the project was to assess existing priorities in terms of countries and to set new quantitative targets.

Figure 5-10 shows the course of the project, which took six months.

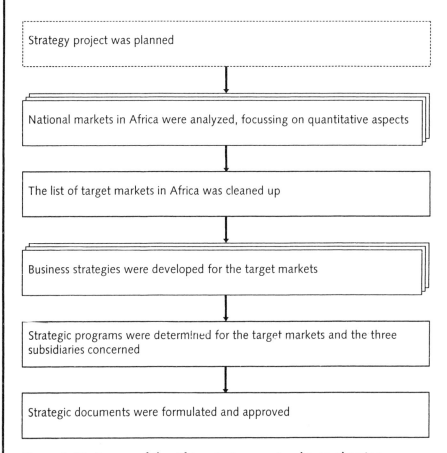

Figure 5-10: Course of the Africa strategy review by an elevator manufacturer

After setting the scope and the timing of the project, analysis of the markets in the various African countries began. Subsidiaries in France, Italy and Switzerland were responsible for this, as it was these companies which had handled the projects there. Using current market data and internal figures and after an initial evaluation of threats and opportunities, the steering committee updated the priorities for the different countries. Next, one of the three subsidiaries was responsible for producing or updating the strategy for each country. After discussing the country strategies, the steering committee put together strategy implementation programs for the country markets and for the three subsidiaries concerned. After this workshop the country strategies were all reformulated according to a single framework and an overall Africa strategy was produced which was approved by the company's board of directors.

If we compare this procedure with the process put forward in Figure 5-8, we see that the project had a more narrowly defined objective. In both analysis and planning only country strategies were discussed; the company as a whole and the product groups were not part of the project. So the steps relating to these could be left out. But assessment of the priority country markets had to be brought into the process. Usually this is not considered a matter for the project because invested capital in the country markets hampers the companies from quickly switching priorities. The elevator manufacturer, however, marketed products in Africa exclusively through dealers, so the company had the ability to shift its focus of activity relatively quickly. Because of this, the extra step in the process was a valuable one.

Finally **Figure 5-11** shows which process seems suitable for which type of company, with the companies classified into the same six types as in Figure 4-4 where standard systems of strategic documents were introduced. Thus the reader can see the connection between the different planning processes and the documents resulting from them.

	One product group in one industry market	Several product groups in one industry market	Several product groups in several industry markets
One geographical market	Simplified process	Standard process as in Figure 5-1	Extended process as in Figure 5-7
Several geographical markets	Standard process as in Figure 5-1	Extended process as in Figure 5-8	Extended process as in Figure 5-9

Figure 5-11: Process types and company types

5.5.3 Adapting the process to deal with specific strategic questions

In section 5.5.1 we saw that, in addition to company structure, a specific strategic question can also demand an adaptation of the process.

There is one specific strategic question of great practical importance, especially for small and medium-sized companies. This is to evaluate foreign markets and, if appropriate, to plan how to open them up. When companies find their home markets stagnating and foreign competitors forcing their way in, often leading to fierce competition and loss of margin, then they will need to develop a strategy for internationalization.

Figure 5-12 shows a process for producing an internationalization strategy. The company we are considering here is active in its home market only and has a number of product groups within the same industry. In cases where the company has only one product group, the process of strategic planning is much simpler. In cases where there are a number of industry markets, the process becomes more complicated.

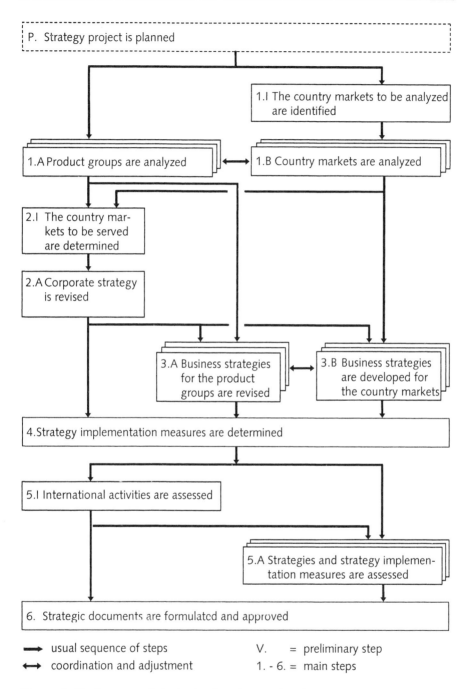

Figure 5-12: Process of strategic planning to develop an
internationalization strategy

As we can see in Figure 5-12, the steps which must be worked through are basically the same as in the standard process. However, in this project some of the problems will become very complex and for this reason the steps have been sub-divided. We thus have three steps which focus specifically on the particular objective of the strategy project, labeled in the figure with the letter I (Internationalization strategy). The outcome of these steps will be decisive for the success of the project:

- In Step 1.I, it is necessary to make a selection of countries to be analyzed. This is necessary because of cost: it becomes very expensive to study in detail a whole range of different country markets. However, it is important not to exclude attractive markets at this stage, otherwise the result of the planning process will not be satisfactory.
- In Step 2.I, it is necessary to determine the foreign markets in which positions will be built up during the planning period.
- Finally, in Step 5.I, the prospective activities in new countries have to be globally assessed. In particular it will be necessary to look again thoroughly at possible risks and at the financing of the strategic implementation programs.

An example of the development of an internationalization strategy can be found in **Inset 5-4**.

Inset 5-4: The production of an internationalization strategy for telephone sets

In the middle of the eighties a medium sized Western European company was producing telephone exchanges for public authorities, switchboards and telephone units. The exchanges generated a large proportion of their turnover in export markets, while turnover for the other two product groups came mainly from the home market. The national post and telecommunications authority was an exclusive customer, renting switchboard and telephone units to their customers. With impending deregulation of the markets for these product groups, the company was looking at considerable falls in turnover and profit margins. Opening up markets in other countries was intended to compensate to some extent for the erosion of the company's position in the home market.

The company management decided to follow a two-phase approach. The first phase was to see the creation of new foreign markets for the company's telephone sets. The second step would be to exploit the new customer relations to market the switchboard systems in these countries, too.

The introduction of a new range of telephones would be the occasion for the leap into export markets. For this reason the development of the internationalization strategy was conducted in parallel with preparations for production of the new telephone models. The steps in developing the internationalization strategy were as follows:

- First there was a quick initial analysis of foreign countries, using technical, cultural and economic criteria to select a number of markets for further analysis: In order to keep to a minimum the need for technical modifications to products, countries were selected where the telephone system had similar technical characteristics to the system in the home country. In view of the fact that language problems can act as entry barriers, only English, French or German speaking countries were considered. The final criterion in the initial selection was that prices for telephone sets should be above the average.
- The initial review threw up five countries which were then analyzed in detail. Using local consultants, the company carried out a strategic analysis of the appropriate telecommunications markets in each country. In addition there was an evaluation of possible partners and initial contacts with them took place.
- In order to concentrate its limited financial and human resources, the company decided to focus initially on two countries where market positions would be built up during the planning period.
- The next step was to produce market entry strategies for these two countries. Once more consultants with knowledge of the local markets were brought in to help.
- The next step was to plan the details and the timing for implementation of the strategy. The programs covered a wide range of tasks from the initial advertising campaign to the putting in place of the logistics for distribution and repair of the telephone sets. To ensure that the company would be present on the

ground, priority was given to negotiations with potential partners.
- Finally the two strategies were reassessed for their feasibility and
financial plans were drawn up covering the five following years.
These were required as a condition for obtaining approval of the
internationalization strategy from the governing board.

A comparison of this process with the standard procedure in Figure
5-12 shows that they resemble each other very closely. The essential difference is that there was no need in the company for a revision of corporate strategy or of the strategy for the product group
of telephone sets. The corporate strategy explicitly planned the
opening up of foreign markets with the telephone sets in the first
phase and therefore did not require revision. There was also no
need to adjust the strategy for the product group of telephone
sets. It had been revised in connection with the production of a
new generation of products and together with the corporate strategy provided the basic framework within which this strategy project took place.

5.5.4   Final remarks

Section 5.5 has been concerned with the question of when and how
to adapt the standard process for strategic planning. It has led us to a
better understanding of the process of strategic analysis and planning.
In Parts III to VI, we now focus on each step and provide recommendations as to the methods and content when working through the
process. To ensure clarity, the structure and most of the content of
Parts III to VI will follow the lines of the basic process as presented in
Figure 5-1.

6   The strategic analysis and planning toolbox

6.1   Important tools of strategic analysis and planning

In Chapter Five, an integrated process for strategic analysis and planning was introduced. In section 5.3, which briefly describes the steps in this process, reference was made to certain well-known analysis and planning tools, such as, the portfolio methods. But many other important tools or methods for strategic management exist, and in Chapter Six, an overview is now given. At the same time, the Chapter shows where and how these methods can be used within the process described in Chapter Five.

The literature on strategic management proposes numerous methods of analysis and planning which can be used to solve more or less closely defined problems. To some extent different terms are in use for the same or similar methods. For example, strengths and weaknesses analysis and competitor analysis are very similar in practice: each of these methods focuses on a company's strengths and weaknesses relative to those of its most dangerous competitors. These two methods are also, to a certain extent, similar to benchmarking, in which company performance in a particular activity is compared with best practice. This may give a company clues as to where it can focus to improve weak points and to maintain company strengths. The company used for benchmarking purposes need not necessarily be a direct competitor, but in practice this is often the case, and here we speak of competitive benchmarking (Miller & Dess, 1996, p. 133).

As there are so many different methods of analysis and planning, it is not easy to give an overview. Our approach in doing so is practical, rather than academic. **Figure 6-1** presents the methods of strategic analysis and planning which, in our experience, can be selected as being the most important. We have proceeded as follows:

- Methods with similar objectives and procedures, and which are not in practice perceived as being different methods are combined in a single category.
- Not included here are methods which focus only on the collection of information, such as the delphi method or other methods in

market research. Similarly, we have excluded statistical procedures for processing data or forecasting, such as regression analysis or the extrapolation of trends. Such methods can be considered as supporting tools which are used in strategic analysis and planning in combination with one of the methods listed in Figure 6-1.

- Analysis of resources
- Balanced scorecard
- Boston Consulting Group portfolio method;
  Market growth - market share portfolio method
- Defining of the strategic businesses;
  Division of the company activities into strategic business fields
  and strategic business units
- General Electrics and McKinsey portfolio method;
  Market attractiveness - competitive strengths portfolio method
- Generic business strategies;
  Generic competitive strategies
- Global environmental analysis
- Identifying strategic success factors;
  Identifying criteria for customer choice
- Industry segment analysis;
  Customer segments and sub-markets analysis
- Market system analysis
- Network of success potentials;
  Network of competitive advantages
- Scenario analysis
- Stakeholder value analysis
- Strategic program planning;
  Implementation program planning
- Strengths and weaknesses analysis;
  Competitor analysis;
  Benchmarking
- Structural analysis of an industry;
  Five forces model
- Structural analysis within an industry;
  Strategic groups model
- Value chain analysis

Figure 6-1: The most important methods of strategic analysis and planning

A description of the tools is not provided here as each is explained in detail in Parts III to Part VI, together with a description of the relevant step in the planning process in which it may be applied. However, what is important here is to see how these methods fit into our strategic planning process. In addition, the tools can also be considered in terms of the three sections of strategic analysis: the global environment, the relevant industries and the company itself. The next section addresses these two questions.

6.2   Allocating the tools to the three sections of strategic analysis and to the steps in the strategic planning process

To give the reader a clear overview, first the strategic analysis and planning tools will be considered in terms of the three sections of strategic analysis. In the second step, we will match them up to the correct steps in the strategic analysis and planning process.

In the strategic analysis, we distinguish three sections: the global environment, the relevant industries and the company itself.

Matching the methods to the three sections is a straightforward matter:

- As well as global environmental analysis itself, the method of scenario analysis can be used to examine the environment, as it also deals with the prediction of developments and future events. Scenario analysis is more sophisticated and provides superior quality, but it is a much more expensive method, and is therefore used only where there is great uncertainty about developments in relevant parts of the environment.
- To examine the relevant industry, we can use all those methods which deal with the market and the relationships between competitors. Market system analysis and industry segment analysis provide a view of the structure of the market. The link between the market and the competitors is made with the identification of strategic success factors; these show the demands that customers have with regard to the market offer. Porter's structural analysis of an industry

uses five forces to explain competitive intensity in an industry (1980, p. 3 ff.). A more differentiated view of the competitive situation can be obtained by looking at strategic groups; this can be done with the help of Porter's structural analysis within an industry (1980, p. 126 ff.).

- The two portfolio methods each allow an analysis of the attractiveness of the industries in which the company competes and of the competitive strength of its various activities. On the basic of this work, the portfolio methods can be used to specify future target market positions for the businesses. With this combination of external and internal aspects, the portfolio methods are attributed to the relevant industries and the company itself.

- The remaining methods of analysis and planning belong in the third section: the company itself. Analysis of stakeholder values clarifies the overriding objectives the strategies must reach. The strength and weakness analysis shows where a basis for the future strategies can be found and what the gaps are which need to be filled or worked around. The definition of the strategic businesses provides a strategic view of a company with different activities and provides a future-oriented basis for strategic decisions at the corporate level. Resource analysis identifies and evaluates the various physical, intangible, financial and organizational resources in a company and its different divisions. It highlights key resources which should be maintained or strengthened. Value chain analysis (Porter, 1985, p. 33 ff.) shows the links between the resources and the market offers. Generic business strategies and networks of success potentials are two tools which allow businesses to plan their future strategy. Finally, the strategic programs will define packages of implementation measures, while balanced scorecards ensure that the strategic goals are respected in daily business.

Fitting these tools into the strategic planning process is less straightforward than matching them to the sections of strategic analysis. The reason for the difficulty lies in the fact that a majority of the methods can be used in a number of different steps. One example is the five forces model, which could be applied in Step One "Strategic analysis", in Step Two "Developing the corporate strategy" and in Step Three "Developing the business strategies". It would, of course, be unwise to use a tool two or three times: this would provide a poor return in terms of the relationship between cost and usefulness. Here we recommend using each method once only, as follows:

- In the strategic analysis in Step One, the principal task of the strategy development team is to put together a basic set of data. For this reason, Step One requires methods which collate and structure data.
- Methods which diagnose opportunities and threats and identify strategic options belong in Step Two and Step Three.
- The tools which are designed to support the implementation of strategies effectively and efficiently are used in Step Four.

Despite these principles, the attribution of the various methods to the steps remains a subjective matter. Our view is that the tools should be used as follows:

- Five methods are recommended for put together a basic set of data in the strategic analysis phase. Global environmental analysis will throw light on the broad environment for the company's activities, while for each business a view of the market as a system is required. The analysis of the market should be further specified by looking at customer demands and identifying strategic success factors. By means of strengths and weaknesses analysis, the company's competitive position can be compared with those of its chief competitors. Finally, the key stakeholder values for the company as a whole must be analyzed.
- To provide a firm basis for defining corporate strategy, it is sometimes necessary to look at future environmental developments in detail. Here scenario analyses can be carried out for the industry markets concerned. In addition, the competitive situation in the industry markets can be examined with structural analysis of industries. Where necessary structural analysis within industry can also be carried out. Following on from the definition of the strategic businesses, one of the two portfolio methods should be used to provide a portfolio analysis and to develop and assess options at the corporate level.
- For the development of business strategies in Step Three, an industry segment analysis is recommended for each industry market. For the businesses, value chain analysis and resource analysis should be undertaken. On the basis of these analyses, for each business the future generic business strategy and the future network of success potentials can be determined.

- Definition and planning of the strategic programs and the specifications for balanced scorecards are tasks which can clearly be allocated to Step Four, in which the implementation measures are fixed.

Figure 6-2 shows the allocation of the eighteen methods to the three sections of analysis and to Steps One to Four of the strategic planning procedure.

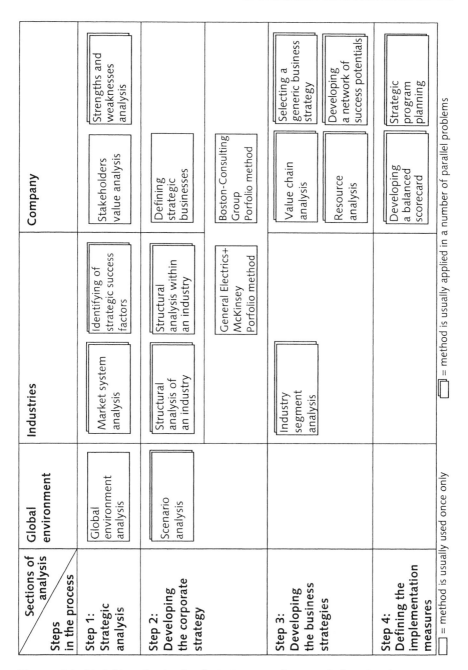

Steps in the process / Sections of analysis	Global environment	Industries		Company	
Step 1: Strategic analysis	Global environment analysis	Market system analysis	Identifying of strategic success factors	Stakeholders value analysis	Strengths and weaknesses analysis
Step 2: Developing the corporate strategy	Scenario analysis	Structural analysis of an industry	Structural analysis within an industry	Defining strategic businesses	
			General Electrics+ McKinsey Porfolio method	Boston-Consulting Group Porfolio method	
Step 3: Developing the business strategies		Industry segment analysis		Value chain analysis	Selecting a generic business strategy
				Resource analysis	Developing a network of success potentials
Step 4: Defining the implementation measures				Developing a balanced scorecard	Strategic program planning

□ = method is usually used once only ⧉ = method is usually applied in a number of parallel problems

Figure 6-2: Matching the tools of strategic analysis and planning to analysis sections and planning steps

Part III

Strategy project planning and strategic analysis

In the proposed process for strategic planning two steps precede the development of strategies. These are (1) the planning of the strategy project and (2) strategic analysis. Although these steps are not essential to the determining of future success potentials, they are worth including because they allow an efficient and thus cost-effective resolution of the problems of strategy formulation in Steps Two and Three. The extra effort invested in the Preliminary Step and Step 1 is normally more than compensated for by the more rapid and less expensive solution of the steps which follow. In addition, thorough project planning improves the quality of the strategies resulting from the project.

Figure III-1 presents the process of strategic planning. The first two steps, which are dealt with here in Part Three, have been outlined in bold.

For these first two steps Part Three presents recommendations both on procedure and on content. There are two chapters:

- Chapter Seven looks at the preliminary step: the planning of the project. We begin by showing why the development of strategies should be treated as a project. We then go on to discuss the different problems to be solved in this planning step.
- Chapter Eight moves on to Step One of the heuristic procedure: strategic analysis. First we show why a strong information base must be established before strategic decisions are made. Next the content and outcomes of strategic analysis are examined. We continue with an overview of important methods of analysis and then go on to a closer examination of the methods which tend to be used most often in strategic analysis. The chapter closes with a number of recommendations on practical matters in carrying out strategic analysis.

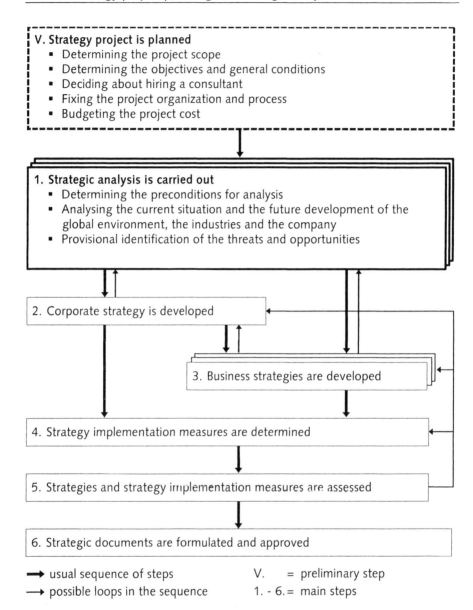

V. Strategy project is planned
- Determining the project scope
- Determining the objectives and general conditions
- Deciding about hiring a consultant
- Fixing the project organization and process
- Budgeting the project cost

1. Strategic analysis is carried out
- Determining the preconditions for analysis
- Analysing the current situation and the future development of the global environment, the industries and the company
- Provisional identification of the threats and opportunities

2. Corporate strategy is developed

3. Business strategies are developed

4. Strategy implementation measures are determined

5. Strategies and strategy implementation measures are assessed

6. Strategic documents are formulated and approved

→ usual sequence of steps   V.   = preliminary step
→ possible loops in the sequence   1. - 6. = main steps

Figure III-1: Strategy project planning and strategic analysis as steps in the process of strategic planning

7   Project planning

7.1   Why strategic planning should be seen as a project

In most companies, short and medium term plans are produced or reviewed on an annual basis. There are usually guidelines or traditional practices which determine at what point in the year planning or updating occurs and how it is done. Because of this experience with short and medium term planning, most managers think of planning as a regular or cyclically occurring activity which proceeds in an almost routine fashion. It would be mistaken to think of strategic planning in this way. Decisions as to which markets to serve, what competitive strategies to follow and what investments to make in resources are too important to be approached in this spirit. All strategic decisions have the following characteristics:

- they deal with complex interrelationships
- they occur at irregular intervals
- they are always unique in their scope, in their questions and in the framework of preconditions to be met
- they have a long-term influence on the fate of the company

This description of strategic decision-making highlights features which are typically used to characterize projects. Approaching strategy development as a project is an obvious step to take first of all because of the good fit of these characteristics. There are, furthermore, good practical grounds for doing so. When a company's management undertakes to define a new strategy, it will not only be confronted with the strategy issues, but will also face methodological problems:

- There are often differing views as to what the documents are, which need to be produced and what they should contain.
- There may be disagreement about the overall procedure and the various analytical methods to be used.
- There may be disagreement too about the quality of the information needed as an input for the strategic decisions. There may be differing opinions about how much data is required to support these decisions, and how much time and money should be allocated to procuring the data.
- The possible decision to use an external consultant can be contro-

versial, as can be the exact scope of his or her role in the strategy development.

If these matters are discussed as they arise, at the same time as the issues themselves, the strategy development process can become inefficient and can lead to unsatisfactory results. Only if the strategy development project is first planned in detail is the strategy development team free to concentrate on the issues.

7.2   Overview of the topics of project planning

There are a number of different factors involved in planning a strategy project and we have therefore divided the planning into a number of subtasks. **Figure 7-1** gives our recommendation for the agenda of the project planning meeting. The results of the meeting should be approved by the person or body that initiated the strategy project and thus form the official project assignment.

The following sections examine the different topics of strategy project planning more closely.

7.3   Determining the project scope

One of the initial questions, which is of great importance, concerns the exact scope and content of the project. In large companies, it would be unusual for all unsolved strategic questions to be dealt with in a single project. Often the project initiator will have divided strategy problems among a series of projects which can take place either in sequence or in parallel. It is also common for strategy projects to focus only on certain specified businesses, product groups or geographical markets.

Drawing on our experience as strategy consultants, in **Figure 7-2** we give a summary of the most typical strategy projects which can arise.

1	Project scope
	1.1 Areas to be included
	1.2 Questions to be addressed
2	Objectives and boundary conditions of the project
	2.1 Objectives of the project
	2.2 Boundary conditions of the project
3	Support from a consultant
	3.1 Basic decision about hiring a consultant
	3.2 Possibly: Tasks of the consultant
	3.3 Possibly: Selection of the consultant
4	Project organization and team
	4.1 Project organization
	4.2 Members of the different committees and working groups
5	Process and milestones
	5.1 Project process
	5.2 Milestones
6	Project budget
	6.1 External costs
	6.2 Internal costs
7	A.O.B.

Figure 7-1: Agenda for a strategy project planning meeting

The figure shows how our approach to strategy development fits each of three categories of strategy project:

- In frames outlined in bold are the two types of project which can be approached using the standard process described in section 5.2.
- The types of project which are in ordinary frames are those which correspond to one of the processes explained in section 5.5.
- For those in frames with broken lines, no specific process has been recommended in Part II. These are nearly all less complex problems than those examined in Chapter Five and the necessary simplification of the process should cause no problems.

	One product group in one industry market	Several product groups in one industry market	Several product groups in several industry markets
One geographical market	Developing a product group strategy	Developing a company strategy and product group strategies	Developing a company strategy, division strategies and product group strategies
		Developing a product group strategy	Developing a division strategy and product group strategies
			Developing a product group strategy
	Developing an internationalization strategy	Developing an internationalization strategy	Developing an internationalization strategy
Several geographical markets	Developing a company strategy and country strategies	Developing a company strategy, product group strategies and	Developing a company strategy, division strategies, product group strategies and country strategies
	Developing a country strategy	Developing a product group strategy and country strategies	Developing a division strategy, product group strategies and country strategies
		Developing a country strategy	Developing a product group strategy and country strategies
			Developing a country strategy

☐ = strategy planning project following the standard process described in section 5.2

☐ = strategy planning project following a process described in section 5.5

⬚ = strategy planning project needing an adaptation of one of the processes described in chapter 5

Figure 7-2: Different types of strategy project and the appropriate methodological approach

7.4   Determining the objectives and boundary conditions of the project

The objective of a strategy project consists in the development of the required strategies. This is the main objective, but it can be useful to prescribe more precise objectives. **Inset 7-1** presents examples of how a project initiator can formulate specific requirements which constitute more specific objectives.

Specific objectives are optional, but in every case the boundary conditions must be identified. If this is not done, much time and money may go into unnecessary analysis and planning. Even more important than the unjustified costs of such inefficiencies will be the damage to motivation that can result.

There are two main types of boundary conditions for the planning process that need to be discussed for every strategy project:
- Mission statement, company culture and overriding objectives: how far must they be respected? Can variations be tested out?
- Finance: what financial means are available to implement the strategies? If, for example, a business can only invest what it has itself earned then there is no point in looking at growth strategies involving the acquisition of large competitors.

Inset 7-1: Examples of specific objectives in strategic projects

- The corporate strategy should produce a list of subsidiary companies which are to be sold off and a list of possible candidates for acquisition. It should also indicate the amount of finance required for the next six years which will have to be borrowed on capital markets.
- The business strategy should make recommendations as to development projects for the next three years and also indicate the level of investments required at the two plants X and Y for the same period.
- The business strategy must establish what increases in turnover and contribution margins can be expected for the next five years as a result of the decision to expand the company's involvement

in Germany. In addition, a budget must be produced for the next five years for necessary investments in marketing and sales.
- The internationalization strategy for Europe must select three target countries in which market positions are to be built up as the first priority. It must also determine which countries should form the second priority group. For all the remaining countries in Europe the strategy must explain the reasons why at present that country cannot be selected as a target market.
- The country strategy for Belgium must explain what the consequences of the closing of the factory at X will be. As a basis for negotiations with the Belgian government, it must also produce recommendations as to what activities in businesses A and B might be transferred to Belgium.

7.5   Deciding whether to hire a consultant

Consultancy firms are frequently used in strategy projects. If this is being considered, it is best to be clear about what functions the consultant should fulfil before choosing one.

As **Figure 7-3** indicates, a consultant can offer contributions at the levels of project management, methodology and the development of the content of the strategies. At each level different tasks to be carried out by the consultant can be identified.

Usually a consultant makes at least some contribution at all three levels. But as it can be seen in the figure, project leadership and the final choice of strategies should not be delegated to a consultant. They must instead be carried out by the managers involved in the project in order to ensure their commitment to the result of the planning process and subsequently to guarantee their support for the implementation of the strategies.

Clear agreement about the consultant's functions facilitates the choice of the appropriate consultant. It also helps to define the contractual arrangements with the consultancy firm selected.

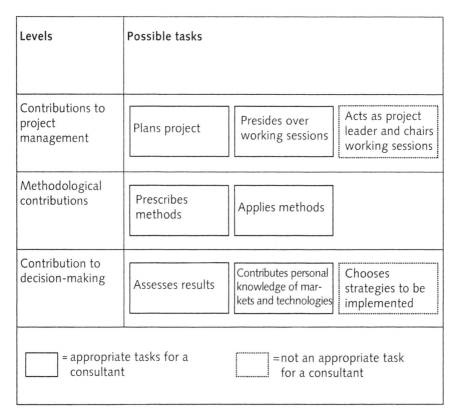

Levels	Possible tasks		
Contributions to project management	Plans project	Presides over working sessions	Acts as project leader and chairs working sessions
Methodological contributions	Prescribes methods	Applies methods	
Contribution to decision-making	Assesses results	Contributes personal knowledge of markets and technologies	Chooses strategies to be implemented

☐ = appropriate tasks for a consultant   ⬚ = not an appropriate task for a consultant

Figure 7-3: Possible functions of a strategy consultant

7.6   Fixing the project organization

A further important subtask in planning a strategy project concerns the project organisation and the appointment of the strategy team.

The project organization depends to a large degree on the scope of the project:

- Where the project is only examining a single business and one geographical market a simple structure is adequate. All that is required are two groups: a decision group and a working group. **Figure 7-4** gives the composition of the groups and their principal tasks.
- If a number of businesses and/or geographical markets are being

examined, then there will have to be a larger number of working groups, working in parallel. These will need to be coordinated by a steering committee, which will also be responsible for synthesizing the results and presenting them to the decision group. **Figure 7-5** presents a recommended organization for such strategy projects.

Decision group
- Project leader
- Members of the board and managers responsible for the businesses included in the project
- Optionally: Selected members of the working group
- Optionally: Consultants

Main tasks
- Determines the objectives and boundary conditions of the project
- Discusses and approves the results of analysis
- Discusses the strategic options and makes the selection
- Approves the final documents

Working group
- Project leader
- Selected members of the management team
- Optionally: Consultants

Main tasks
- Carries out strategic analysis
- Determines and assesses the strategic options
- Formulates the strategic documents

Figure 7-4: Project organization for simple strategy projects

In choosing the project team the following rules should be respected:

- The project leader and the leaders of the working groups should be the line managers responsible for the businesses being analyzed and planned. If, for example, one of the companies in a diversified internationally active group is producing a business strategy, the project leader should be the chief executive of that company. In such a situation it is desirable too that the country managers reporting to him should lead the working groups developing the country strategies. Having the same persons responsible for planning and for implementing the strategies is desirable from the point of view of motivation and increases the likelihood that the strategies produced will be concrete and realizable.
- Larger strategy projects require a project coordinator who is freed

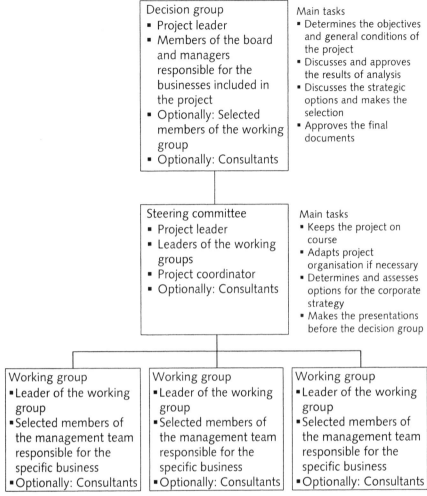

Figure 7-5: Project organization for complex strategy projects

from some of his normal duties for the duration of the project and is asked to give a considerable amount of his time to the project. This is required for him to be able to manage project duties such as organizing meetings, managing documentation and keeping the

project on schedule.
- The members of the working groups must be chosen with care. They need to meet three requirements. First, they must cover a wide range of knowledge: in order to determine the future direction of the company, thorough knowledge of marketing, technology, and finance is necessary. Secondly, every working group must include expertise on the methods of strategic analysis and planning. Often this can only be guaranteed by bringing in consultants. Thirdly, the group needs to have working time at its disposal. This third requirement means that in addition to senior and junior managers, trainees can be usefully included in the working groups.

7.7   Fixing the process and the milestones of the project

The planning of a strategy project also requires fixing the process and the deadlines for the completion of each stage.

It can happen that a company already has a procedure for running strategy development projects which is proven and accepted. If not, this book is of course intended to be of assistance:
- Section 5.2 presented a recommended standard process with seven stages.
- Section 5.5 showed how this standard procedure can be adapted according to the specific situation of the company.

These two sections should thus provide a good basis for defining the project process.

Once the process has been fixed, deadlines for each step must be set. A brisk pace is desirable, but there is no point in being too ambitious: most project group members will also have their regular duties to perform during the project and will therefore not be able to devote themselves entirely to strategic planning.

Inset 7-2 gives the course of a strategy project for producers and distributor of beer and non-alcoholic drinks operating at a national level.

Inset 7-2: Course of a strategy project in a company producing and distributing beer and non-alcoholic drinks

The company in question was created at the beginning of the nineties through a merger between two competitors. At the time the project began, the company produced and sold a number of beer brands on the home market. It also owned a range of different mineral water springs. Soft drinks were also produced at these sites and the product range contained both own brands and brands produced under license. The company was also a wholesaler distributing a full range of beverages.

As a result of the merger, a strategy project was undertaken to define the future direction and to provide the strategic foundation for the organization of the new company. In the first phase the project team concentrated on corporate strategy. In the second phase a strategy for non-alcoholic drinks was developed, with the development of a strategy for beer being deferred. The managers of the various breweries continued to follow their existing brand strategies. The wholesaling activity did not have any existence as a separate organizational unit at the time the project began. The various operations were either directly under the control of the group management or were subordinated to one of the breweries. Building on the corporate strategy, a restructuring project for the drinks wholesaling activities was also undertaken in Phase Two, with the aim of reorganizing it into a single unit.

Figure 7-6 shows the course of the project. As you can see, both phases of the project largely followed the standard process described in Chapter Five. In Phase One no business strategies had to be developed, so there is no step for this in the figure. In addition, the strategic analysis could be concluded quickly since the only data that had to be obtained was that required for the portfolio analysis and planning and this mainly proceeded on the basis of internal information. In addition, the development of strategies for non-alcoholic drinks in Phase Two followed the process described in Chapter Five. However, in Phase Two, unlike Phase One, the group not only determined the overall corporate strategy of the division, but also developed the business strategies for the brands and product groups.

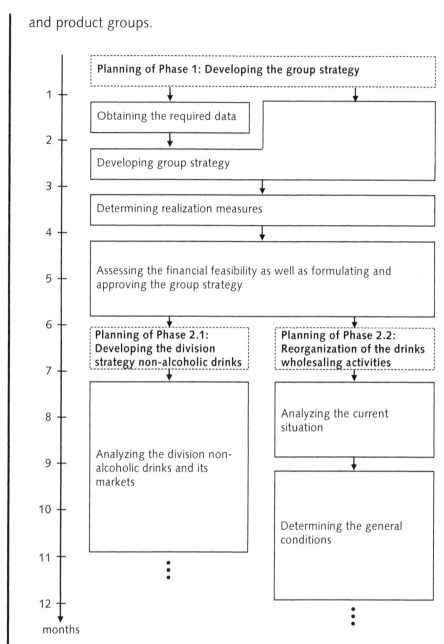

Figure 7-6 : Steps in the strategy project for a drinks group

7.8   Budgeting the project cost

The final task in project planning is budgeting for the cost of the project. The strategy project can be budgeted in the same way as other company projects and the company will usually already have existing guidelines as to how this should be done.

The budget should take into account the totality of the costs involved in producing the strategies. Costs arising from the implementation of the strategies are not included in the working budget for the analyzing and planning process. They have to be determined in the strategic decisions during Steps 2 to 4 of the process.

Inset 7-3 gives the budget for an internationalization strategy project for a producer of telephone sets.

Inset 7-3: Budgeting for the development of an internationalization strategy for a producer of telephone sets

In the middle of the eighties Company A was a medium sized company producing telephone exchanges for public authorities, switchboards for companies and telephone sets. The exchanges generated a large proportion of their turnover in export markets, while turnover for the other two product groups came mainly from the small home market. The national post and telecommunications authority was an exclusive customer, renting the telephone sets to their customers. With impending deregulation of the markets for these product groups, the company was looking at considerable falls in turnover and profit margins. Opening up markets in other countries was intended to compensate to some extent for the erosion of the company's positions in the home market.

Figure 7-7 presents the budget plan for the development of an internationalization strategy for telephone sets.

We would like to add the following brief notes on this budget:
- The total budget seems high, and therefore there is a great

temptation to dispense with those services provided externally. A great deal of money could be saved, in particular, by dropping the consultants for the target overseas markets. But it is vitally important to resist this temptation. The cost of using consultants should be seen in the context of the high investments required for market entry and the accompanying risk.

- As the example shows, the internal costs incurred by the strategy project are so high that there is good reason to budget them. Our example assumes a monthly average salary of $6,000 for the managers involved. Counting 13 monthly salaries, 40% extra for social costs and a working year with 2,200 hours, this means that the internal cost per hour per employee is $50.

	Internal costs per working hour at $50	Strategy consultants	Consultants for overseas markets
Phase A: Selection of overseas markets to be investigated	15,000	10,000	
Phase B: Analysis of five overseas markets with good potential for success	45,000	20,000	250,000
Phase C: Selection of two or three markets to be targeted during the planning period	10,000	5,000	
Phase D: Development of country strategies for markets selected in Phase C	30,000 to 40,000	10,000 to 15,000	60,000 to 90,000
Phase E: Planning of implementation measures	20,000 to 30,000	10,000 to 15,000	20,000 to 30,000
Phase F: Critical reassessment of strategies and approval by the board	15,000	10,000	
Total costs excluding travel and other expenses	135,000 to 160,000	65,000 to 75,000	330,000 to 370,000
		530,000 to 605,000	

Figure 7-7: Project budget for the development of an internationalization strategy for telephone sets

8   Strategic analysis

8.1   The need for strategic analysis before strategies are developed

Strategic analysis is the first step in our process, placed before the development of corporate strategy in Step Two and the development of business strategies in Step Three. There is no denying, however, that it is rather difficult to carry out strategic analysis independently of the development of the strategies. So before dealing with the content and methodology of strategic analysis, let us first see why strategic analysis is the first separate step in our process.

Information is only required to the extent that it is needed to answer strategic questions. It is only the information relevant to identifying and evaluating strategic options which is necessary. From this point of view, we would not wish to place strategic analysis as a separate independent step at the beginning of the process of strategic planning. However, practical experience has shown that there is a body of information which will, with all probability, be necessary for the development of strategies. To collect this data in one concentrated move at the outset, before the determining of strategies, is more efficient, both in terms of time and money, than trying to put together the data during later stages, in a number of different steps.

However there are two disadvantages in having a separate Step One for strategic analysis before strategy development:

- On the one hand it can turn out that information collected in Step One is not relevant for determining strategies and has thus been collected to no purpose. But here experience suggests that this will apply to relatively little of the information collected.
- On the other hand it can happen that the basic set of information does not contain all the data needed for the development of strategies. If important information is not available when we come to determine strategies, the missing analysis will have to be carried out during the later phases of development of corporate and business strategies. How large these extra information needs are will depend on the particular strategic questions and options.

8.2   Content and conclusions of strategic analysis

As we have seen, it is through strategic planning that the long-term development of the company and its businesses is determined. For this to be possible, an overview is required of the global environment, of the relevant markets and of the company concerned. So strategic analysis must provide a variety of types of information.

The analysis is thus divided into three sections: the global environment, the industries concerned and the company itself.

The environment can be considered under five headings:
- economic conditions and developments
- social and cultural developments
- ecological developments
- technological change
- political and legal developments

Documenting changes in the global environment must involve analysis of the regulatory bodies. These include state institutions, employers' and industry groupings, trade unions and consumer organizations. Information provided by these groups must be integrated into the five categories for the environmental analysis.

The most complex field for analysis is the industry. Following Porter (1980, p. 5 and p. 32 f.), we define an industry as a group of companies offering similar products and services and thus in direct competition with each other. Industry analysis is divided into three categories:
- buyers' market
- competitive situation
- suppliers' markets

As large companies are often active in more than one industry, parallel analyses will be required for each industry.

The third area for analysis is the company itself. According to Johnson and Scholes (2002, p. 145 ff. and p. 156 ff.), there are two aspects:
- stakeholder demands
- processes, resources and competencies

A stakeholder is an individual or a group with an interest in the company (Freeman & Reed, 1983, p. 89). Important stakeholders are shareholders, employees, customers, suppliers, and the general public.

While stakeholder demands can be documented for the company as a whole, even when dealing with large diversified companies, processes, resources and competencies always have to be analyzed separately for each industry.

Strategic analysis culminates in the identification of threats and opportunities, both at the level of individual activities and for the firm as a whole. However, this is intended to be merely a provisional assessment of the company's situation, which will be reassessed and further specified during Steps Two and Three of the strategic planning process.

Figure 8-1 summarizes the information presented in this section so far.

As the goal of the analysis is the recognition of threats and opportunities, it follows that a view of the situation based on the past is not sufficient. Threats and opportunities lie in the future. Identifying threats and opportunities therefore absolutely requires that the analysis should examine not only past developments but also future ones. In this connection, it is useful to look far into the future, well beyond the planning period itself. How far this should extend will depend on the individual case; it is not possible to set a fixed general time period valid in all cases, whether for planning or for analysis. The reason for this lies in the purpose of strategic planning: what we have to do is to plan measures for the maintenance and construction of strategic success potentials. The time period for these measures depends on the industry and the company. For example, an electricity company will require a longer period covered by analysis and a longer planning horizon than a management consultancy firm. **Figure 8-2** shows the differences between these two types of company.

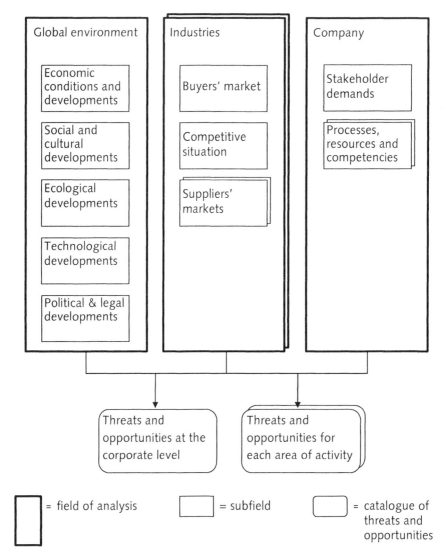

Figure 8-1: Content and outcomes of strategic analysis

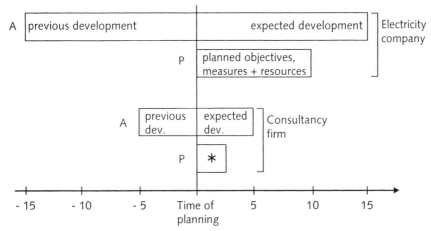

A = period covered by analysis
P = planning horizon
* = planned objectives, measures + resources

Figure 8-2: Strategic analysis and planning periods for an electricity company and a management consultancy firm

8.3 Description of the applied methods

8.3.1 The choice of the methods applied in strategic analysis

In strategic analysis in Step One it is a matter of providing a picture of the current situation and of possible developments. Less important are the assessment of the situation and the identification of options. So the methods to be used should focus on collating and structuring data. Five concrete methods are recommended for use at this stage:

- global environmental analysis
- market system analysis or analysis of the value creation process
- identification of strategic success factors or identification of criteria for customer choice
- strengths and weaknesses analysis or competitor analysis or benchmarking
- stakeholder value analysis

We will now present each of these five methods.

8.3.2 Global environmental analysis

Global environmental analysis focuses on developments in the company's environment, identifying trends which could have a major impact on the company's situation.

With an objective such as this, the method has a very wide scope. It is
this which constitutes the main danger: its application requires some
limits, otherwise in an extreme case it will produce no more than a
superficial prognosis for the future of a country or of the whole world.
Clearly a result like this cannot make a substantial contribution to the
development or assessment of strategies. A global environmental
analysis which aims to provide a framework of conditions for the development of strategies and clues to the assessment of strategies can,
following Aeberhard (1996, p. 118 ff.) be carried out in four steps:

1. The first step is to determine the objects of analysis: which elements
   in the environment will influence the development of the company? For larger companies active in different industries and geographic areas, normally a number of important elements will be
   identified, while companies concentrating on one specific market
   typically will have to select only a small number of elements. In
   simple cases there may be only one aspect to consider, for example
   a proposed change in legislation, such as the repeal of a law requiring the checking and servicing of oil storage tanks. For companies
   carrying out this work the global environmental analysis perhaps
   needs only to consider how this change will affect demand and
   prices.
2. For each of the elements selected in Step One, the developments
   up to the present and the current situation have to be described:
   concisely but with precision. Where relevant, quantitative data
   should be provided. For example, a power station based on coal
   would provide the figures for coal consumption for the past twenty
   years together with those for current coal reserves in the ground.
3. Facts about the past and present form the basis for prognoses
   about the future. How this prognosis is expressed will depend on
   the particular object of study and on what information is available
   for the past. The prognosis for the future may be limited to qualitative statements, but techniques for the extrapolation of trends can
   also be used. Prognoses produced with quantitative techniques

have to be checked carefully, for if a change in trends goes unrecognized, there may be a false basis for strategy development. For example it would be mistaken to extrapolate into the future the existing trend in demand for oil tank servicing if the repeal of the law requiring this will affect future demand.

4. Step Four should bring together the different data to produce an overview of future environmental development. At this stage it is necessary to consider the interactions between the trends identified how each development may influence the others. Trends may cancel each other out or may reinforce each other's effects. For example, in looking at the demand for potatoes in central and northern Europe, stagnation in population growth will increase the effects of lower per capita consumption. However, in the same region, the stagnation in population growth is not an important factor for the market for voice and data communication services. Here per capita demand is increasing sharply and there is overall growth.

8.3.3   Description of the market system

After examining the global environment of the company next we must look at the industry or industries concerned. First, for each relevant industry market, we need to capture the market system. In situations where there is a simple market structure, instead of a description of the market system, the value creation chain of the industry can be described.

Perhaps some readers will question the necessity of describing the market system. While it is true that most of those involved in the strategy project will know the market structure from their daily work, this analysis is nevertheless useful. There are two reasons for this: first, the members of the strategy group will establish a shared view and common language. Secondly the method provides a strategic view of the situation.

Kühn (1997, p. 20 ff.) recommends a five-step procedure:

1. First identify the markets whose systems are to be described. For a regionally based book retailer with a number of branches there is

only one market, whereas a diversified investment product company will only obtain a satisfactorily differentiated picture if it looks at each industry market separately. If the company operates internationally some of these industry markets will require to be analyzed country by country.

2. In the second step the boundaries of the market must be precisely defined, both geographically and in terms of products and/or services. It is important to define the relevant market rather than the served market. For example, the regionally based bookstore chain would include the nearby shopping center in its examination of the market and would also include new electronic media products.

3. Then for each market the actors must be identified. Generally what this means is:
   - the company and its competitors
   - the trade channels, perhaps separated into wholesalers and retailers,
   - the end consumers, typically divided into segments
   - external influencers of the market like consumer organizations, journalists etc.

4. On the basis of these elements the fourth step is to present the market as a system. **Figure 8-3** provides an example: the beer market in Switzerland in the mid-nineties.

5. Finally an estimate of the flow of goods, either in terms of quantity or money value, must be given. Figure 8-3 gives quantities in millions of litters. In order that the trends can be seen clearly in the chart, forecast values must be included alongside the current figures.

8.3.4   The identification of success factors

A strategic success factor is a variable which has an important effect on long-term success. As well as a number of general success factors which apply in all industries, each industry has its own industry-specific success factors (see **Inset 8-1**). The success factors are important because they reveal the dimensions of competition. It is in these important dimensions that competitive advantages can be constructed. For this reason it is important that the success factors of the

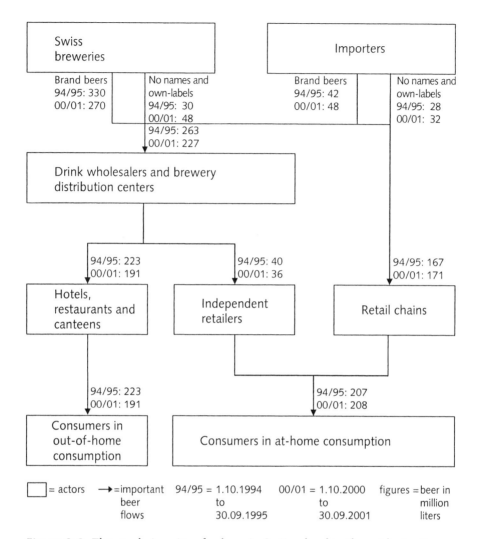

Figure 8-3: The market system for beer in Switzerland in the mid-nineties

industry or industries concerned are identified during strategic analysis.

Our approach builds on the work of Grant (2002, p. 95 ff.) and Heckner (1998, p. 161 ff.) and we recommend a six-step process:

1. First, determine the industries for which the strategic success factors must be identified.

2. For each industry, identify and evaluate user demands in respect of the offer. It is recommended to include both existing customers and non-customers. Information can be collected through semi-structured interviews or in workshops.

3. Parallel to this, for each industry an internal working group must determine the dimensions which govern the competition between different competitors. The main focus should be on what causes the company to win or to lose a sale. It is the answer to this question which reveals the competitive advantages and disadvantages of the company and the underlying industry - specific success factors.

4. In the fourth step the results of the two previous steps are compared. This produces a new overall list of industry-specific success factors. The two approaches to the identification of success factors usually do not lead to identical lists. There are two reasons for this: first the customers look at success factors at the level of the offer while the internal group normally concentrates on success factors at the level of resources. The second reason is that customer demands can sometimes be met in different ways. Quality, for example, may be important for customers, but this 'quality' can be provided partly through advertising or good customer relations. Customers systematically underestimate the influence of certain elements of the marketing mix and thus certain success factors will not be thrown up when the customers are researched. This fourth step, in which the results of Steps Two and Three are synthesized, requires a certain level of expert knowledge.

5. Next the various industry-specific success factors must be classified into two groups: standard success factors and dominant success factors. This distinction is important for planning the elements of the marketing mix (Kühn, 1997, p. 44 ff.): the dominant success factors are those which allow the possibility of differentiation from the competitors while standard success factors indicate dimensions in which a certain level has to be attained. An industry usually has only few dominant success factors and a larger number of standard success factors.

6. The importance of industry specific success factors can change. Therefore, especially for the dominant success factors, we need to ask ourselves whether their influence is likely to increase or decrease over time. The trends identified in the global environmental analysis should be brought into this discussion. In certain circum-

stances the emergence of new success factors must be recognized, for example, one thinks of the effects of e-commerce on booksell-ing.

Determining industry-specific success factors is an intellectually de-manding task. If both customers and non-customers are included, which we recommend, the analysis will also be expensive and time-consuming. The resultant success factors, however, form an important basis for analysis of strengths and weaknesses. They are also impor-tant for the formulation of business strategies in Step Three.

Inset 8-1: Two kinds of success factors

At the beginning of the sixties, Daniel (1961, p. 81 ff), who was working on the design of information systems, observed that a company's success was dependent on a small number of factors. His concept was later applied to strategic planning by Leidecker and Bruno (1984, p.23 ff).

In strategic planning it is important to distinguish between general success factors and industry-specific success factors (Kühn & Grünig, 2000, p. 92 ff.):

- General success factors are valid in all industries. Their effect on success is constant; they remain valid at all times. Because of this broad validity, general success factors are defined in a relatively abstract way.
- Industry-specific success factors apply to a more or less closely defined industry. Their effect on success may change over time. In comparison with general success factors they apply in a much more limited area and they are therefore generally given a more concrete definition. **Figure 8-4** shows the industry-specific suc-cess factors for steel producers and grocery retailing chains (Grant 2002, p. 98).

Empirical studies have tried to identify both general success factors and also industry-specific success factors. However, research which tries to identify industry-specific success factors suffers from two disadvantages:

- The results are valid only for a limited period, and the length of this period cannot be predicted.
- The results are relevant only for a limited number of companies.

Industry-specific success factors generally have to be identified by the companies themselves, as part of strategic analysis.

Success factors for grocery retailing chains	Success factors for steel producers
• Low cost operation requires •• operational efficiency •• scale-efficient stores •• large aggregate purchases to maximize buying power •• low wage costs • Differentiation requires •• large stores to allow wide product range •• convenient location •• easy parking	• Cost efficient through scale-efficient plants • Low cost location • Rapid adjustment of capacity to output • Low labor costs • In special steels and some special uses, scope for differentiation through quality

Figure 8-4: Industry-specific success factors for grocery retailing chains and steel producers

8.3.5 Analysis of strengths and weaknesses

With the help of strengths and weaknesses analysis (or competitor analysis, or benchmarking), we evaluate the company in comparison with competitors: market positions, market offers and resources are compared. In this way we can recognize where the fundamental elements for the future strategies lie and what the weaknesses are which must be either worked around or overcome.

We propose a five-step approach to strengths and weaknesses analysis:

1. First determine the areas of company activity which require a strengths and weaknesses profile. The answer to this important first question depends on the extent to which the company is diversified

and the geographical markets in which it operates. In a diversified company strengths and weaknesses analysis should be carried out for each division. It is also possible that a separate analysis will be required for each geographical market.

2. The greatest difficulty in strengths and weaknesses analysis is in determining the criteria for assessment. These criteria must be strategically relevant, both for the current situation and for the future. As we saw, the success factors fulfill this condition of strategic relevance. We therefore recommend basing the list of criteria on the industry specific success factors.

3. In Step Three the competitor or competitors to be included in the analysis must be determined. The strongest direct competitors should be selected.

4. In Step Four the data must be obtained. Usually much of this data is already available, for example in sales reports or competitors' publications. In some cases it can be worthwhile to consult industry experts or carry out customer research. In practice this fourth step is often omitted. The reason is that the members of the project team feel that they know the company and its competitors well enough already to be able to make a direct assessment of strengths and weaknesses. But experience shows that the knowledge in the strategy project group, not only about the competitors but even about their own firm, often has important gaps and can also be distorted by vested interests.

5. In Step Five the strengths and weaknesses profiles of the company and its strongest competitors are developed and compared. **Figure 8-5** presents a form which can be used to carry out this task. On the vertical axis, we find the criteria arranged according to the three categories of success potential. As Figure 8-5 is intended as a general tool, the criteria are formulated in a rather abstract way. On the horizontal axis, a nine-point scale is proposed for measuring the strengths and weaknesses of the company and its competitors. **Figure 8-6** shows the strengths and weaknesses profiles of two internationally operating manufacturers of hair products. As we can see, the criteria for assessing the market offers and the resources of the two competitors are based on the industry specific success factors and therefore more specific than the criteria in Figure 8-5.

Criteria \ Assessment	1	2	3	4	5	6	7	8	9
Market position									
• market share									
• change in market share									
• company image									
• profitability									
Market offer									
• scope of product range									
• depth of product range									
• quality of products									
• price									
• supplementary services									
• speed of executing orders									
Resources									
• ground and buildings									
• assets									
• financial strength									
• structures and processes									
• patents and licences									
• company name and brands									
• marketing and sales competencies									
• production and sourcing competencies									
• research and development comp.									
• quality and cost control competencies									
• management competencies									
• flexibility and capacity for change									

1 = very weak   3 = weak   5 = average   7 = strong   9 = very strong

Figure 8-5: Strengths and weaknesses analysis matrix

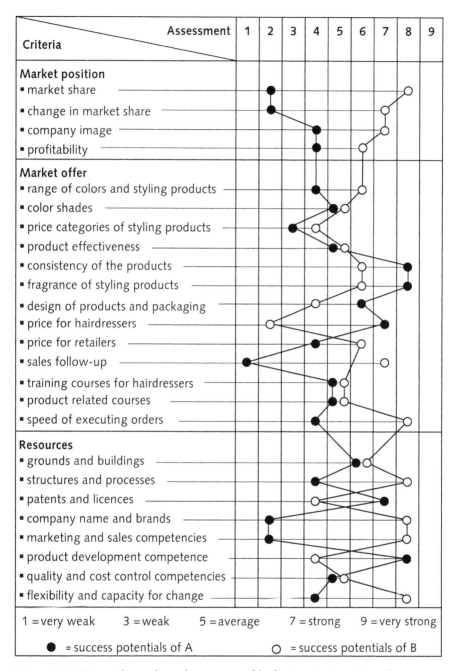

Figure 8-6: Strengths and weaknesses profile for two internationally operating manufacturers of hair products

8.3.6   Stakeholder value analysis

The purpose of strategies is to ensure that companies reach their overriding objectives. This usually means ensuring the survival of the company and the long-term production of a reasonable profit. If these are the only overriding objectives, then a stakeholder analysis is unnecessary and can be dispensed with. This is true, for example, if the only overriding objective is to maximize shareholder value. However, if shareholders are willing to make economic sacrifices in order to promote social, political, ethical or environmental goals, then these values must be made explicit. Non-economic aims, such as, for example, the protection of work or the pursuit of an environmentalist agenda, are only possible if the company's continuing existence is secure. Such aims therefore do not replace the pursuit of profit, they simply constrain it.

To analyze and harmonize values a three-step procedure is recommended (Aeberhard, 1996, p. 198 ff.; Ulrich, 1978, p. 51 ff.):

1. First the stakeholder groups to be included in the analysis must be identified, and representative individuals selected. The number of stakeholders involved will be greater or smaller according to the kind of owners and the size of the company. Management should always be included.
2. Next the values of these persons need to be collected, either in written form or orally. **Figure 8-7** can be a useful starting-point for this. It presents seven value dimensions and a number of different possible responses. It is important that all persons involved in the value analysis should share a common understanding of the terms used in this scheme and so an introductory session is necessary to make this clear. Individual value profiles can then be produced.
3. The final step is to hold a workshop at which the various different value profiles are compared and the differences discussed. In this way, possible conflicts can be uncovered. Sometimes it is even possible to harmonize the values. But if this cannot be achieved, it is the task of the project leaders to determine which values will be those that govern the development of strategies.

Dimensions	Possible answers				
Distribution of profit	As little as possible	Stable but modest	According to results, but tending to be modest	According to results, but tending to be high	As high as possible
Attitude to risk	As much security as possible	Low-risk activities acceptable		High-risk activities acceptable	Willing to take very high risks
Pursuit of social aims	Only if it does not affect financial performance	With small financial sacrifices		With large financial sacrifices	As long as the company's existence is not threatened
Relationship to government	Negative defensive positioning	Non-political		Politically active with a specific agenda	Maximum support and subordination to state
Pursuit of environmental concerns	Only if it improves financial performance	Only if it does not affect financial performance	With small financial sacrifices	With large financial sacrifices	As long as the company's existence is not threatened
Attitude to suppliers	Maximum value for money		Good value for money but with responsibility		Cooperation and partnership
Attitude to customers	Maximum profit on sales		Good profit on sales but with attention to genuine customer satisfaction		Cooperation and partnership with attention to genuine customer satisfaction

Figure 8-7: Scheme for developing value profiles

8.4   The process of strategic analysis

8.4.1   Overview of the process of strategic analysis

Strategic analysis is the first and often the most expensive step, in terms of both time and finance, in the strategic planning procedure. It requires three closely linked steps. An overview of these is given in **Figure 8-8**. Step 1.1 is described in detail in the next Section 8.4.2. This is the step which is decisive in determining the scope and quality of the strategic analysis. In contrast, Steps 1.2 and 1.3 are described only briefly in Section 8.4.3, as the application of the methods concerned has already been discussed and readers are familiar too with determining opportunities and threats.

8.4.2   Determining the preconditions for analysis

In Step 1.1 the areas to be analyzed are determined and then the methods to be used are specified. In this way the preconditions are set for effective and efficient realization of the analysis.

The markets and activities to be analyzed can be derived from the company's structure. The analysis usually focuses on the global environment, one or more industry markets, and the company itself. **Inset 8-2** illustrates how the market must be defined for a producer of babyfood.

The cost of obtaining and evaluating data for each industry market analyzed is potentially high, irrespective of the company's actual turnover or market share in that market. For this reason, less important areas of activity should not be included in the analysis. It is a good idea to fix a value for turnover or profit, either current values or values to be reached within three to five years, and to exclude activities likely to fall below this figure. In many cases a figure between 5% and 10% will be appropriate to determine which activities should be included in the analysis.

1.1 Determining the preconditions for analysis
   ▪ Determining the markets and activities to be analyzed
   ▪ Determining the methods and the resulting data quality

↓

1.2 Analyzing the current situation and the future development of global environment, industries and company activities
   ▪ Analyzing global environment with global environment analysis
   ▪ Analyzing the industry markets with market system analysis and identification of strategic success factors
   ▪ Analyzing the company activities with strengths and weaknesses analysis and, if necessary, stakeholder value analysis

↓

1.3 Provisional identification of opportunities and threats
   ▪ Provisional identification of the opportunities and threats at corporate level
   ▪ Provisional identification of the opportunities and threats for each activity

→ usual sequence of steps

Figure 8-8: The process of strategic analysis

Inset 8-2: Determining which market to analyze for a producer of baby food

The company concerned is a family business based in the south of Germany which produces and markets baby food. There are two product groups: ready cooked baby food for children between 6 and 18 months packaged in glass jars and dry cereal products packed in bags to which water or milk is added prior to consumption. The company has significant market share in each product category. The question was whether to limit the analysis to these two product groups. Once it was realized that competitors offering the whole range of baby food products enjoy competitive advantages as a result of the positive synergies between the product groups, the right decision was taken, namely to look at the whole baby food market with five product groups: milks, cereals, jars, biscuits and juices.

With internationally active companies there is also the question of whether to analyze the served industry markets by carrying out a separate analysis for each country market. If there is one global market with international competitors then this is unnecessary. This is the case, for example, for wholesalers of raw materials or in the container transport business. In contrast, for companies marketing medicines, the analysis would have to be country by country, as the structure of the markets can differ greatly from one country to another. In addition, there exist in this industry important competitors who only operate within one country or a limited number of countries. Global pharmaceutical companies will, however, probably wish to group countries into regions in order to obtain an overview of the situation.

The areas of activity selected will form the framework for determining the methods of analysis. This is the second problem within Step 1.1. **Figure 8-9** indicates the methods to be used for the six different types of company. Stakeholder value analysis does not appear here as in practice it is only rarely of relevance.

The different methods of analysis provide the data required for an assessment of the currently realized strategies and in order to develop strategic options. The quality of the data received from analysis will therefore influence the quality of strategic decisions. In addition the collection of data is generally the one task in a strategy project which requires most time and involves the greatest cost. It is therefore a good idea to set a target quality level for the data before starting the analysis. The following levels can be aimed at:

- Level I: Subjective assessments: Data collected on the basis of discussion in working groups and a small number of interviews with members of the board.
- Level II: Subjective assessments plus analysis of existing (secondary) data: As in Level I, but supplemented by systematic assessment of existing data from both internal and external sources.
- Level III: Subjective assessments, analysis of existing data and qualitative interviews: As in Level II, but supplemented by a certain number of interviews with customers, non-customers, and independent experts with knowledge of the markets concerned.
- Level IV: Subjective assessments, analysis of existing data,

	One product group in one industry market	Several product groups in one industry market	Several product groups in several industry markets
One geographical market	• For the whole company: •• global environment analysis •• market system analysis •• identification of strategic success factors •• strengths and weaknesses analysis	• For the whole company: •• global environment analysis •• market system analysis •• identification of strategic success factors •• strengths and weaknesses analysis	• For the whole company: global environment analysis • For every industry market/company division: •• global environment analysis •• market system analysis •• identification of strategic success factors •• strengths and weaknesses analysis
Several geographical markets	• For the whole company: global environment analysis • For every country market/country organization or for the whole company: •• market system analysis •• identification of strategic success factors •• strengths and weaknesses analysis	• For the whole company: global environment analysis • For every country market/country organization or for the whole company: •• market system analysis •• identification of strategic success factors •• strengths and weaknesses analysis	• For the whole company: global environment analysis • For every industry market/company division: •• market system analysis •• identification of strategic success factors •• strengths and weaknesses analysis In certain cases the three analytical methods applied to industry markets/company divisions must be carried out separately for each country market/country organization

Figure 8-9: The application of methods in strategic analysis

qualitative interviews and representative market studies: As in Level III, but supplemented with one or more representative market research studies focusing on important industry markets.

The considerable jumps in cost between the levels mean that in practice companies often choose the lowest level. This happens, for example, when a company's top managers go off for a seminar to develop the strategies. Here the danger is that some of the strategic problems will go unrecognized. A strategy review should be based on objective facts and we therefore recommend that the data should at least reach Level II: Usually the data for the market trends and market share developments is satisfactory, in this case, but what is missing is the equally important qualitative information about market-specific success factors and the success potentials of competitors. For this reason it is often a good move to carry out a limited number of interviews with customers, non-customers and other persons outside the company, and by this reach Level III. The representative market studies which would be required to attain the highest level in data quality are, however, rarely necessary. The considerable cost involved can only be justified in consumer markets where the psychological positioning of the market offers is very important. This is the case, for example, with cosmetics, soft drinks, and exclusive fashion wear.

To sum up, Level I generally does not provide a satisfactory basis for strategy planning and Level IV is only required in exceptional cases. Thus the choice generally falls between Level II with secondary data research and Level III with qualitative interviews.

8.4.3   Carrying out the analysis

Step 1.2 involves the use of methods which have been determined in step 1.1. Section 8.3 showed how each method is used.

Step 1.3 represents a provisional assessment which looks at opportunities and threats at the corporate level and for each of the activities included in the analysis. It is important that the diagnosis is clearly understood to be a provisional one. As the toolbox of strategic analysis and planning in Figure 6-2 shows, additional methods of analysis will be used in the development of corporate strategy and of business strategies in Steps 2 and 3. They may correct, extend or make more precise the opportunities and threats established here in Step 1.

Threats and opportunities are identified by comparing
• environmental developments and market developments with
• strengths and weaknesses of the company.

An opportunity arises when a change in the environment, especially in a market, aligns with an existing or potential strength within the company. In contrast, threats arise when environmental developments cannot be effectively anticipated because they come up against weaknesses in the company. **Inset 8-3** shows important threats and opportunities for a Swiss cigar manufacturer in the mid-eighties.

Inset 8-3: Threats and opportunities for a Swiss cigar manufacturer in the mid-eighties

The company has a wide range of products which are distributed under various brands and product names in Switzerland and Germany. In the middle of the eighties the product type which accounted for much of the turnover and the contribution margin was the stumpy cigar. This sells mainly in Bavaria and Switzerland to older, more conservative consumers, living in rural areas. The demographic structure of the demand for these products means that market volume is declining and the company's turnover is falling constantly despite its market domination.

In the mid-eighties the decline in turnover for their principal product led the management to undertake strategic analysis.

Figure 8-10 presents the most important threats and opportunities as a summary of the analysis.

Environmental development

Stumpy cigars are smoked mainly by older men in rural districts and because of demographic trends this customer segment is declining

Weakness

The company has more than 75% of its turnover in stumpy cigars.

Threat

If effective counter measures are not taken, the company will suffer a dramatic relative and absolute loss in market share in the cigar market

Environmental development

The cost of launching and supporting a brand is rising continually

Weakness

The company has a large number of brands and numerous product names for its different products

Threat

The company increasingly finds itself without sufficient resources to promote its different brands and product names

Environmental development

Younger, urban consumers of cigars have a significant preference for cigarilos. This is, besides expensive Havana - type cigars, the only product group within declining cigar market which is enjoying some slight growth

Strength

• The company owns the cigarillo brand Kuba which until now has not been heavily promoted. The brand name and lettering are attractive, especially to younger consumers.
• Good customer relations and a strong sales team allow the company to introduce or promote products quickly
• The company has available a large overall budget for advertising and product promotions.

Opportunity

Concentrate sales and marketing on the cigarillo brand Kuba

Figure 8-10: Environmental developments, strengths and weaknesses and resulting threats and opportunities for a cigar manufacturer

Part IV

Developing corporate strategies

Part IV deals with the development of corporate strategies. The corporate strategy must guarantee that the company will direct its activities at attractive markets where it can build or maintain an advantageous competitive position. The corporate strategy thus determines the long-term orientation and development of corporate activities.

The corporate strategy is the prime strategic document. In order to fulfil this function it must specify:

- the businesses the company will continue to operate, the new businesses it will set up and those businesses, if any, which the company will withdraw from
- the target competitive positions which the various businesses will have to achieve in their respective markets
- the amount of the investment which will be made in order to maintain or enlarge the strategic businesses.

The production of the corporate strategy is one of the two central steps in the process of strategic planning. **Figure IV-1** shows how the tasks involved fit into the overall process of strategic planning.

Part IV has four chapters:

- Chapter 9 deals with the identification of the strategic businesses. This involves specifying a limited number of product-market combinations with important turnover or contribution margins. The strategic view which results from this will guide all the remaining deliberations with regard to strategic planning.
- Chapter 10 presents two of Porter's models. These models provide an assessment of the future competitive intensity of markets in which strategic businesses compete. The models are known as the Five Forces model, and the concept of strategic groups. Although competitive intensity is important in assessing the attractiveness of markets, Porter's models do not provide help in assessing and

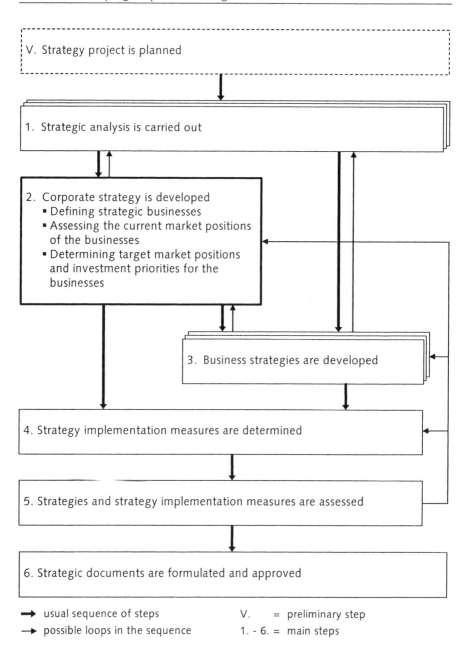

Figure IV-1: The development of corporate strategy as a step in the process of strategic planning

determining current or target competitive positions of the businesses.

- Chapter 11 introduces portfolio methods. These allow strategic businesses to be assessed and planned in terms of both the market attractiveness and the competitive position. The methods allow an assessment of individual businesses and of the overall portfolio of businesses within a corporation. They also offer a basis for determining long-term target market positions and investment priorities for the businesses. Chapter 11 focuses particularly on the two principal portfolio methods, the market growth-market share method and the industry attractiveness-competitive strength method.
- Chapter 12 concludes Part IV with an account of how the methods introduced in Chapters 9-11 can be applied in the development of a corporate strategy and outlines the corporate strategy development process.

9 Defining the strategic businesses

9.1 The strategic business as a three dimensional construct

The primary purpose of corporate strategy is to build up and maintain competitive positions. Before these can be defined, however, there must be clear agreement about the markets, offers and resources they will encompass. The link between the competitive positions on the one hand, and the market offers and resources on the other hand, is made with the help of the notion of the strategic business.

A strategic business is a three dimensional construct which identifies a particular market, specific market offers and specific resources.

Market offer is to be understood in a wide sense, including not only the central products and services, but complementary services, price conditions and so on. The offer includes all the various measures within a marketing mix. It is important to understand that when identifying strategic businesses, it is not only differences in the basic products or services that must be taken into account, but also differentiated use of other elements of the marketing mix. This is, for example, the case for the VW group: it has not only VW, but also Seat and Skoda. And these three brands of vehicle have much more differentiation in the equipment of their cars, in pricing, in advertising, and so on, than in basic product features.

Businesses must be defined independently of the existing organizational structure. Although it can happen that a strategic business will correspond to an organizational unit, it is very important to understand that businesses and organizational divisions are quite different things. The definition of businesses must be based on markets, market offers and resources, whereas company structure is often based on quite different criteria. It is also clear that the definition of strategic businesses, and the formation of a corporate strategy based on these businesses, will often require a review of organizational structure (Chandler, 1962, p. 14). **Inset 9-1** gives an example of a firm where the definition of strategic businesses led to a reorganization.

Inset 9-1: Definition of strategic businesses in a textile company

In the seventies a substantial Swiss textile company found itself in circumstances where it felt obliged to re-examine its strategy. At the time the firm had two main types of market offer: 1. Jersey fabrics for producers of fashionable women's wear, 2. Yarns, sold in part to their own jersey factory but most of which were sold to other fabric manufacturers.

The jersey fabrics were sold principally in the US and Western Europe while the yarns were sold to companies in Switzerland and the countries bordering on it (Germany, France & Italy).

Thus two strategic businesses were proposed:

- Manufacture of jersey fabrics for women's wear (Europe and US)
- Manufacture of yarns for weaving mills and knitwear manufacturers (Switzerland and neighbouring countries)

During a review of business strategies it became clear that, in the area of information processing, the company had significant competitive advantages: qualified employees and leading edge hardware and software. These advantages were not fully exploited in the service of the existing businesses. The head of the computing department, known for his initiative and technical knowledge, had already begun to fill spare capacity by offering computing services to other firms in the region. The future for computing was looking extremely positive so the strategy project group decided to test whether the provision of computing services to companies and public sector organizations could be a possible third strategic business. The review was favorable and the computing center was separated from the rest of the company and set up as an independent business. Its turnover soon reached figures comparable to those of the other two businesses. It continues to exist today, in the form of a consulting company, while the two former core businesses are no longer operating.

Let us finally note that not every business deserves to be seen as a strategic business and incorporated into strategic planning. In line with the requirement that in strategic planning we focus on the company as a whole and on important sections of the company, it follows that businesses are only to be brought into the process of strategic planning if they are important for success. Generally this means that the business must have the potential to generate a significant proportion of the profit of the corporation.

9.2   Two types of strategic business

When formulating strategic guidelines for one particular business, it is important to know whether these require to be adjusted to the guidelines for any of the other businesses. For example, it may be that a business which is not profitable in the long term cannot simply be sold off or run down, because the production costs of a profitable second business depend on maintaining capacity in a common production facility. Or it may become necessary to align the competitive strategies of two businesses with different brands in the same market so that competition between them is minimized. In order to highlight the importance of the independence or dependence of businesses, we distinguish two types of strategic business: strategic business units and strategic business fields.

The type of business which has a significant need for coordination with other businesses will be called a strategic business unit. In section 9.1, we put forward three dimensions which determine businesses: markets, offers and resources. For the formation of business units it is above all the second dimension, the market offer, which is of importance. A business unit produces an individual offer.

Figure 9-1 gives an overview of the most important criteria in determining the strategic business units of a company, together with simple examples. We should note that in practice often different criteria may produce quite similar results: product-related criteria (1 - 4) and customer-related criteria (5 & 6) are in fact two sides of the same coin.

Criteria	Examples
(1) Products which can be differentiated as technically distinct	Soft drink producer: • Business unit: cola drinks • Business unit: lemon drinks
(2) Products which can be differentiated according to their use	Pharmaceutical manufacturer: • Business unit: treatment of heart disorders • Business unit: treatment of influenza
(3) Products which can be differentiated according to their position in the industry value chain	Footwear manufacturer and trader: • Business unit: footwear manufacturing • Business unit: retail outlets for foot-wear
(4) Products or services which can be differentiated according to brand or marketing	Cigarette manufacturer: • Business unit: brand A • Business unit: brand B
(5) Differentiation according to customer type	Coffee roasting: • Business unit: retail to private customers • Business unit: supply to hotels, restaurants, etc.
(6) Differentiation according to market segments	Producer of mattresses: • Business unit: high priced products for quality and image oriented customers sold under the company's own prestigious brand • Business unit: low priced products for price-conscious customers sold under own-labels

Figure 9-1: Criteria for the definition of strategic business units

In practice, business units always have a specific market positioning or marketing mix. But the requirement for strategic relevance means that not every product group with its own market positioning or marketing mix has the weight of a strategic business unit.

As we have seen, strategic business units produce an independent market offer. On the other hand strategic business units possess limited autonomy as regards served markets and/or resources. For this reason business units normally require adjustments to other businesses:

- Two business units are active in the same market and may damage each other through their competitive activity. In the worst case they may cannibalize each other's sales. Here strategies that have not been mutually adjusted bring the threat of strong 'negative synergies' in sales.
- Two business units use the same resources and are therefore dependent on each other, either in their cost structure or in their product quality. This is the case, for example, if they are only able to afford highly qualified specialists by sharing the costs involved. Here strategies that have not been mutually adjusted bring a loss of synergies in costs or quality.

Strategic business units, therefore, produce an independent market offer but require to be coordinated with other businesses in respect of markets and/or resources. In contrast, the strategic business field is largely autonomous: strategic business fields do not share either markets or resources with other businesses.

In practice, however, absolute autonomy is rare. The criterion of independence, especially in resources, must therefore not be applied too strictly. We can still speak of strategic business fields as long as these have independent use of the resources which are relevant to their competitive advantages. It is also possible in some cases for companies to reorganize so that shared resources are divided and business units are thus deliberately transformed into business fields. This is worth doing when the gain in motivation or performance can be expected to offset the possible losses in cost or synergies arising out of the division of the resources. This kind of move is not usually considered during the initial definition of strategic businesses but may come up later in the course of the discussion and evaluation of strategic options.

It is important, too, to note that strategic autonomy should not be taken to suggest financial independence. For example, one strategic business may be able to count on an initial infusion of cash from other businesses in the company. Alternatively, the company's corporate strategy may require a strategic business to produce a positive free cash-flow in order to finance investment in its other strategic businesses. Strategic autonomy always operates within financial limits, since financial resources are always limited.

Figure 9-2 presents the relationship between business units and business fields. For simplicity's sake, we distinguish only two strategic business units. It should be noted that:

- Situations 1 - 3 show the three possible types of need for coordination that may be necessary between business units in terms of markets and resources. The need for harmonization means that together they represent a business field. Thus there is often a hierarchical relationship between the two types of business, with the business field being made up of a number of business units.
- In those cases where business units are found to be largely independent in both markets and resources they can be upgraded to business fields as in Situation 4.

We can now present definitions of the two types of strategic businesses.

A strategic business field is
- a business which contributes critically to the success of the corporation
- and whose strategy can be planned independently
- because it has an independent market offer and
- because it does not to any significant extent share markets and/or resources with any other business in the corporation.

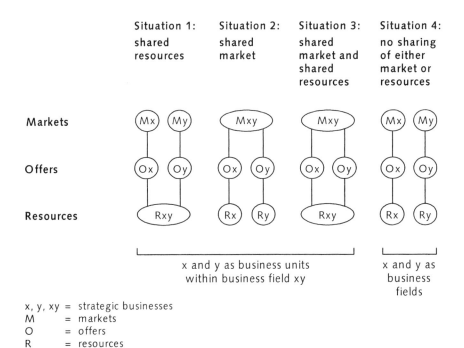

Figure 9-2: The need for coordination between strategic businesses

A strategic business unit is

- a business which contributes critically to the success of the corporation
- with its own independent market offer
- but whose strategy must be adjusted to those of other business units within the corporation
- because they operate in the same market and/or share the same resources.

The definition of strategic business fields as relatively independent parts of the corporation indicates that there is only a weak level of interdependency and potential for synergy between them. A business field is thus a company within the company. Strategic business units on the other hand either represent a particular market offer within a strategic business field, or in the case of a small company, a particular market offer within the company. With their market-based interdependency and/or shared resources they are relatively closely bound to the other business units in the business field or in the small company. This creates potential for synergies which must be uncovered and exploited.

Figure 9-3 presents the differing degrees of autonomy of business fields and business units for a company with three strategic business fields of which two are subdivided into different strategic business units.

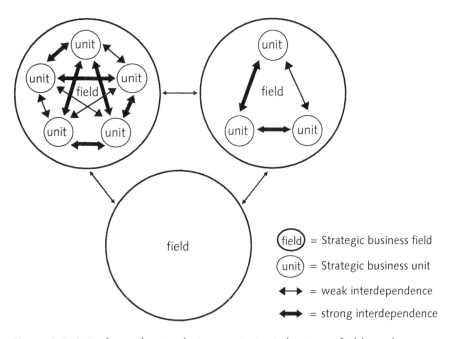

Figure 9-3: Interdependencies between strategic business fields and strategic business units

9.3   Constellations of strategic business fields and strategic business units

We can identify four different constellations for strategic business fields and units. In three out of the four cases we can find numerous examples in practice, while the remaining case is rare and is included here only for the sake of completeness.

Constellation 1 represents a company that cannot be subdivided either into business fields or business units. This type of company operates in a single market with a unified marketing mix and a single product group. Examples include small shops, such as boutiques selling clothing and stationery shops. Medium-sized companies which fall into this category would include a firm of joiners operating in one region only or the producer of a regional newspaper. Certain specialized larger firms like Benneton and Coca-Cola, belonged in this category in the early years of their development.

Constellation 2 comprises companies that have no more than one business field, but this business field can be divided into a number of business units. There are three sub-types of this constellation, which is very common in today's business world:

- In Constellation 2A the business units market their products independently but use the same resources. For example, a producer of tinned food may sell its own brand through independent retail outlets while at the same time cooperating with a large retail chain abroad and supplying it with products which will be sold under a private label or as unmarked products.
- Constellation 2B represents the reverse situation. The different business units have independent resources, but their marketing must be closely coordinated. This is the case when, for example, a manufacturer of skiing equipment takes over a smaller competitor but then continues to produce and market its products separately. In order to limit competition between the two companies, their marketing must be coordinated.
- Constellation 2C is a combination of the first two. There are synergies both in marketing and resources. For example, in the Swiss watch manufacturing industry there are a number of small assemblers producing differing ranges of models with the same production facilities and these are sometimes marketed under several different brand names. In these cases there must be coordination both in the production and the market positioning between the different business units.

Constellation 3 is rare in practice. The companies concerned can be divided into business fields but these remain so homogenous that they cannot be further subdivided into business units. An example is a medium sized company which provides cranes for unusually difficult construction projects and also specialized transport services for dangerous substances.

Constellation 4 represents the most complex case. A company has a number of business fields which can be subdivided into business units. Most large chemical manufacturers and manufacturers of industrial goods fall into this category, as do large diversified food producers.

Figure 9-4 gives an overview of these constellations of strategic business fields and strategic business units.

9.4   Defining strategic businesses

Before the current strategic situation can be evaluated and strategic goals formulated, the strategic businesses of a corporation must be defined. This represents the first stage in the process of developing a corporate strategy.

For the definition of strategic businesses the following steps are required:
- Identifying and classifying of existing market offers.
- Determining the strategic business units.
- Grouping business units into business fields according to market and/or resource interdependencies. Possible upgrading of business units to business fields.

In the first step, the objective is to identify existing market offers and classify them according to similarities or hierarchical relationships. What is required is to achieve a systematic overview of important turnover generating activities, for both the present and the future. Normally the initial strategic analysis should generate enough knowledge about the interrelationships between markets served, market offers and resources to produce this list of market offers.

In the second step strategic business units are determined. To do this,

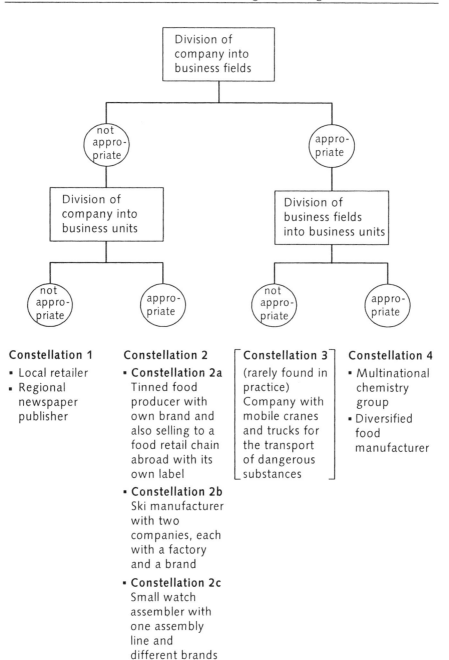

Figure 9-4: The four constellations of strategic business fields and strategic business units

it is necessary to group together all those products or services which meet similar needs and have, or ought to have, a similar market positioning.

As we saw in section 9.3 above, a business also requires a certain minimum size to be of strategic importance. To evaluate the strategic relevance of businesses, it can be useful to choose a quantitative criteria; for example, a specific percentage of company turnover, which the business should achieve in the future in order to be of strategic importance. This minimum percentage must be subjectively assessed by the planners. In practice, values between 3% and 5% have often been found useful. Estimates regarding the future are always uncertain, and so it is wise to regard any figure used as a rough guideline only, rather than a strict criterion. Turnover is the principal criterion, but here too flexibility is needed. Where businesses have strong potential as regards contribution margin or profit, it can be appropriate to classify them as strategically important, even though the percentage of company turnover they represent may be low.

If it is found that a business unit is not of strategic relevance then it may be possible to incorporate it into a larger unit with similar products. Manufacturers of pharmaceuticals and agrochemical goods very often have a number of related product types in one business unit.

In Step Three the business units are grouped into business fields or upgraded to the status of business fields. To do this the market-related and/or resource-based interdependencies between the business units must be carefully examined.

- Where a strategic unit has no essential interdependencies with other units and is thus relatively independent in the market served and in resources, it can be upgraded to a business field. This is, however, an exceptional situation. In general, business units will be combined into business fields.
- Where there are considerable synergies between business units in markets served and/or resources used, they form together a single business field.
- In some cases there will be strong synergies between all the activities within a company. Here the company has a number of different business units, but these all form a single business field. This case corresponds to Constellation 2 in Figure 9-4.

Experience shows that in practice it is often difficult to decide whether a market or resource relationship between business units is sufficiently strong to justify grouping the business units into a business field:

- Sometimes it is difficult to decide whether or not two market offers are in competition and therefore whether or not the activities of the two business units should be coordinated. In these cases the decision should depend on the extent to which the offers are substitutable for the fulfillment of customer needs and on the degree to which the customer segments overlap.
- Resource dependencies should be interpreted in a restricted sense. They may be said to exist only when the resources concerned are of great importance for the achievement of essential success potentials or the avoidance of important competitive disadvantages.

In particularly difficult cases one can use as the acid test the question of whether the sale of a business would threaten the existence or the value of one or more of the remaining businesses. Where the answer is in the affirmative, the business concerned should be regarded as a business unit.

After the identification of strategic businesses it is sometimes necessary to redefine the working groups responsible for the planning of the business strategies.

Inset 9-2 illustrates the thinking behind the definition of businesses for a diversified medium-sized company in the agricultural sector.

Inset 9-2: Definition of businesses for an agricultural company

This medium-sized family-owned company is based in the Pfalz area of Germany. In 1996 the corporate strategy was reviewed in view of the rapid changes in the agricultural sector (shrinking markets, internationalization, mergers and acquisitions) which had led to much tougher competition. The board of directors was unsure which parts of the business to develop in order to survive and to maximize their success. Here are their main conclusions in the attempt to define an initial business structure.

The company produces pesticides, seeds and animal health products. In addition it is established as a retailer of agricultural ma-

machinery and also owns a medium sized vineyard.

Pesticides and seeds are marketed throughout Germany by an efficient sales organization. In view of the strength of the competition (competitors include internationally active multinational corporations like Dupont, BASF and Bayer) the market share obtained represents an astonishing success. Although the company develops and produces pesticides in its own central facility, some 50% of pesticide turnover is obtained with products from foreign firms, for which the company has exclusive distributing rights. In contrast, the seeds are developed and produced entirely in the central facility.

There is a separate organization for veterinary products. An independent sales and distribution organization markets these to veterinary surgeons, to manufacturers of animal feed products and to livestock farmers: pig and poultry farmers and producers of calves for veal.

The agricultural machinery business is a regional operation with five outlets for sales and customer service in the wine growing region of Rheinhessen and Pfalz. To the small and medium sized agricultural firms which predominate in this region it offers a wide range of machines from different manufacturers. The company's vineyard is highly reputed for its white wines: Riesling and Silvaner. The customers are principally up-market restaurants, wine bars, and a number of companies and private clients interested in exclusive wines. Sales are concentrated in the local area and in three major cities: Munich, Berlin and Dusseldorf.

Figure 9-5 and **Figure 9-6** display the results of Step One in defining the strategic businesses:
- Figure 9-5 gives an overview of how the turnover is divided, presenting figures for the five main product groups.
- Figure 9-6 presents the turnover for pesticides in the three main product categories and then according to the crops. Crops are also used to subdivide the turnover in seeds.

Product groups	Turnover for 1995 in millions of DM	Market growth trend	Market share trend
pesticides	60	↘	↗
seeds	22	↗	→
animal health products	25	↗	→
agricultural machinery	12	↘	↗
wine	2	→	→

Figure 9-5: Turnover structure of the agricultural company

Product groups	Total market size 1995 in millions of DM	Turnover for 1995 in millions of DM	Market share trend
pesticides	1540	60	
herbicides	940	25	
▪ wheat	450	15	↘
▪ maize	160	–	–
▪ sugar beet	200	5	→
▪ rape	100	3	→
▪ potatoes	30	2	→
fungicides	490	35	
▪ wheat	380	10	↗
▪ fruit/grapes	70	15	↗
▪ potatoes	40	10	↗
insecticides	110	–	–
seeds	710	22	
wheat	250	12	↘
maize	350	–	–
sugar beet	110	10	↗

Figure 9-6: Detailed turnover structure for pesticides and seeds

As turnover statistics show, the company has a large number of different products, each with individual market positioning. Several of them have only a small turnover.

With regard to strategic relevance, it was decided to adopt 10% of turnover (12 million DM) as the figure which a strategically relevant business should be currently contributing or be able to reach in the future. The use of this relatively high figure meant that wine was not eligible, and required the grouping together of pesticide and seed products. As their marketing and distribution was largely shared, some product groups with large turnover within pesticides and seeds were not considered as separate businesses. This produced the following list of business units as the result of Step Two:

- pesticides (60 mil.)
  - herbicides (25 mil.)
  - fungicides (35 mil.)
- seeds (22 mil.)
- animal health products (25 mil.)
- agricultural machinery (12 mil.)

It would also be possible to arrange the hierarchy in pesticides differently, putting the types of crop first, with, for instance, wheat as the main category, subdivided into herbicides and fungicides. But this was rejected as inappropriate, not corresponding to the realities in the industry.

Step Three, the identification of business fields was now a relatively simple affair. The main categories all offer their products in different markets, although they do share a common type of customer. This fact is of secondary importance, as the competitive arena is different in each case; there are no relationships between the different product types as far as the competitors are concerned.

However seeds and pesticides share resources to an important degree and are therefore strategically interdependent. Herbicides and fungicides are also closely related in terms of markets, as they are faced with essentially the same competitors.

Figure 9-7 displays the initial business structure, which was the result of these considerations. In this case it also turned out to be the structure finally adopted, since it was decided that it would be too expensive to provide independence of resources for pesticides and seeds.

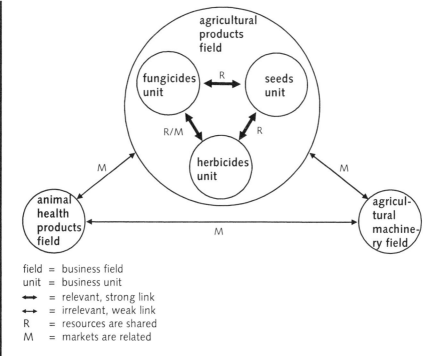

field = business field
unit = business unit
⟷ = relevant, strong link
⟷ = irrelevant, weak link
R   = resources are shared
M   = markets are related

Figure 9-7: The business structure in the agricultural company

10 Assessing relevant industries with the help of competitive intensity models

10.1 Basic reflections on the assessment of competitive intensity

The model for assessment of a current or target market position proposed in Chapter Three has two sides:

- assessment of the attractiveness of the industry relevant to a particular strategic business (= assessment of market aspects) and
- assessment of the possibilities for building a strong competitive position with this business (= assessment of competitive strength)

The models proposed in this chapter are intended to help strategic planners to assess one of these two aspects. They help to evaluate the attractiveness of the industry markets served by strategic businesses. The models are based on the idea that certain features of the industry structure determine the expected intensity of competition and thus the average margin which competitors will be able to achieve. The average margin represents the attractiveness of the industry and is of great importance in determining the profit which a business can be expected to make in the long term. This line of reasoning reflects what is known as the market-based view, and this is explained in **Inset 10-1.**

Two models for the prediction of competitive intensity will now be described, both of which were developed by Porter:

- the Five Forces model for broad analysis of an industry (Porter, 1980, p. 3 ff.), and
- the strategic groups model for identifying and analyzing specific sectors within the industry (Porter, 1980, p. 126 ff.).

These models can be used in a two-step analysis of the attractiveness of an industry for any particular strategic business.

In the first step, the Five Forces model is used to obtain a broad view of the structure of an industry and, based on this, to forecast the expected level of competitive intensity. The current and future values are collected for five features which Porter identified as central determinants of competitive intensity. In relatively uniform competitive situations, that is in industries where the competitors are all of

Inset 10-1: The market-based view

The market-based view is derived from findings in Industrial Economics, a sub-discipline within Economics. The market-based view uses the following line of reasoning:

- Market structures have a strong influence on the abilities of companies to act and on the chances of success from these actions.
- Success depends on the competitive behavior adopted by a company. However, companies or businesses are not free in the choice of their actions, but more or less constrained by the structural framework.
- The success of a company or business is therefore dependent on both market structure and competitive behavior. The relative importance of the two factors depends on the industry.

This central line of reasoning is known as the structure-conduct-performance paradigm.

The market-based view focuses on the first factor, the industry structure, which is considered on two levels:

- Structural analysis of industries explains the competitive intensity and the average rate of return of an industry in comparison to the average rate of return across all industries.
- The variance in profit levels among companies within a single industry is usually much greater than the variance in the average return for different industries (cf. Rumelt 1987, p. 141 f.). This phenomenon cannot be explained by looking globally at an industry; a more detailed structural analysis is required. The industry is therefore divided into groups of suppliers with similar competitive positions and strategies. The groups with attractive positions are protected against the other competitors in the industry by entry barriers. This is what allows them to maintain their above average profits over the long term (Porter, 1980 p. 126 ff.).

approximately the same size and offer comparable products, this broad view will already enable a judgment as to whether the market is attractive enough to justify the investment required to build up or defend a market position. This would be the case, for example, for the steel industry, wheat wholesaling or cigarette manufacturers.

However, where an industry brings together competitors of varying strengths and sizes, offering different products and/or using different manufacturing processes, the broad overview may sometimes be misleading. Consider, for example, the watch-making industry. Manufacturers of luxury watches have strong competitive positions and good future prospects, but over-capacity and lack of potential for differentiation among their products has brought fierce competitive pressures on the assemblers of medium-priced articles. Where industries have this sort of heterogeneous structure it is useful to follow up the initial analysis with a structural analysis within the industry, based on the strategic groups model. Clusters of competitors are identified with similar competitive strategy. Closer analysis will then focus on two areas: the cluster in which the strategic business is now situated (assessment of the current strategy), and clusters which reveal an attractive margin and which might become target clusters (assessment of strategic options). In the analysis of the clusters, great attention will be given to the question of how far entry barriers impede access to these groups for competitors from other clusters or other industries. For example, for the producers of luxury watches the exclusive brand image is a particularly effective barrier to new entrants. These brands have been built up with heavily resourced campaigns over very many years. For a newcomer, the task of acquiring in a relatively short time the same prestige as an established brand is almost impossible.

10.2   Analyzing industry structure with the Five Forces model

10.2.1 The basic concept underlying the Five Forces model

Industry structure analysis, or to be more precise, analysis of the competitive structure in an industry, seeks to explain why the average return is higher or lower in a particular industry, compared with others. The underlying reasoning is as follows:

- The competition between competitors in an industry can be described in terms of five forces or characteristics of the industry structure. The competitive intensity therefore varies according to the different constellations of these five forces.
- These then indicate whether the average rate of return for the industry under consideration is higher or lower than the average for all industries.

Figure 10-1 presents Porter's model in schematic form showing the interaction between the determinants of competitive intensity. The five forces are: (1) the bargaining power of buyers, (2) the bargaining power of suppliers, (3) the threat of new entrants to the market, (4) the threat of substitute products and services and (5) the rivalry between firms (Porter, 1980, p. 3 ff.).

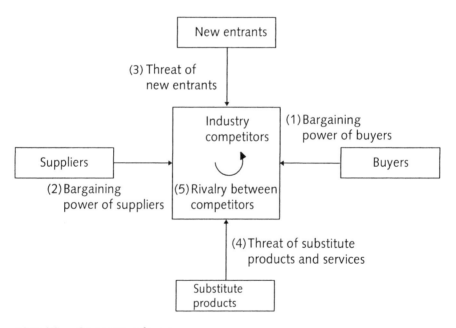

(1) to (5) = Competitive forces

Figure 10-1: Porter's Five Forces Model
(adapted from Porter, 1980, p. 4)

Competitive intensity increases, and the average industry return falls, when the bargaining power of buyers and suppliers is high, the threat from new entrants and substitute products is high, and the rivalry between firms is intense. These five competitive forces depend in their turn on other structural characteristics of the industry.

10.2.2 Areas of application

The Five Forces model Porter conceived primarily as a framework for assessing the quality of industries and for determining points of departure for the improvement of competitive strategy (Porter 1991, p. 97 ff.). Here we are concerned with the first of these two applications.

The Five Forces model is suitable for assessing both existing markets and potential new markets being reviewed as strategic options. It is particularly suitable for the industries of business fields. But in a modified form, it can also be used to assess sub-industries of business units. In addition, an analysis with the Five Forces model can be carried out inexpensively using the collected experience of the company.

Although it may seem useful to apply the model to review all relevant industries, in practice it is principally used to assess selected industries. Two main types of use predominate:

- Predicting the development of the margin in important existing business fields where there are signs that competitiveness is increasing.
- Assessing the attractiveness of a target industry for the potential creation of a new strategic business. In cases where the new business is envisaged as an acquisition or where there is little existing knowledge of the industry in the company, the Five Forces model, with its limited requirement for information, allows a robust assessment of market attractiveness.

In these two types of case, Porter's model can always be recommended. But in view of the low cost of the exercise, every strategy project should consider the option of using the model to conduct a general review of the competitive situation in all relevant industries.

10.2.3 Procedure

Using the Five Forces model to carry out a structural analysis requires the following three steps:

1. definition of the industry to be analyzed
2. description of the current competitive situation
3. prediction of the development of the competitive forces and the changes this will bring in competitive intensity and thus in profit margin

The above assumes that it is previously determined which industries will be subject to analysis.

Step One is the definition of the industry to be analyzed. This step guarantees that before discussion of competitive strengths begins, there will be a clear understanding as to which companies or other organizations have to be included and under which of the five forces.

Where a company has more than one business field, the various markets these serve are usually to be considered as industry markets in Porter's sense of the term. Take for example a graphics and media firm with a newspaper, book publishing, printing and book shops. This company is active in four industries. In each of the four it faces different competitive forces, and is thus confronted with a different competitive intensity. In this case therefore, it is appropriate to carry out four separate structural analyses.

Often, however, the activities of a company are concentrated within a single business field, divided among a number of business units. Resource-based and market-related links between these units mean that, in the majority of cases, they belong to the same industry. In this situation, it is necessary to determine whether one structural analysis is sufficient, or if it would be useful to analyze the different sub-industries related to the business units.

Step Two, the description of the current competitive situation, usually requires a great deal of time. In this step, the factors which influence the five competitive forces must be examined. Here it is sensible to analyze them in the order in which they were presented above in Figure 10-1:

(1) The bargaining power of buyers

(2) The bargaining power of suppliers
(3) The threat of new entrants
(4) The threat of substitute products
(5) Intensity of rivalry between firms

This order is to be preferred because of the interdependencies between the factors. Thus the danger of new entrants is, for instance, considerably reduced if the buyers are in a strong position and are holding down margins in the industry. As the chart shows, it is the rivalry between existing firms that is to be considered last of all, as it is influenced to a considerable degree by the other four factors.

Figure 10-2 shows the most important factors of influence to take into account when assessing the five competitive forces. The figure also shows which tendencies lead to harder competition in the industry and therefore produce an unattractive position for a business (Porter, 1980, p. 5 ff.)

Step Three is intellectually the most demanding. It is necessary to predict the long term development of the competitive forces and the changes this will bring in competitive intensity and in profit margin. Usually it is sufficient to concentrate the discussion on those competitive forces identified in Step Two as being of key importance. For pharmaceutical producers, for example, the bargaining strength of suppliers and the threat of substitute products are both likely to be of little significance. In this industry, however, it is necessary to examine the significant changes which might occur in the strength of the buyers, for example through a further concentration within the health insurance providers, or through government pressure on health spending. The same is true for the threat of new entrants, where the possibility of the entrance of generic producers needs to be examined.

In tackling the second and third steps, it is useful to refer to the findings established during strategic analysis, especially the global environmental analysis and the market system analysis.

Competitive factors	Values which may raise competitiveness within an industry
(1) The bargaining power of buyers	
Degree of concentration of buyers	high
Costs of supplied products and services as a proportion of the total costs of the buyers	high
Degree of standardization of products and services	high
Degree of importance of supplied products and services for the quality of buyers' products and services	low
Technological and financial possibilities for buyers to integrate vertically	high
Market transparency for buyers	high
(2) The bargaining power of suppliers	
Same dimensions as listed above for (1)	the reverse of the values for (1)
(3) The threat of new entrants	
Lack of bargaining power of buyers and suppliers typically tends to increase the danger of new entrants.	
Access to distribution channels	easy
Customer loyalty to suppliers	low
Cost to customers of switching suppliers	low
Minimum turnover required	low
Capital required by new entrant	low

Figure 10-2: The most important competitive dimensions and how they may produce intense competition

Competitive factors	Values which may raise competitiveness within an industry
Absolute cost advantage of established companies	low
Legal requirements or restrictions	negligible
(4) The threat of substitute products and services	
Performance of substitute products and services	better than industry products and services (*)
Cost of substitute products and services	lower than industry products and services (*)
(*) Long-term survival of the industry is in doubt if both of these two conditions are met.	
(5) Intensity of rivalry between existing firms	
Overall rivalry between existing firms tends to increase if there is strong bargaining power of buyers and suppliers and if there are increased threats from new entrants and substitute products.	
Number of existing firms	large
Market agreements between existing firms	not present
Customer segments with specific needs	negligible
Market growth	stagnating or declining
Industry-specific investments	high
Cost of withdrawal from the market	high
Range of other markets that existing resources would allow the firms to move into	limited

Inset 10-2 gives the industry structure analysis for a small capital goods producer and the far-reaching consequences which flow from it.

Inset 10-2: Structural analysis of the industries for a capital goods producer

In 1991 Messrs. J and M bought S-Tech., a firm based in the Bern region. At the time, this company had a turnover of 4.75 mil. Swiss francs. The company had three areas of activity, which were each analysed in turn using Porter's model for industry structure analysis.

Of the three businesses, by far the greatest turnover, 3.25 mil. Swiss francs, came from sales of smaller machines for pick & place of printed circuit boards. Industry analysis produced the following picture of the market for these products:

- The machines were all produced for a single customer, who sold them on under his own brand name and who thus enjoyed a great deal of bargaining power.
- The components used were standard parts offered by many suppliers, so that the suppliers had insignificant bargaining power.
- The contractual arrangements with the only customer were such that it was unlikely that he would switch away from S-Tech to a different supplier. For this reason the threat of new entrants was examined not in terms of possible rival suppliers to that customer, but rivals in the market where their customer sold the products on. The machines that the company had developed and was now producing were designed for the assembly of SMD boards. In 1991, these boards, onto which components are soldered, represented a new technology with great potential for growth. Accordingly large corporations were also interested in producing such machines. Panasonic, Philips and Siemens had all already entered the market or announced their intention to do so and further powerful competitors could be expected. The management of S-Tech doubted, moreover, that their single customer would find a niche which would allow it to escape the worst effects of the entry of powerful new competitors.

- The most important substitute product for SMD board in 1991 was the older through hole board, into which components had to be inserted. These products did not represent an important threat.
- Rivalry between competitors was likely to intensify, with both a price war and a technological race in which the larger pick & place machine producers with their greater development budgets would have a long-term advantage.

Thus for the S-Tech. the overall future for this product group, automatic pick & place machines for assembling printed circuit boards, was considered bleak.

The five forces analysis gave a much more positive result for the second business, machines for processing cables, which had a turnover of 1.35 mil. Swiss francs in 1991.

- At the time the analysis was carried out, 100% of production was exported through a Swiss agent. So for this product group too there was a large degree of dependence on a single customer. However, in contrast to the pick & place machines, here the matter could be corrected fairly simply. The company retained all the rights to its products and could export directly. This would have the advantage of establishing closer contacts with the end-users as well as reducing the bargaining power of the customer.
- Suppliers of standard parts for the machines had little bargaining power.
- The market in which the company was operating was for smaller benchtop machines and would not be attractive to new entrants. This was a niche market of limited volume and with modest potential for growth. In addition, a large investment would be necessary to enter the market considering the annual contribution that could be expected.
- Two substitute products were identified. Cables can always be cut and stripped by hand. Here however, low investment is accompanied by high labour time and costs which are considerable even for operations in countries where labour is cheap. The second substitute was terminating machines, which were already available in 1991. These machines both cut and strip the cables and also mount the electrical connectors at each end. Their dis-

advantage is that they are much more expensive and less flexible, being designed for specific applications and only usable in assembly line production. S-Tech had benchtop machines which could be used either for assembly lines or in workshop production.
- The limited number of competitors meant that it was not difficult to get an overview of the market. Rivalry with competitors was judged to be tolerable. In addition, direct competition between rival products was to a large extent mitigated by the possibilities for product differentiation; this also meant that competition was not exclusively focused on price.

Movement detectors based on radar technology produced a modest turnover of 150,000 Swiss francs per year. The view of future prospects produced by analysis of the market did not look too promising:
- The movement detectors were sold to manufacturers of automatic garage doors and mobile warning light systems for building sites. For the customers these detectors did not seek to exert great pressure on prices for these components.
- Suppliers, too, were not a source of pressure on costs. As for the

	Pick & place machines	Cable processing machines	Movement detectors
Bargaining power of customers	÷ ÷	÷ → +	+
Bargaining power of suppliers	+ +	+ +	+
Threat of new entrants	÷ ÷	+	++
Threat of substitute products and services	+	0	÷ ÷
Intensity of rivalry between existing competitors	÷ ÷	+	0
+ + = situation or trend very favorable to S-Tech.			
0 = situation or trend neutral for S-Tech.			
÷ ÷ = situation or trend very unfavorable to S-Tech.			

Figure 10-3: Overview of industry structure analysis for the three businesses of S-Tech

other businesses, S-Tech only required standard products.

- As these movement detectors depended on the old form of radar technology, the danger from new entrants was practically nil. In fact, some competitors had already abandoned the market.
- New sensor technology represented a great threat. Systems based on this technology had already been introduced and were not only cheaper to produce, but also more reliable, and ecologically less damaging.
- The limited number of suppliers of radar-based movement detectors meant that rivalry between firms was small. By 1991 competition was no longer within the industry but between these products and the superior substitutes.

Figure 10-3 provides an overview of the three analyses for the company's businesses. It led to a radical decision by the new owners. They chose to gradually withdraw from production of two of the product groups and to concentrate exclusively on the machines for cable processing. The turnover statistics presented in

Turn-over / Year	Pick & Place machines		Cable Processing machines		Movement detectors		Total	
	in mio. Swiss francs	%	in mio. Swiss francs	%	in mio. Swiss francs	%	in mio. Swiss francs	%
1991	3,250	68	1,350	29	150	3	4,750	100
1992	1,750	32	3,650	66	100	2	5,500	100
1993	1,650	25	4,900	74	50	1	6,600	100
1994	1,400	14	8,550	86	0	0	9,950	100
1995	2,050	16	10,850	84	0	0	12,900	100
1996	550	5	10,750	95	0	0	11,300	100
1997	0	0	15,300	100	0	0	15,300	100
1998	0	0	18,350	100	0	0	18,350	100

Figure 10-4: Turnover development of the businesses of S-Tech 1991 to 1998

Figure 10-4 show how their decision to focus on the business with the best competitive position was rewarded. Turnover in this business multiplied more than tenfold in the period from 1991 to 1998 and now far outweighs turnover lost from giving up the two other areas. In terms of profitability, the position looks even better. As the remaining business produces higher contribution margins, the decision to go for focus has much improved the profit situation.

10.3   Analyzing structures within industries with the Strategic Groups model

10.3.1 The basic concept underlying the Strategic Groups model

Examining competitive intensity in an industry with the Five Forces model provides an explanation of higher or lower industry rates of return compared to the business average. But in many industries average return is not a significant indicator because the variation among the returns of different competitors is too high. There are many industries where this variation is considerably higher than the variation between industry averages (Rumelt 1987, p. 141 f.). In such cases internal industry analysis can help to explain differing rates of return within an industry.

Internal industry analysis is based on the following line of reasoning:
- In most industries the competitors can be allocated to strategic groups based on similarities in their competitive position.
- The differing competitive positions are not all equally attractive, but the groups with strong positions are protected against the potential entry of other competitors to their groups by mobility or entry barriers.
- Differences in profitability within an industry can be explained partly in terms of the existence of these strategic groups in which the competitive positions of the attractive groups are protected.

A large proportion of the variation in returns cannot, however, be explained by the concept of strategic groups. It has to be attributed to individual competitive advantages in offers and resources (Hansen &

Wernerfelt, 1989, p. 399 ff.).

Figure 10-5 (Porter, 1980, p. 153) gives the strategic groups for the chain saw manufacturing industry. The figure shows the following points:

- The two most important competitive dimensions in this industry are channels of distribution and quality image.

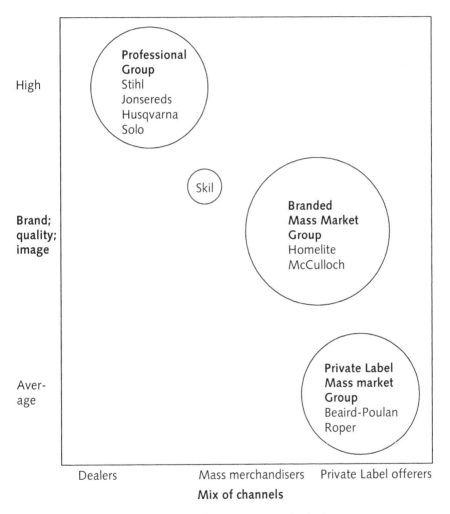

Figure 10-5: Strategic groups in chain saw manufacturing
(adapted from Porter, 1980, p.153)

- One competitor, Skil, is in a strategic group by itself.
- The different sized circles indicate differences in turnover between the four strategic groups.

10.3.2 Areas of application

Carrying out a structural analysis within an industry is usually much more expensive than is a global industry analysis with the Five Forces model. Structural analysis within an industry should therefore be restricted to a review of selected industries when global analysis with the Five Forces model has not been able to provide a clear picture of the current and future competitive situation. This is normally the case when different groups of competitors are following different competitive strategies.

10.3.3 Procedure

Before moving on to a description of structural analysis within an industry, we should note that from the mid seventies, the formation of strategic groups within an industry has been the focus of a large number of studies (see Homburg & Sütterlin, 1992, p. 635 ff. for an overview). Most of this work is based on empirical investigations evaluated with the help of mathematical and statistical models. The cost and effort involved in such investigations is considerable and can only be justified for corporate purposes in a few exceptional cases. Usually there will be preconditions, in terms of time and money, which will allow only a much simpler procedure, relying on the evaluation of existing data, and sometimes also incorporating the results of consultations with a limited number of industry experts. It is this order of procedure that we will now describe; it provides satisfactory results and has a good cost-benefit ratio.

The suggested procedure assumes that global industry analysis has been completed. The following steps are required:

1. Identifying the most important competitive dimensions.

2. Determining the positions of all the important competitors as regards these dimensions.
3. Identifying of the strategic groups.
4. Determining barriers to mobility and entry; review of the five forces for groups of strategic interest.
5. Assessing the difficulties of overcoming the barriers to entry to the most strategically attractive groups and of possible forms of retaliation.

The first task is thus to identify the most important competitive dimensions. This does not require a great deal of time, but it is of great importance for the quality of the analysis. Experts on the watch-making industry, for example, have revealed that competition in this industry is based on seven factors (Heckner, 1994):

- retail distribution
- wholesale distribution
- quality and price
- production depth
- marketing approach (pull or push)
- type of product (chronometers, fashion jewelry etc.)
- mechanism and display (mechanical, quartz analog, quartz digital)

Competitive dimensions can be identified by building on the knowledge already available: market-specific success factors and the results of the application of the Five Forces model are of great value in this.

The second task is to determine the positions of all the important competitors as regards these dimensions. How many firms need to be looked at will depend on the industry concerned. In the relatively heterogeneous watch-making industry, for example, with many important medium sized companies in addition to a number of large manufacturers, some fifty firms would have to be included (Heckner, 1994).

The third step is to identify the strategic groups. It is usual to form the groups on the basis of two competitive dimensions, so that the strategic groups can be represented visually by a two-dimensional chart using competitive dimensions which seem particularly important in accounting for performance differences in the industry concerned.

According to Porter (1980, p. 152 f.) these

- should not correlate with each other, and
- should be related to mobility barriers

In many cases, proceeding to a direct definition of the groups will provide a plausible view of the competitive situation in the industry. But for industries where there are a number of different competitive parameters that could be used for the formation of strategic groups, it can also be useful first to discuss different ways of forming the groups and then select the best solution. The formation of groups will always require a measure of judgement. Where there is doubt about the groups, we recommend forming a larger number of small groups. If it then appears that two such groups largely share identical barriers to entry, these can be amalgamated into a single group.

Figure 10-6 displays strategic groups in the watch-making industry (Heckner, 1994). The parameters chosen present a plausible account of the competitive situation in this industry according to the requirements we have already presented:

- The dispersion of the strategic groups over the whole chart suggests that the two dimensions are not correlated.
- The two dimensions, production depth and quality/price are both linked to important barriers to mobility. A producer of private label watches requires only a modest degree of investment in production, while the creation of a large manufacturing operation requires a substantial initial investment in both plant and expertise. There are also great barriers to entry to the luxury segment and the high price segment. Technical ability and good design are not sufficient; a very large and sustained investment in marketing would be needed in order for a brand to acquire the prestige status required.

Step Four involves determining barriers to mobility and entry. For reasons of cost, this step is normally confined to strategic groups which are particularly interesting because

- an existing business is in that group, or
- the group shows an attractive average rate of return and is therefore being considered as a strategic option.

In identifying entry barriers we are usually looking at values for previously identified competitive parameters within the industry. What is

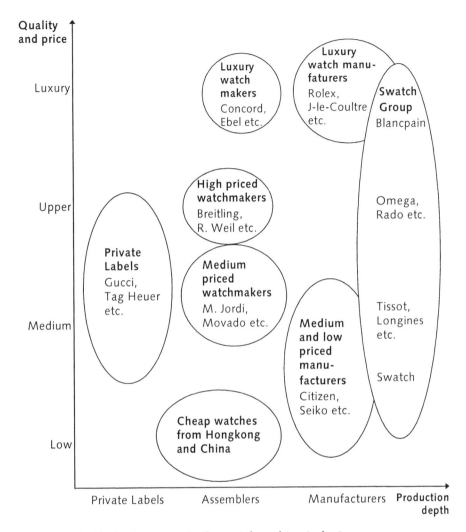

Figure 10-6: Strategic groups in the watch-making industry
(adapted from Heckner 1994)

important is that these should be set as precisely as possible. For example in electronics, aviation electronics or avionics is an attractive strategic group, which is protected by a number of entry barriers. One important barrier is the requirement to be able to deliver replacement devices to any international airport in the world within 24 hours. Overcoming this entry barrier requires considerable investment and brings labour costs which in turn require a relatively high turnover.

This is one of the reasons why there are only a limited number of electronics companies operating in the avionics market.

The effect of mobility barriers in protecting against new direct competitors usually explains the greater part of the difference in profitability between different strategic groups. But there are other factors contributing to profitability differences. In the market for beer, for example, small regional companies are more at the mercy of the large distributors than are large breweries with strong established brands. Because of this it is also necessary to review the results of the industry analysis carried out in the previous step for any interesting strategic groups.

After the most important barriers to entry have been identified, these must be compared with the profitability of the groups concerned. If there is a correlation between high rates of return and specific barriers that are seen as difficult to overcome, then we can be confident of having identified the essential barriers to the entry of new competitors. Where this is not the case we must go back to Step 3 and check whether a different way of forming the groups can be found.

The final step is to assess how difficult it would be to overcome the barriers to entry to the most attractive strategic groups and what forms of retaliation might occur. This demanding task will be that much easier if the entry barriers have been closely specified.

Experience in many different industries has shown that hard technological barriers are generally more at risk than softer factors such as brand images. For example, high precision and long product life used to be important entry barriers to Swiss machine manufacturing, but these have now largely disappeared. In contrast to this, the producers of luxury watches have maintained their position, despite the fact that competitors have bridged the technological gaps, because brands like Rolex and Jäger-le-Coultre have considerable prestige which can only be built up over many years.

11 Determining strategic objectives with the help of portfolio methods

11.1 The basis of portfolio methods

The use of the term portfolio implies an analogy to investment portfolios in stocks, bonds and so on. In strategic planning, as in finance, the objective is to make an overall assessment of investment opportunities and to determine the composition of the future portfolio.

Portfolio methods normally use two criteria, or sets of criteria, which are independent of one another and different in focus. These are (1) criteria for assessing the attractiveness of the markets served by the businesses and (2) criteria for assessing the relative strength of each business in comparison with the competing companies.

In both cases, in assessing markets, and in assessing competitive strengths, the criteria used must allow a comparative judgement of all the various businesses, even in highly diversified companies. Therefore only criteria which have general validity should be used to assess and compare all possible types of business. For this reason, general determinants of long - term business success, such as market growth, market share, product quality, human capacities, financial power, and so on, are the principal criteria used.

Portfolio methods make it possible to assess for both existing and proposed positions of businesses.

After positioning all the businesses in the portfolio, a strategic overview of corporate activity is achieved. This permits an evaluation of the strengths and weaknesses of the strategic business portfolio as a whole. In particular it is possible to assess the central question of how well the existing portfolio is balanced. On this basis the target positions of the businesses can be planned.

The development of portfolio methods has been greatly advanced by management consulting firms using them to battle for a strong competitive position in the lucrative market for strategy consulting:

- The first consulting product of this type was the well-known market growth-relative market share portfolio method developed by the Boston Consulting Group (BCG). With its easily understandable principles for assessing strategic businesses it was quickly adopted by the business world (see, for example, Hedley, 1977, p. 9 ff.). The names coined by BCG for the different categories of businesses: cash cows, stars, question-marks and dogs have long since formed part of the everyday language of corporate life.
- Criticism of the relatively simple Boston method for assessing businesses, which uses two criteria only, led to a spate of suggestions for more complex methods. One of the most popular of these is the industry attractiveness-competitive strength portfolio method, which was developed by the McKinsey company and first tried out on General Electrics (see, for instance, Thompson & Strickland, 1996, p. 252 ff.). The well known PIMS studies provided an important spur to the development of this portfolio method, showing that success in strategic businesses is dependent on a number of general success factors which can be used as criteria in assessing the value of a strategic business. **Inset 11-1** provides a brief account of the PIMS research project and its most important findings.

In sections 11.2 and 11.3 the two portfolio methods mentioned above are each introduced in turn, after which in section 11.4 we look at how to carry out portfolio analysis and planning. As the procedure to be used for each of the two methods is almost the same, we deal with the two together in a single section.

Inset 11-1: The PIMS program

PIMS (Profit Impact of Market Strategies), was started by General Electrics. The research began in the early sixties and has been pursued since 1975 at the Strategic Planning Institute. It uses a large data bank with quantitative information relating to more than 2,500 strategic businesses in companies all over the world and covering all industries. For each business more than 200 quantitative indications are available for each year of operation. The data is collected annually by means of a standardized questionnaire. Multiple regression analysis is the principal statistical tool used to identify success factors.

Thirty-seven independent variables can explain some 80% of the variance of the dependent variable ROI. Nineteen determining factors allow an explanation of about 70% of the variance of the dependent variable free cash-flow. Seven variables have particularly strong influence on ROI and free cash-flow:

- A high absolute and relative market share in a served market has a positive influence on both ROI and free cash flow.
- A high market growth correlates positively with absolute profit, has a neutral influence on ROI, but has a negative impact on free cash flow.
- Value added per employee, also called productivity in PIMS, has a positive effect on both ROI and free cash flow if it is above the industry average.
- Quality of products and services, measured in relative terms compared to competitors, correlates positively with both ROI and free cash flow.
- Product differentiation relative to competitor's products has an effect which is dependent on market share. With a strong market position, differentiation has a positive influence on ROI and free cash flow. If the market position is weak, the effect of differentiation cannot be predicted.
- Vertical integration has different effects according to the types of markets. In mature and stable markets, increased vertical integration has a positive effect on ROI and free cash flow, while the same tendency will have a negative effect in markets growing, declining or lacking stability.
- High investment intensity, defined as the sum of tangible assets and working capital divided by turnover, correlates negatively with ROI and free cash flow.

The general success factors identified by PIMS can be used to evaluate businesses. The results of the PIMS program have therefore, contributed to the development of portfolio methods.

11.2   The market growth - market share portfolio

11.2.1 Portfolio matrix

The market growth - market share portfolio matrix has two axes: the vertical axis represents real market growth and the horizontal axis relative market share. Usually the relative market share is determined in comparison with the position of the strongest competitor in the market.

Each axis is divided into two sections:

- For the vertical axis (market growth) we suggest using the average growth rate of the world economy as the mid-point which separates the sectors. Alternatively, if a corporation's activities are focused on one industry or one region, the average real market growth of that industry or region is recommended.
- The horizontal axis (relative market share) is divided using the relative market share of 1.0 as the mid-point. This creates a division which allows only one competitor per market to be positioned to the right of the dividing line.

As shown in **Figure 11-1**, the businesses placed in the resulting four squares of the matrix are usually labeled dogs, question marks, stars and cash cows. These labels are more or less self-explanatory.

The selection of real market growth and relative market share for the two axes is usually justified in terms of the implications of the market life cycle and the experience curve. **Inset 11-2** explains the relation between these two models and the axes of the BCG portfolio.

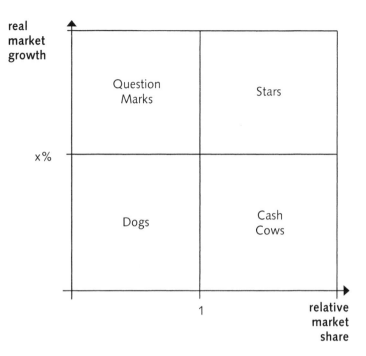

Figure 11-1: The Boston Consulting Group portfolio matrix

Inset 11-2: Market life cycle and experience curve as the basis of the BCG portfolio method

Real market growth as a criterion for assessing industry attractiveness is generally justified in terms of the implications of the market life cycle. **Figure 11-2** shows the typical development of a market. Usually the life cycle is divided into five phases. For a number of reasons, competitive intensity increases during the phase of maturity and will usually be very high in the phases of saturation and degeneration; comparable product offers, competitive pricing and increasing marketing expenses lead to shrinking margins. Growth in market share can only be achieved at the expense of competitors. Investment during this phase, and in the succeeding saturation phase, is less profitable and often confined to replacement investments. The saturation phase may be extremely prolonged, so in the context of long-term strategic planning, it is not necessary to assume a reduction in market size.

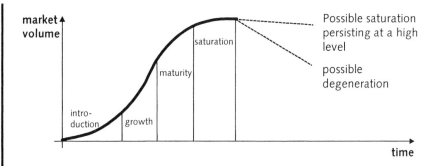

Figure 11-2: The market life cycle

Relative market share, the second dimension, is chosen on the basis of the implications of the experience curve, an empirical model based on findings across a wide range of industries. To quantify the experience curve, accumulated production output is used to measure experience, the independent variable of the model. The average cost per unit of output is the dependent variable. According to the experience curve, with every doubling of accumulated output there is a potential for a reduction in real costs of added value per unit of 20 to 30%. **Figure 11-3** presents the experience curve in graphic form. The main conclusion to be drawn is as follows: relative market share, defined as market share in comparison with one's strongest competitor, is of great strategic importance. If a company has a higher relative market share, it usually produces

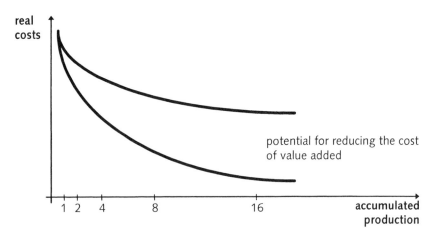

Figure 11-3: The experience curve

more units and thus achieves a larger accumulated output. This in turn creates a potential to reduce costs which, when used, leads to cost advantages over competitors with lower relative market share. These advantages can be used in a number of different ways. For example, the extra margin can be used to lower prices or to increase advertising in order to gain sales at the expense of competitors. Alternatively the better margin can be retained to produce a higher cash-flow which then can be diverted to other businesses to build up a strong position in a different market. In general, higher relative market share can lead to a better margin which in turn creates opportunities to realize attractive strategic options.

11.2.2 Norm strategies

The characterization of the four sections of the matrix suggests strategies which businesses in each area will typically follow. These are called norm strategies and their main characteristics are indicated in **Figure 11-4.**

In the basic BCG method, the choice of a strategy depends strictly on the position of a business in the portfolio matrix. But in certain cases these norm strategies can be problematic as strategic guidelines; each market situation is different, and one must take into account the specific strengths and weaknesses of the businesses concerned. The norm strategies for question marks and dogs in particular must always be reviewed critically and will in many cases be replaced by more suitable strategies. The norm strategies for stars and question marks should also not be applied blindly, but usually they provide sensible guidelines for determining target market positions and investment priorities.

The heterogeneity of demand in many markets means that even market positions with a relative market share lower than 1 can be attractive in the long term. This is always the case when a strong position has been built up in a particular customer segment or in a specific product type. Companies in second, third or far lower places in the competitive hierarchy may nevertheless dominate certain segments or

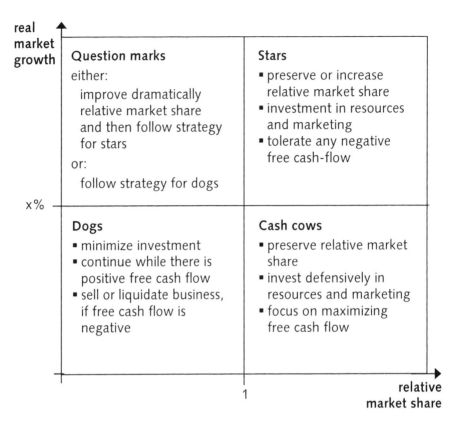

Figure 11-4: Norm strategies in the Boston Consulting Group portfolio

product areas and these companies can often justifiably follow a cash cow or star strategy. Many industries provide examples of this, including the markets for cars and for cigarettes. In both of these markets a number of competitors can maintain attractive market positions because of uniquely profiled market offers.

The norm strategies apply in principle only to strategically independent businesses without mutual dependencies, what we have called business fields. When a portfolio includes strategic businesses with important resource and market synergies, that is business units, the norm strategies must be reviewed particularly carefully. In such cases, we must take into account the impact of these strategies on the costs and market positions of other, related business units belonging in the same business field.

11.2.3 Recommendations for the portfolio as a whole

The original sense of the term portfolio implied a balanced collection of investments. As well as norm strategies for the individual businesses, therefore, there will also be recommendations which apply to the portfolio as whole. The basic objective is to create a portfolio with a balance between mature cash producing businesses and future-oriented businesses which require investment. This ensures, on the one hand, that the company is investing in markets which promise to be highly attractive in the future, and on the other hand, that the businesses in mature markets will be self-financing or may produce a free cash-flow which can be invested in other businesses (Grant 2002, p. 482f.).

The cash cows in the portfolio matrix must produce a considerable proportion of the revenue of a corporation. In addition, the portfolio matrix must include stars, which will be the high-turnover, cash-producing businesses of the future. A few question marks are also desirable, as they give the corporation room for maneuver. They may attract investments or furnish free cash-flow. Dogs are not wanted; they do not produce cash, neither do they have any future potential.

Figure 11-5 presents three examples of unbalanced portfolios, together with one which is suitably balanced. The first portfolio lacks businesses which will guarantee long term survival. The cash cows which are currently achieving a financial surplus are accompanied by only a single question-mark. This is operating in an industry with positive market growth and which is therefore attractive for the future, but the business has a poor competitive position. The second portfolio has numerous options for the future but lacks businesses providing the free cash-flow needed to exploit the potential of the stars and question marks. The third portfolio is not satisfactory at all, either in terms of current free cash-flow or future potential. The fourth presents a sensible balance between businesses generating funds and those which require funds.

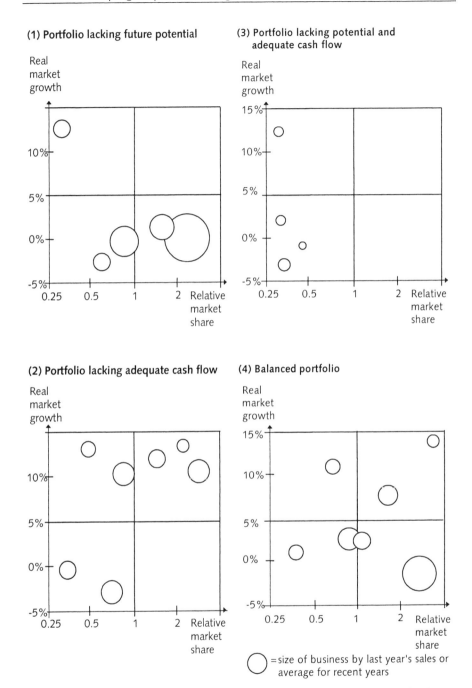

Figure 11-5: Examples of business portfolios based on the BCG method

11.3   The industry attractiveness - competitive strength portfolio

11.3.1 The portfolio matrix

In contrast to the BCG approach, the industry attractiveness - competitive strength portfolio is more complex:

- The two single quantitative criteria which define the position of a business in the BCG portfolio matrix, real market growth and relative market share, are here replaced by a wider set of quantitative and qualitative criteria.
- The four sections of the BCG portfolio matrix give way to a scheme with nine squares

It should be noted that whereas the Boston Consulting Group portfolio uses two criteria derived from the theoretical models, in this portfolio method any plausible criteria may be incorporated. Although this approach allows a more differentiated assessment of strategic businesses, there is a risk of more subjectivity.

Researchers have developed a number of differing sets of criteria (see for example Johnson & Scholes 2002, p. 288, and Thompson & Strickland 1996, p. 253). One of the most interesting is proposed by Hill & Jones (1992, p. 281 f.). It consists of two sets of seven criteria, as shown in **Figure 11-6**.

It is important that the assessments of businesses in this portfolio are carried out analytically. A brief, intuitively based assessment procedure will not only lack precision, but such a procedure almost inevitably leads to manipulations based on political considerations within the firm. In line with personal interests, individual businesses will be positioned either too favorably or not favorably enough. We therefore recommend that an analytical procedure is used, as follows (Hill & Jones 1992, p. 281 f., Thompson & Strickland, 1996, p. 248 ff.):

1. Determining the assessment criteria.
2. Determining the relative importance of the criteria by attributing to each a relative weight; the total of the relative weights for each of the two sets of criteria must be 1.

Criteria for assessing industry attractiveness	Criteria for assessing competitive strength
Industry size	Market share
Industry growth	Technological know-how
Industry profitability	Product quality
Capital intensity	After-sales service
Technological stability	Price competitiveness
Competitive intensity	Low operating costs
Cyclical independence	Productivity

Figure 11-6: Hill & Jones criteria for assessing industry attractiveness and competitive position
(adapted from Hill & Jones 1992, p. 281 f.)

3. Rating each business on each of the criteria, using a standardized rating scale.
4. Calculating industry attractiveness and competitive position by multiplying the values for each criterion by their weightings and adding the resulting products.

Figure 11-7 proposes a scheme for establishing the industry attractiveness and competitive strength of a business, based on Hill & Jones's criteria.

The vertical and horizontal axes of the industry attractiveness-competitive strength portfolio are each divided into three sections, corresponding to high, medium and low values. This produces nine squares which are grouped into four areas, as shown in **Figure 11-8**:

- The three squares at the top right (2.3, 3.2 & 3.3) are labeled 'investment and growth'. Their strong industry attractiveness and competitive strength justify investment and an extension of activity.
- The three squares at the bottom left (1.1, 1.2 & 2.1) share a combination of low or medium industry attractiveness and low or medium competitive strength. For businesses which fall into these squares a harvest strategy is the most appropriate. Where there is no prospect of a positive free cash-flow, the businesses should be sold or liquidated. This group of squares is labeled 'harvest or divest'.
- Square 1.3 represents the 'cash cows' in the McKinsey and General

Assessment criteria	Weighting of criteria	Unweighted value		Weighted value
Industry attractiveness of the business				
(1) Industry size	0.15	on scale from 1	2	0.3
(2) Industry growth	0.15	(totally unattractive)	4	0.6
(3) Industry profitability	0.2	to 4 (very	4	0.8
(4) Capital intensity	0.1	attractive)	3	0.3
(5) Technological stability	0.1		4	0.4
(6) Competitive intensity	0.2		2	0.4
(7) Cyclical independence	0.1		4	0.4
Industry attractiveness overall	1.0	---		3.2
Competitive strength of the business				
(1) Market share	0.3	on scale from 1	2	0.6
(2) Technological know-how	0.1	(clear competitive	4	0.4
(3) Product quality	0.1	weakness) to 4	3	0.3
(4) After-sales service	0.1	(clear competitive	2	0.2
(5) Price competetiveness	0.2	strength)	1	0.2
(6) Low operating cost	0.1		1	0.1
(7) Productivity	0.1		1	0.1
Competitive position overall	1.0	---		1.9

Figure 11-7: Analytical procedure to establish industry attractiveness and competitive strength of a business

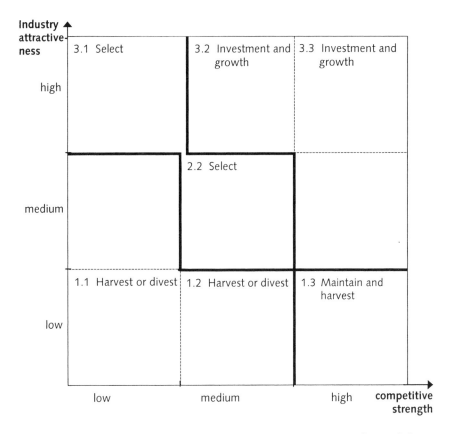

Figure 11-8: The industry attractiveness - competitive strength portfolio matrix

Electric Portfolio. The appropriate strategy for businesses of this square is to maintain them and to realize free cash-flows.
- The two remaining squares, the center one (2.2) and the top left hand square (3.1), are labeled 'select'. For businesses falling into these areas, either option is possible. A more detailed analysis should reveal whether or not it would be favorable to invest in the businesses concerned.

This grouping is different from what is conventional in the literature (see for example Thompson & Strickland, 1996, p. 226) where the bottom right hand corner square (1.3) is generally attributed to the select group. This view is difficult to accept; in practice the combination of low industry attractiveness and strong competitive strength requires investments to hold the strong position and the harvesting of the free cash-flow produced by such businesses.

It can be helpful to use the BCG matrix to check the validity of the industry attractiveness - competitive strength portfolio. To do this seems especially important when a industry attractiveness-competitive strength portfolio is based on a summative evaluation of the current positions of the businesses. Alternatively, instead of setting up a BCG portfolio in parallel to the industry attractiveness-competitive strength portfolio, the two methods can be combined within a single matrix. One way in which the two approaches can be combined is explained in **Inset 11-3.**

Inset 11-3: Combining the two portfolio methods

It can be interesting to combine the two methods by incorporating information from the BCG method into the industry attractiveness - competitive strength portfolio matrix. For every business located in one of the nine boxes the relevant real market growth and relative market share are indicated with arrows. **Figure 11-9** gives an example.

This presentation makes it possible to recognize any lack of correspondence between industry attractiveness and real market growth on the one hand, and competitive strength and relative market share on the other. For example, in the business field C we have high industry attractiveness alongside a real market growth of only 3%. In business field B, while the competitive strength is rated as average, relative market share is only 0.2. In addition, for the planning period a marked rise in competitive strength is expected, but the relative market share will rise only insignificantly, to 0.25. These discrepancies must be accounted for and the factors must be listed which have led to the differences between the values for the quantitative parameters (real market growth and relative market share) and the qualitative ones (industry attractiveness and competitive strength).

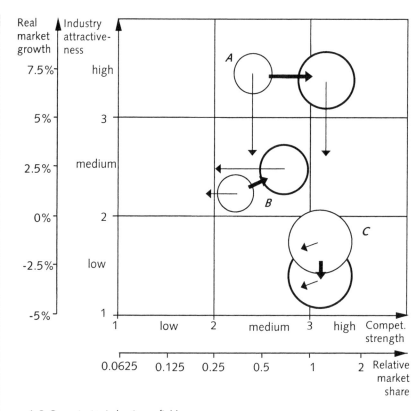

A,B,C = strategic business fields

○ = turnover current position

○ = turnover target position

➡ = changes in the positions of the
        business fields during the
        planning period
→ = positions of the business fields
        in terms of real market growth
        and relative market share

Figure 11-9: Portfolio plan combining the two methods

There are two essential advantages to supplementing the industry attractiveness-competitive strength portfolio method in this way with the 'hard facts' of the BCG method:

- There is often a danger that the current and target portfolio positions for businesses will be manipulated for company - internal political reasons. This effect can be effectively countered if the two quantitative criteria (real market growth and relative market share) are applied on the basis of real data. Proceeding in this way reveals discrepancies between qualitative and quantitative assessments which will have to be accounted for.

- The application of the BCG criteria is useful in order to assess whether the portfolio is financially balanced, which is always difficult to judge for an industry attractiveness - competitive strength portfolio.

11.3.2 Norm strategies and recommendations for the portfolio as a whole

As in the BCG portfolio, the positions of the businesses lead to general recommendations for strategies. The norm strategies for the industry attractiveness-competitive strength portfolio are presented in key words in **Figure 11-10**. As with the norm strategies for the BCG portfolio, these are not to be applied uncritically, but must be reviewed carefully and given specific form.

As with the BCG approach, a balance in the portfolio between businesses producing cash and those requiring investment is suggested. But in the industry attractiveness-competitive strength portfolio this recommendation is less easy to apply: the link between the types of business and their potential for free cash-flow is less clearly established.

A balance in the industry attractiveness-competitive strength portfolio must be achieved first of all between the businesses in the group labeled investment and growth and those in square 1.3 at the bottom right, which are the equivalent of the cash cows in the BCG portfolio. A well-balanced portfolio will not include too many businesses from other areas, because in many cases these represent businesses which neither produce cash, nor help to assure the future of the corporation.

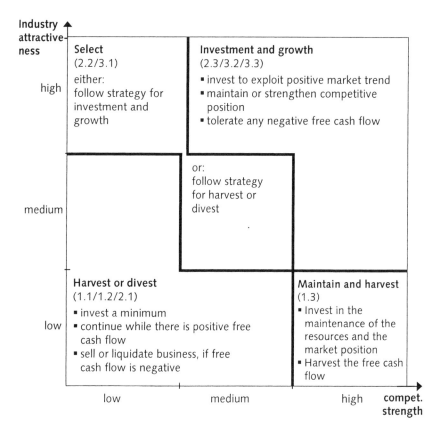

Figure 11-10: Norm strategies in the industry attractiveness - competitive strength portfolio

11.4   Portfolio analysis and planning process

11.4.1 Overview of the process

Portfolio techniques are appropriate only in cases where the corporation (or an important part of a big company), whose strategy is being reviewed, has a certain degree of heterogeneity. If there are only one or two business fields or business units, a picture of the strategic situation of the company can be obtained without resorting to portfolio methods.

Although the two portfolio methods described above are technically different, the basic approach and the general objectives of the methods are the same. The portfolio analysis and planning process can therefore be defined identically for the application of the two methods.

For portfolio analysis and planning the following five step process is recommended:

1. Preliminary methodological decisions.
2. Definition of the current portfolio.
3. Forecast of the future market growth or industry attractiveness, according to the chosen method.
4. Analysis of the current portfolio
5. Planning of target portfolio and target market positions

The five steps will be described in detail in the following sections.

11.4.2 Preliminary methodological decisions

Before commencing the portfolio analysis and planning process, two methodological decisions are required.

The first decision concerns the selection of the portfolio method to be used. If we limit our discussion to the methods presented above, there are three possibilities:

- BCG portfolio.
- Industry attractiveness - competitive strength portfolio.
- Both of these in parallel or in combined form.

In general the BCG portfolio is to be preferred: it is simpler and less open to subjective factors. The fact that the method is limited to two criteria can be compensated for during the development of business strategies.

The second decision required concerns the number of portfolio plans. This problem is usually solved rapidly. For example, consider a watch manufacturer with four strategic business units; these will be accommodated in a single portfolio. A graphics firm with the three strategic business fields "graphic design", "photolithography" and "printing", the last of these subdivided into four business units, also presents no difficulties. Here the "graphic design" and the "photolithography" and the four business units within "printing" can be accommodated within a single portfolio. The need for more than one portfolio arises if more than ten to twelve businesses need to be included in the planning. As **Figure 11-11** shows, a portfolio with more than ten businesses is likely to be confusing and no longer helpful in providing a clear picture of the strategic situation of the company.

If the number of strategic businesses is more than a certain figure, it becomes necessary to use more than one matrix. For example, for a

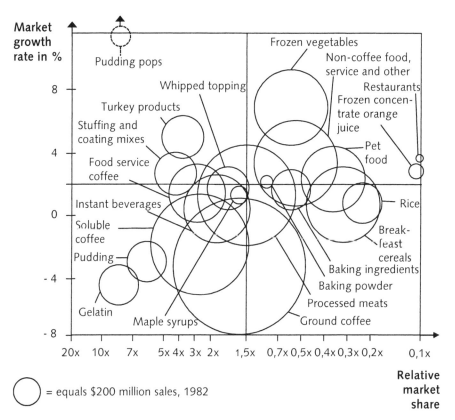

Figure 11-11: Market growth - market share portfolio of General Foods Corporation 1982
(Collis & Montgomery, 1997, p. 19)

chemical corporation operating in four industries, pharmaceuticals, fertilizers, paints and vitamins, with different product groups in each of them, it would be appropriate to use five portfolio matrices on two hierarchical levels. At the top level there would be a portfolio with the four business fields or divisions. At the second level there would be a separate portfolio presenting the business units within each division.

What follows is based on the usual choice of a single portfolio plan.

11.4.3 Description of the current portfolio

The current portfolio is established in a three stage process.

First, the markets served by the businesses have to be precisely defined, both geographically, and in terms of products and services. These specifications provide the basis for identifying the quantitative information necessary to establish the current position of the businesses.

Next the current positions of the businesses are determined. The necessary technical background to this has already been presented above.

Third the importance of the businesses must be indicated. This is usually done by drawing circles in which the size of the circle indicates the amount of turnover generated by the business.

We suggest basing the description of the current portfolio strictly on data for developments up to the current situation and specifically not to include forecasts or visions of future developments. A clear separation between experienced reality and predicted developments helps to restrict subjective bias in the definition of the current position of businesses. It also helps to clarify what the planners are talking about when they analyze the opportunities and problems linked to the current business portfolio.

11.4.4 Predicting changes in real market growth or industry attractiveness

Predicting changes in market growth or industry attractiveness serves two purposes:
- It produces information which is needed to assess the current portfolio, in particular to evaluate the viability of cash cows and dogs.
- It prepares the way for the discussion of strategic options and the definition of the planned strategy.

Depending on the type of business, the forecasting period should cover from five to ten years. This period is determined by the binding effect of investments and the number of years during which resources need to be exploited to yield a good return.

11.4.5 Analysis of the current portfolio

The analysis of the current portfolio comprises two main tasks:
- The evaluation of the current portfolio as a whole, mainly judging the balance between mature cash producing businesses and future oriented businesses and
- a preliminary examination of the suitability of adopting norm strategies considering the specific situations of the different businesses in the portfolio.

For a discussion of what is important in carrying out these tasks see sections 11.2.2, 11.2.3 and 11.3.3.

11.4.6 Planning the target portfolio and target market positions

The analysis of the current portfolio should reveal threats and opportunities related to the portfolio as a whole and to individual businesses. The recognition of an unbalanced portfolio, with a cash cow in a declining market, or a star whose development cannot be financed, or a question mark with an uncertain future, or other problem areas, is the starting point for discussions leading to alternative target portfolios and to specific objectives for the individual businesses.

Generally it is advisable to produce two or three different alternatives for the target portfolio. Often the discussion in strategy planning groups leads inevitably to these different alternatives. But if this does not happen, then there must be a conscious effort to find more than one possibility. Often options can be found in different concentrations of future activities.

In many cases the discussion of different target portfolios produces clear preferences for one alternative. If this is not the case, an in-depth evaluation is recommended. This normally means developing business strategies, at the least for those businesses whose target portfolio positions have been the subject of controversy in the project group. Working out specific business strategies before finalizing the corporate strategy certainly complicates the planning process. But it may often be a good investment in helping to avoid the setting of unrealistic portfolio targets. One should also remember that it is typical for heuristic problem solving to include loops in the path to the overall solution.

In any event, even if a specific target portfolio seems feasible and clearly superior to other solutions, we recommend complementing the stated objectives of the businesses in terms of relative market share or competitive strength with estimates concerning the development of free cash flow or cash drain for the businesses. Although it is often difficult to develop such estimates, not to do so would mean that the financial feasibility of the proposed corporate strategy remains uncertain and this could jeopardize its implementation.

11.4.7 Portfolio analysis and planning in a retail group

Inset 11-4 now presents an account of the portfolio analysis and planning in a retail group based in the east of Switzerland.

Inset 11-4: Portfolio analysis and planning in a retail group

Baer is a large department store in downtown St Gallen which has belonged to the family of the same name for three generations. Offering a full range of goods, it has been able to preserve its dominance in the region **Figure 11-12** presents the range of goods sold and estimates for current turnover.

The store's competitors are large hypermarkets on the one hand, and small specialized shops on the other. Currently the store enjoys 24% of a total market for the St Gallen urban area worth an estimated 800 million Swiss francs. Its largest competitor has a market share of 19%. The average real market growth across all product groups is estimated at approx. 3%, while the growth rate of the Swiss economy is about 5%.

With an eye on the increasing ecological awareness among consumers the owners of the store accepted an offer of franchising rights three years ago from The Body Shop Levy in Zürich for the three cantons of St. Gallen, Appenzell and Thurgau. The Body shop stores sell cosmetic products based on natural substances

product group	turnover in mil. CHF
textiles, clothing and shoes	70
cosmetics and toiletries	10
food	20
household goods	40
sports goods	25
home electronics	20
fashion jewellery and accessories	2
books and magazines	2
flowers	1
miscellaneous	2
total turnover	192

Figure 11-12: Product groups and turnover in the Baer department store

which have been developed without experiments on animals. Body Shops have been opened in Rohrschach, Wil and St. Gallen, and the turnover figures for the three shops confirm the Baer Group management's positive assessment of the market. With market growth of 10% for natural cosmetics, the Body Shops last year had turnover figures of 0.8 mil. Swiss francs in Rohrschach, 1.0 mil. Swiss francs in Wil and 1.5 mil. Swiss francs in St. Gallen.

Some years ago the owner of the store at that time, Fritz Baer, decided to make his advertising department independent of the store, hoping to widen its horizons and foster a more entrepreneurial mode of thinking among the employees. The agency which was set up, Kreativ, at first only accepted outside work in order to use temporary overcapacity, but for ten years now has been competing vigorously for external contracts and these now constitute 60% of its turnover of 2.4 mil. Swiss francs. With overall spending on advertising stagnating in this region, there is now a bitter struggle for business. With a market share of 7% for the region, Kreativ is around 3.3 times smaller than its strongest competitor, a national agency, based in Zurich.

Figure 11-13 shows how these activities within the Baer Group can be classified into strategic business fields and strategic business units. As can be seen, the fashion jewelry and accessories, books

Strategic business fields	Strategic business units
Department store	Textiles, clothing and shoes
	Cosmetics and toiletries
	Food
	Houshold goods
	Sports goods
	Home electronics
Body Shops	-
Advertising agency Kreativ	-

Figure 11-13: Strategic business fields and business units in the Baer Group

and magazines, flowers and miscellaneous have all been excluded from consideration as their low level of turnover makes them strategically irrelevant.

The Boston portfolio method was adopted and the various business fields and business units incorporated into a single portfolio plan. **Figure 11-15** presents the current portfolio and **Figure 11-14** gives the data on the basis of which it was established.

The uncertainty of the economic situation makes it difficult to predict future real market growth. Predictions are based on subjective assessments by the management for the coming five years:

- The department store expects an overall growth of around 2%. The predictions are particularly low for food and textiles, where zero growth is forecast. Cosmetics and household goods can expect 2% growth. Sports goods expect to continue their growth trend of about 8% per annum. Home electronics remains a positive area but the predicted growth of 10% is less than that of previous years.
- According to the management, growth in the market for natural cosmetics will also tail off and settle at around 8%.
- The region's stagnation in advertising expenditure will continue and zero growth is predicted for the advertising sector.

Management discussion of the target portfolio focused on the two businesses with low relative market share. Two options were considered, investing in the advertising agency and the business unit 'food' in order to gain increased market share or abandoning these businesses in order to concentrate resources on activities which were better placed for future success. Because of the high competitive intensity in advertising and food, both of which were in saturated markets with no growth, the management decided to give up these businesses. After adopting this basic principle the next task was to specify target relative market share for the businesses that would remain:

- The appeal of the department store for consumers should be maintained. By reviewing the product range, and through

Strategic business fields and business units	Relevant area	Unconsolidated turnover in mio. CHF	Turnover of the strongest competitor	Relative market share	Average real growth rate for the last three years
Department store	St. Gallen Urban area	192	150	1.30	0.03
Textiles, clothing and shoes		70	85	0.82	0.00
Cosmetics and toiletries		10	13	0.77	0.03
Food		20	100	0.20	0.01
Household goods		40	24	1.67	0.04
Sports goods		25	16	1.56	0.08
Home electronics		20	20	1.00	0.12
Body Shops	East Swiss	3.3	1.1	3.0	0.10
Advertising agency Kreativ	East Swiss	2.4	8.0	0.30	0.00

Figure 11-14: Data concerning the current portfolio for the Baer Group

intensive advertising and a thorough renovation of the sales floors, the current relative market share of 1.3 would be preserved. For textiles the range would be expanded and a higher market share achieved; with an unusually wide range of branded goods, especially jeans, shoes and sports wear, it was hoped to reach a relative market share of 1.0 or better. Sales of food would be dropped in favour of a shop-in-the-shop solution in which the space would be rented out to an established delicatessen retailer, which would in turn increase the appeal of the store as a whole. Within cosmetics and toiletries, the area of make up would be expanded and a limited range of perfumes would be introduced. This should maintain the current competitive position. In household goods the aim was also to hold the current leading position. For home electronics and sports goods the ever expanding range of products and the high market growth

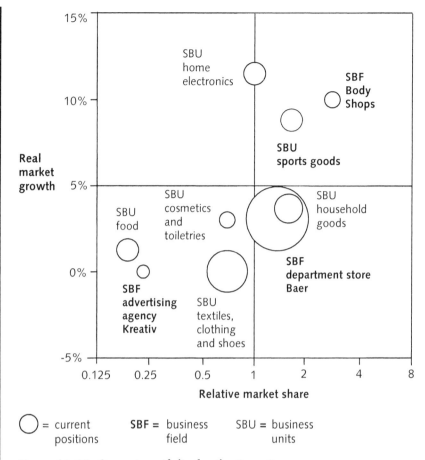

Figure 11-15: Current portfolio for the Baer Group

rate demanded considerable investment in marketing and in ex-
tending the product range. In these two areas the current leading position should at least be maintained.

- The successes with the Body Shops encouraged the owners of
  the group to plan two more such stores in Frauenfeld and in
  Kreuzlingen, one to be opened next year and one the year after
  that. With no serious competition in the area of natural cosmetics, relative market share could be expected to grow to 4.0.
- The advertising agency would be bought out by the management, with the Baer Group undertaking to give its advertising
  contracts exclusively to this agency for a period of three years.

Figure 11-16 presents the target portfolio for the Baer Group.

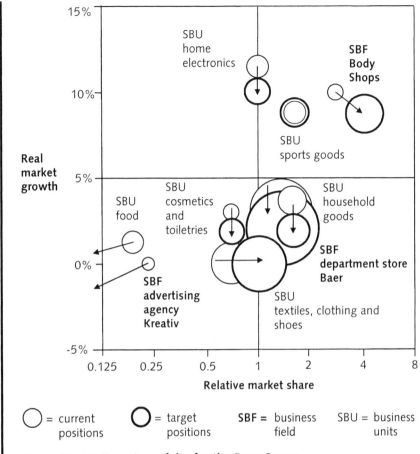

Figure 11-16: Target portfolio for the Baer Group

12　The corporate strategy development process

12.1　Overview of the process of developing a corporate strategy

The development of corporate strategy constitutes the second step in the process of strategic planning. Producing and evaluating corporate strategy options is a complex undertaking, which is divided into a number of subtasks. **Figure 12-1** gives an overview of the process we recommend. In line with the nature of heuristic methods, certain loops are built into the process.

In sections 12.2 and 12.3 the first two tasks are discussed, defining the strategic businesses (task 2.1) and describing the current corporate strategy (task 2.2). Since Chapter Nine, Ten and Eleven have already dealt in detail with the content of these steps, the sections provide no more than a number of reminders with brief additional remarks.

Section 12.4 offers a more detailed account of the development of strategic options on the basis of an assessment of the current strategy (task 2.3). It addresses the question of defining the breadth or focus of corporate activities and looks at a number of fundamental strategic choices for developing businesses: internal growth, strategic alliances, mergers and acquisitions. Possibilities for diversification are also considered.

The final task in the process described in Figure 12-1, the provisional formulation of the planned corporate strategy (task 2.4), does not require detailed commentary. But we would like to underline that, once Step Two of the overall planning process has been accomplished, it is important to produce a clear written account of the results, in order to use this as a basis for the development of business strategies in Step Three. The resulting document should also facilitate the final formulation of the planned strategies in Step Six of the overall planning process. The fact that the planned corporate strategy, as formulated in task 2.4, should be regarded as provisional, is a logical consequence of the heuristic planning process, of the nature of the assessment criteria and of the available information at this stage

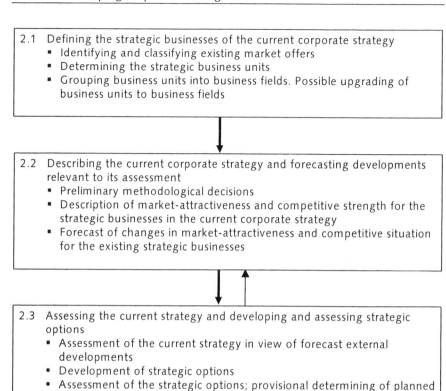

2.1 Defining the strategic businesses of the current corporate strategy
- Identifying and classifying existing market offers
- Determining the strategic business units
- Grouping business units into business fields. Possible upgrading of business units to business fields

2.2 Describing the current corporate strategy and forecasting developments relevant to its assessment
- Preliminary methodological decisions
- Description of market-attractiveness and competitive strength for the strategic businesses in the current corporate strategy
- Forecast of changes in market-attractiveness and competitive situation for the existing strategic businesses

2.3 Assessing the current strategy and developing and assessing strategic options
- Assessment of the current strategy in view of forecast external developments
- Development of strategic options
- Assessment of the strategic options; provisional determining of planned corporate strategy

2.4 Provisional formulation of the planned corporate strategy

 usual sequence of steps    possible loops in the sequence

Figure 12-1: The process of developing a corporate strategy

of the planning process. It is often difficult to evaluate whether the strategic goals expressed by the corporate strategy are realistic without knowing more about the business strategies to be followed by the different businesses. The process of development of the business strategies gives more and more concrete insight into the nature and sustainability of competitive advantages and so makes it possible to evaluate the feasibility of the planned corporate strategy. This means that as a result of business strategy planning in Step Three of the overall planning process, the corporate strategy may have to be adapted, partially altered or completely reviewed.

12.2   Defining the strategic businesses

A systematic approach to defining the strategic businesses (task 2.1) is presented in Chapter Nine, and, as Figure 12-1 indicates, is included in the corporate strategy planning process without requiring any adaptation. The commentary here need only refer to two points of special importance:

- For the assessment of the current corporate strategy and the development of strategic options it is vital to distinguish between the relatively autonomous business fields and the business units, which are much more closely linked to other businesses. With business fields, far-reaching options can be envisioned, such as involving the business in a joint venture, or selling off the business altogether. But when considering options like this for strategic business units, market or resource links with other business units must always be taken into account. For example, selling off a product group which shares resources with other business units generally leads to a less efficient use of production facilities, marketing capacities or other resources and this means higher costs for the businesses which remain. To give another example, involving a business unit in a joint venture with a strong partner, when its market is linked to that of other business units, can have the effect of weakening the competitive position of the other businesses operating in the market.
- It is also an important principle that the definition of strategic businesses produced as the outcome of subtask 2.1 is regarded as provisional. The strategic options to be developed and assessed in the final step of the corporate strategy planning process (task 2.3) will nearly always lead to some change in the structure of strategic businesses. Depending on the result of the planning decisions, the number of strategic businesses may increase and enlarge the strategic scope of the company. In addition it can be useful to develop new product groups within a business field and in this way create new strategic business units. Introducing new business units within a business field can be strategically useful, either to use current resources in a more efficient way and so cut unit costs for existing businesses, or to respond to the needs of different customer groups to try to keep potential new competitors out of the market. Finally it can prove useful to upgrade business units to business fields or downgrade business fields to the status of business units. Upgrad-

ing business units may promote entrepreneurial thinking and responsibility or induce a more flexible approach to the market. Downgrading means that two or more business fields, which previously enjoyed autonomy, are combined into a new strategic business field. With this, potential for synergies can be used and reduced costs and increased profit will be the result.

The provisional definition of the strategic businesses is the basis for the description of the current corporate strategy and for forecasting the developments in task 2.2.

12.3   Describing the current strategy and forecasting developments relevant to its assessment

Task 2.2 begins with preliminary methodological decisions. They concern two questions:

(1) the choice of specific methodological tools for the description of the current corporate strategy; since it is more efficient to describe and assess the current corporate strategy with the help of the same tools, this decision determines at the same time the methods applied in step 2.3.
(2) the question of whether specific models or methods should be used to forecast developments in market attractiveness over the following years.

Concerning the methodological tools to describe and, in step 2.3, to assess the current corporate strategy, the following recommendations are made:

- The reasons for choosing or not choosing a particular portfolio method are discussed in section 11.4.2. But it is important to emphasize that portfolio methods are appropriate only where the portfolio of strategic businesses has a certain degree of complexity. Where there are three or fewer businesses, it is sufficient to produce a written description of the strategic position (the competitive strength and the attractiveness of the served markets) of these businesses.
- In order to achieve a deeper understanding of the market attrac-

tiveness, it is often helpful to use Porter's two models, the Five Forces model of competitive intensity and the model of strategic groups both described in Chapter Nine, especially for strategic businesses which are in a critical position or need an in-depth evaluation for some other reason.

• Describing and evaluating competitive strength is a difficult task. It consists principally in judging whether advantages in the market offer are based on sustainable advantages in resources. The detailed evaluation of market offers and resources is one of the main tasks in planning business strategies. But some estimate of the resource situation is also necessary in order to assess the current corporate strategy and to develop strategic options.

The importance of resources for strategy formation has been established by extensive research, **Inset 12-1** provides a summary of this work, known as the resource-based view.

Inset 12-1: The resource - based view
(Kühn & Grünig, 2000, p. 141 ff.)

Whereas the market-based view can be summed up by the structure-conduct-performance paradigm, the resource-based view is expressed by the resources-conduct-performance paradigm:

• A company's resources are the basis of its strategic success. These resources have come into existence over a long period or have been consciously constructed.

• Resource advantages allow companies to produce offers which are differentiated from those of their competitors.

• Market success is the result of competitive advantages at the level of both offers and resources.

Figure 12-2 presents the two paradigms of the market-based and the resource-based view.

In the resource-based view, the term 'resources' must be understood much more broadly than its everyday meaning suggests. Apart from plant, equipment, finance and human resources, resources include:

Market-based view: structure-conduct-performance paradigm	Resource-based view: resources-conduct-performance paradigm
Structure: When building businesses, firms choose industries and strategic groups. The structure of these markets and groups defines the possibilities for achieving success	**Resources:** Companies obtain over time, either by good fortune or by planned measures, resources which are unique and not available to competitors.

Conduct: Firms use these possibilities by choosing a competitive strategy and building the required resources	**Conduct:** The use of these resources to create products or services meeting customer requirements in specific markets leads to permanent competitive advantages

Performance: Differences in long-term performance can be explained by industry and group attractiveness together with the realized competitive strategy	**Performance:** Long-term differences in success can be explained in terms of the use of unique resources to create products meeting customer needs.

Figure 12-2: Market - based view and resource - based view paradigms

- Organizational structures and management tools
- Patents and licenses
- Corporate image and brand image
- Quality and size of the customer base
- Corporate culture
- Competencies in the company

Assessing the strategic value of resources is a central problem in the resource-based view. According to Barney (1991, p. 99 ff.) a resource must have four characteristics in order to produce sustained competitive advantages:

1. Rarity: the value of resources depends on restricted availability. Is it possible for a competitor to buy in a resource which he does not possess? The most valuable resources are often those which are closely linked to brands, like McDonalds, Coca Cola and Marlboro. These leading brands have enormous value. Strong corporate cultures, like that of McKinsey, are also unique resources.

2. Ability to meet customer needs: the resource must have the capacity to be transformed into benefits. This is an essential condition. Even if the resource's availability is restricted, it has no value if it cannot be used to produce products or services which meet customer needs.

3. Imperfect imitability: a resource must be difficult for the competitors to initiate. The network of stores owned by Migros is an example. Even if billions were invested, it would be very difficult for a competitor to create such a network of shops in prime locations covering the whole of Switzerland.

4. Imperfect substitutability: the resource must resist substitution. Technological developments often lead to substitution of resources. For example, the skills for producing propellers lost much of their value fifty years ago when jet aircraft were produced.

Fairly rough forecasts of changes in market attractiveness and competitive situation are often sufficient as a basis for assessing the current strategy. Expert opinion based on the data gathered in strategic analysis is therefore usually enough to prepare the planning decision of step 2.3. But of course, it can sometimes be helpful to use more sophisticated forecasting methods, such as scenario analysis to obtain greater insight into important market dimensions or the expected behavior of competitors. Scenario analysis occupies a prominent place in the planning literature and enjoys wide acceptance among larger companies facing complex and uncertain planning problems. **Inset 12-2** provides a short introduction to this rather demanding diagnostic instrument.

Inset 12-2: Scenario analysis
(Lanner, 1999a)

Scenario analysis was first developed by the Rand Corporation for the planning of military strategy. The method began to be adopted by companies for strategic planning at the beginning of the seventies, when the oil crisis of 1973-4 highlighted the limits of existing planning tools. Royal Dutch/Shell successfully pioneered the technique and it allowed the company to predict the oil crisis and to plan appropriate reactions earlier than competitors (Reibnitz, 1987, p. 11 ff.).

By a scenario we mean
- a possible future constellation of elements in the company's environment, together with
- the developmental trend which leads to this situation

Figure 12-3 presents a way of representing scenarios visually in the form of an expanding cone (Reibnitz, 1987, p. 30). As time moves forward away from the present, the range of possible constellations increases: the cone expands. Figure 12-3 presents three scenarios:
- The so-called trend scenario is the simple result of the continuation of present developmental trends into the future.
- Scenario 1 is another possible path of development. If this line of development is more favorable to the company than Scenario 0, the company may try to influence the environment in this direction. While the opportunities for small and medium-sized companies to influence their environment are limited, large international companies do have the power to influence environmental trends.
- Scenario 2 at first follows Scenario 1 but then an event intervenes which affects subsequent development. From the point of view of the company this is an undesired effect - the event is seen as a disturbance - and so counter-measures are planned in this scenario which steer development back in the desired direction of Scenario 1.

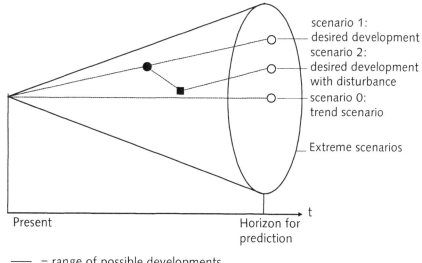

= range of possible developments
= development of scenario
= disturbance
= beginning of counter-measures

Figure 12-3: Tracking of scenarios
(adapted from Reibnitz, 1987, p. 30)

- The diagram shows that companies in a dynamic environment should not base their planning on a single prognosis of future development, as the range of variation for future developments is large. The purpose of scenario analysis is to illustrate the range of possible future developments and, on the basis of these, to develop alternative paths for company development.

Scenario analysis can be seen as consisting of the following sub-tasks:

- The subject of the study and the questions to be addressed must first be defined. Scenario analysis is a costly procedure and can only be justified where there is clear agreement about the focus and purpose of the analysis.
- Next, the most important factors must be identified which can influence the subject of the study, and a framework must be created, linking these factors together. Both qualitative and quantitative factors must be included. As a consequence of the

presence of qualitative factors, the different variables usually cannot be linked in a purely mathematical way. But the ways in which they influence each other can usually be described

- Next for each variable the possible developments must be identified.
- These possible developments for different variables are now grouped together in bundles of related possible developments.
- For each bundle of possible developments, the resulting scenario must be described as concretely as possible. It is important to state explicitly the events which form part of the scenario.
- If it is possible to influence these future developments to a certain extent, appropriate measures must be sketched out. Generally this is only possible for very large international companies. In the proposed procedure for corporate strategy planning in Figure 12-1, decisions concerning such measures are part of task 2.3.

The preliminary methodological decisions determine the content of the two subsequent procedural steps of task 2.2, the description of the strategic position of the businesses in the current corporate strategy and the forecast of developments affecting market attractiveness and competitive position. The most widely used models and methods are described in Chapters Ten and Eleven. Based on our experience in strategy planning, we would like to add one further recommendation here. In order to prevent a mixing of more objective facts and managerial decisions, we suggest interpreting task 2.2 as an activity which aims to produce a well structured and well founded information base but will not yet include evaluations of current strategies and strategic options. A clear separation of the two tasks helps to recognize and limit the influence of any subjective values and departmental interests which might bias the results of the planning process.

12.4 Assessing the current strategy and determining the planned strategy

12.4.1 Preliminary remarks

While tasks 2.1 and 2.2 prepare the ground for corporate strategy planning, task 2.3 comprises the genuine planning decisions. It is the key task in the corporate strategy planning process. This does not mean that tasks 2.1 and 2.2 are not important for the quality of the result of the planning process. The input from these tasks to a large extent determines how well founded the decision processes are and thus how well-founded is their outcome, the corporate strategy.

As indicated in Figure 12-1, task 2.3 comprises (1) the assessment of the current strategy, (2) the development of strategic options and (3) the assessment of these strategic options. In the following, these three procedural steps will be addressed separately in sections 12.4.2 to 12.4.4. But of course one should bear in mind the interdependence of these questions and the heuristic nature of the planning process: in practice the planners will sometimes need to review earlier decisions in the light of what is learned in the subsequent steps.

12.4.2 Assessment of the current strategy

The current corporate strategy should be assessed on two levels:
- The planners should make an overall assessment of the strategic value of the current portfolio of business fields and business units and
- examine threats and opportunities for the strategic positions of the individual businesses.

The assessment on both levels should not be done for the current situation, but should anticipate the future trend in market attractiveness and competitive intensity.

To assess the portfolio as a whole the project group should judge the balance between major cash producing businesses and growth gener-ating businesses, in which the company will need to invest to ensure its future. The steps required are analogous to what is presented in Chapter 11 in the section on portfolio methods and therefore does not require further comment here.

Assessment of the future competitive position of the different busi-nesses is carried out under the assumption that there will be no change in strategy pursued. Two aspects must be evaluated:

- First the competitive situation in the industry markets served by the businesses must be assessed. Normally the information base estab-lished in task 2.2 will provide an indication of the growth rates, the expected competitive intensity and the trends in the profit margins, both for the industries as a whole and for specific strategic groups within industries. On this basis the project group should be able to identify and describe market-based threats and opportunities which are of strategic importance.
- However it can be very useful to assess the available resources too. This may provide a better understanding of how stable the com-pany's competitive positions are and of what possible changes might occur in the competitive positions at the level of the market offer when competitors can imitate or substitute the key resources needed to create these. In addition sustainable strengths in specific resources can offer companies opportunities to generate innovative market offers and diversify into new and attractive markets. The approximate assessment of resources required in task 2.3 essentially means that a summative qualitative comparison is made between the company and its principal competitors in terms of technological and marketing skills. In quantitative terms, the available financial means within the company for product development and market-ing must be compared with the budgets of competitors. Very often production is of less importance, both quantitatively and quantita-tively, as in many industries there is the possibility of outsourcing.

The assessment of the current strategy should finally produce three results:

- a list of businesses which can expect success by continuing with their current strategy
- a list of businesses which require a reassessment of strategy

- a judgement as to whether the existing portfolio of businesses is sufficient or whether new areas of activity should be researched.

12.4.3 Development of strategic options

(i) Two types of options

At the corporate level two different types of options can be distinguished: the planners may both develop options for the future portfolio, and develop options for businesses so they can reach their target positions in the future portfolio.

In section 12.4.3 these two tasks are each discussed in turn.

(ii) Options for the future portfolio

Based on the assessment of the existing portfolio and the current businesses, it is now possible to produce and assess options for the future portfolio. In generating and assessing options for the future portfolio two basic questions must be answered. The first of these concerns the breadth of corporate activity. Where the breadth of the current portfolio is judged unsatisfactory, the question also arises as to which new areas the company should diversify into.

As regards the breadth of company activity, a number of different positions are possible. The range of possibilities goes from tightly focused companies, like Schindler, which concentrates on the production, installation and maintenance of elevators, right up to conglomerates like General Electrics, with the broadest imaginable range of activities in both capital goods and consumer products. An example of a company taking a middle course is Feldschlösschen, which produces beer, mineral water and soft drinks and is also a drinks wholesaler.

Determining the optimal breadth of company activities is naturally a crucial matter. A number of different theoretical approaches have been developed and very many empirical studies have been carried out which attempt to throw light on this question. **Inset 12-3** summarizes findings from this research.

Inset 12-3: The optimal breadth of company activity
(Palich, Cardinal & Miller, 2000)

Determining the optimal breadth of activity of a company has been an important research area for more than three decades. Palich, Cardinal and Miller have produced a summary of this research (2000, p. 155 ff.).

In the first part of their article the authors present theoretical models which attempt to explain the relationship between success and degree of diversification. Reviewing the various proposals which have been made, they put forward three hypotheses as possible explanatory models:

- The linear model
- The inverted U model
- The intermediate model

Figure 12-4 presents the three hypotheses. The linear model assumes that a company's competitiveness rises as company activity increases in heterogeneity. The arguments underlying this hypothesis refer to market power and access to lower prices in internal factor markets. The other two hypotheses assume that where a company diversifies into a related field, businesses will share resources and will therefore be able to realize economies of scope. In the inverted U model these advantages can be eroded when companies diversify too widely because of exponentially increasing management and coordination costs and inefficiencies in internal resource allocation. This hypothesis thus assumes that there is an optimal degree of diversification. The intermediate model, in contrast, proposes that in the transition from related to unrelated diversification advantages and disadvantages will balance each other out and performance remain unchanged.

In the second part of the article, the authors carry out a meta-analysis to test the inverted U model empirically. They identify 82

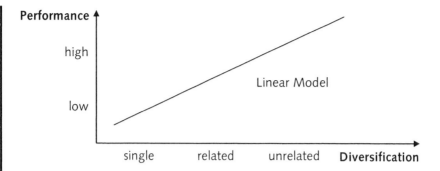

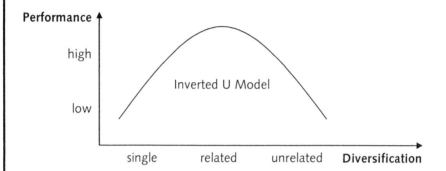

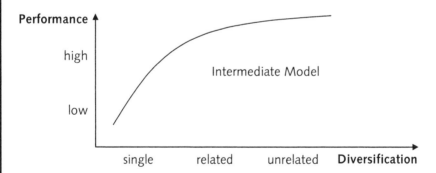

Figure 12-4: Three models explaining the success of diversification
(Palich, Cardinal & Miller, 2000, p.157)

different empirical studies on diversification, of which about two-thirds prove suitable for their meta-analysis. In order to avoid the problem of data being counted twice, they eliminate all data that authors cite from other studies.

The meta-analysis presented considerable methodological difficulties, as the studies included operationalize the problem in different ways and work with different statistical approaches. There is not space here to consider this in detail. Nevertheless, the results are clear. Regardless of which measure of performance is used (growth, ROI, ROS or others), the inverted U model is validated. For company managers, the finding is that neither a very narrow nor a very wide field of activity is optimal for success. The optimal degree of diversification may well be hard to identify, but it is located where businesses use the same resources and economies of scope exist. This may happen most often when a number of businesses are active in the same industry market. However, it is also possible that activities in different markets can bring positive synergies. But here the different businesses must share strategically important resources.

If the current portfolio is not sufficient for the future, diversification possibilities must be identified and assessed. Following Miller and Dess (1996, p. 244 ff.), we can distinguish between three forms of diversification: vertical, horizontal and geographical. Within each of the three there are a number of possible variations:

- For vertical diversification the question arises as to whether to invest in the preceding or succeeding step in the value creation chain.
- For horizontal diversification, in principle any industry in which the company is not already active is available as a choice.
- For geographical diversification, the field of activity can be extended by including any new region or country where the company is not currently operating: If the corporation has more than one business field, it will be necessary to decide which business fields will build positions in new markets.

Although, in practice, the room for maneuver among alternatives will always be somewhat restricted, nevertheless the search for possibilities to widen corporate activity often leads to a number of options which are very different from each other, and this fact makes it difficult to compare and judge them. The large number of failed attempts at diversification can mainly be attributed to the difficulty in evaluating options.

Miller and Dess (1996, p. 265 ff.) make a number of interesting observations on the subject of the assessment of strategic options. **Figure 12-5** gives six motivations for diversification, which, according to these writers, are most often cited in support of a diversification move. Miller and Dess recommend assessing diversification options primarily in terms of criteria which correlate positively with the ability to create shareholder value. The diagram in Figure 12-5 orders the criteria according to their capacity to create this value. The following criteria seem to be the most important:

- the possibility of exploiting existing core competencies. Valora's strategy is an example confirming this: the company only diversifies into industries where it can use its competencies in consolidation or multiplication
- potential to increase market power
- the degree of common use of infrastructure, such as transport and warehousing arrangements, strong store locations etc.

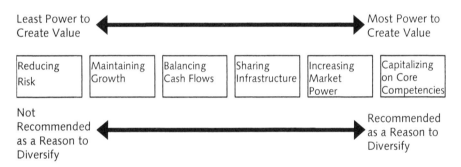

Figure 12-5: Reasons for diversification and their assessment according to Miller & Dess
(adapted from Miller & Dess, 1996, p. 267)

Less valid, according to Miller and Dess, is an evaluation of a diversification option simply in terms of its effects on portfolio balance, growth or risk reduction. While these are all desirable outcomes, they are not in themselves sufficient criteria in order to distinguish a poor diversification option from a good one. Assessing synergies in terms of market and/or resources is clearly much more suitable for this purpose.

(iii) Options for establishing the future portfolio

Until now we have looked at options for optimizing the future portfolio. We now turn to the question of how to achieve the target portfolio. Usually a better portfolio cannot be created at a stroke: a number of specific strategic measures will be required for the different businesses.

There are three categories of business for which specific strategic measures will be required: those to be newly established, those to be expanded and those to be divested. Those businesses which are required to hold their position during the planning period will not need to develop strategy variants within the framework of corporate strategy. Normally it will be sufficient for these businesses to discuss strategic options on the level of business strategy, in order to maintain and defend competitive advantages at the levels of market offers and resources. We will come back to these questions in Part Five of this book.

There are basically three ways of establishing a new business: acquisition, alliance, and building a new business from scratch (Miller & Dess, 1996, p. 254 ff.). **Figure 12-6** matches these to the three different types of diversification, vertical, horizontal, and geographic. We have included recent examples from European companies in the matrix proposed by Miller & Dess (1996, p. 245). The following advantages and disadvantages can be attributed to the three types:

- The advantage of an acquisition is that a new business, with the necessary know-how, is quickly in place. The risks lie in an overly optimistic assessment of the company acquired, too high a price for the acquisition, and problems of integration (Miller & Dess, 1996, p. 254 ff.).
- One main advantage of alliances and joint ventures lies in the fact that partners usually have complementary skills and resources and this reduces the learning period for the new business and brings down the associated costs. The downside is the considerable risk of conflict between the partners. This risk is much reduced, according to Miller & Dess (1996, p. 259 ff.) if three conditions are fulfilled: First clear agreements must be made as to the mission, activity and

Type of diversification / Path of diversification	Vertical diversification	Horizontal diversification	Geographic diversification
Acquisition	Takeover of pharmaceuticals producers by Galenica, a pharmaceuticals wholesaler	Purchase of Foto-labo by the Valora group	Systematic buying up of foreign producers of elevators by Schindler
Alliances and joint ventures	Feldschlösschen's stake in railroad catering up to the mid-nineties	Cooperation between Mercedes and Swatch to produce a new small car	Joint venture between Schindler Holding Co. and the Chinese government to enter the Chinese market for
Growing the company from scratch	The setting up of a network of car dealers by the auto importing company Emil Frey AG	The manufacture of telephone hand-sets by the Swatch group	The establishing of production and marketing companies outside Switzerland by the Swatch group

Figure 12-6: Types of diversification and paths to diversification
(adapted from Miller & Dess, 1996, S. 245)

tasks of each partner. Second neither partner should think in an excessively legalistic way and seek to protect itself with complex contractual arrangements. Third neither partner should be planning to cheat the other. In cases where alliances or joint ventures involve a sharing of strategically important skills, the danger exists that resource strengths will be eroded as know-how and technical skills are transferred to the partner company, which is often a competitor (Kühn & Grünig, 2000, p. 162 f.).

- It is relatively rare for companies to succeed in diversifying by growing new businesses from scratch within the company: the building up of necessary competencies and resources is slow, expensive, and full of risk. An impressive example is the failure of the Bührle company in its attempt to set up a new business in the market for anti-plane missiles. Although the company had a strong market position in its anti-plane cannon business and the new product group was thus seen by management at the time as a diversification into a related product market, the project brought the company to the brink of extinction. The investment required exceeded by many times the planned budgets and the final product was a weapon system that proved so inferior to its competitors that it was virtually impossible to sell.

If the aim is to strengthen the market position of an existing business, this can be achieved through internal growth, acquisitions or a strategic alliance. But these three possibilities must be assessed differently here than earlier when they were considered as paths to diversification:

- The chances of improving market position through internal growth are usually better than are those of growing an entirely new business. Industry knowledge and technological skills are already present. In addition, it is possible to proceed in small steps, thus reducing the risks. However, it is vital not to underestimate the costs of growing an existing business on its own. As with diversification, here too, where the aim is to strengthen an existing market position, acquisitions offer the possibility of reaching one's goal rather quickly. Moreover, candidates for acquisition are likely to be better known than in the case of a diversification move, which reduces the risk. Another positive fact is that with the acquisition a competitor disappears from the market, changing sides. But the integration of a former competitor always involves risks because of the different culture and values of the acquired company. Most often, however, rivals are simply not available for sale, or resist take-over. This drives up the cost of acquisition, often making the purchase uneconomic.
- A strategic alliance or joint venture is rarely a sound option where the aim is to strengthen an existing market position. Unless severe financial difficulties force a company into this option, the participation of a partner in an existing business can hardly be justified. Management and decision making processes are more time con-

suming and expensive and this will not be offset if - as is often the case - there are only limited gains in skills or in the reduction of risk.

Improving a portfolio is hardly ever a matter of just building new businesses and developing existing businesses. Active portfolio management almost always involves divestments. Following Hill & Jones (1992, p. 301 ff.) the three options here are sale, harvest and liquidation:

- Sale provides a rapid solution, and businesses may be bought up by competitors or by its current management. The disadvantage is that it is difficult to predict how much cash such a sale will generate. There is usually only a limited number of potential buyers and obtaining a good price often depends on whether there is more than one buyer with a genuine interest, so that competition ensues.
- When it is difficult to get a reasonable price for a business, a harvest strategy is often the best choice. **Figure 12-7** shows the course of the development of free cash-flow for a business in which a harvest strategy is followed with success (Hill & Jones, 1992, p. 302). As only the barest minimum is now invested in marketing, product development, and infrastructure, free cash-flow initially rises strongly. However, the lack of investment will bring loss of market share and lead to a slump in free cash-flow. The success of a harvest strategy often depends on whether the management can be motivated for this thankless task. It is also important to conceal the

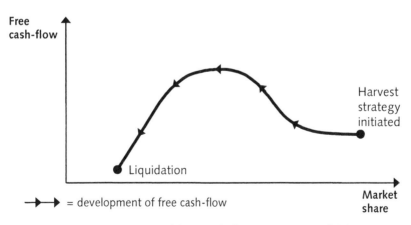

Figure 12-7: Development of free cash-flow in a successful harvest strategy (adapted from Hill & Jones, 1992, S. 302)

strategy from customers for as long as possible and to provide a so-
cially and financially acceptable program for the close-down of the
strategic business.

- As experience shows, liquidation should only be chosen when neither of the other two strategies is possible. Liquidation not only
  means writing off fixed and current assets, but also typically brings
  extra costs in redundancy arrangements and environmental clean-
  ups.

12.4.4 Assessment of the strategic options

As has been shown, strategic options for achieving a target portfolio
are normally no more than approximate indications of strategic measures needed. They very often open up a wide spectrum of possibilities
- possible merger-partners to sustain growth, possible buyers of business to be divested, possible investments - which can only be evaluated when a specific opportunity has been identified. This means that
the assessment of corporate strategy options at this stage of the planning process will often have to remain somewhat vague and therefore
provisional.

The assessment of strategic options should basically use the same
criteria recommended for the evaluation of the current strategy: the
future attractiveness of the markets served and the strength of competitive positions which can be reached once the envisioned strategic
measures have been successfully carried through. But of course, the
evaluation will contain much more uncertain aspects, since strategic
options at the level of corporate strategy very often lead into unknown territory where the planners lack experience and data to
ground their judgments.

Normally concrete date on investment costs, possible earnings and
cash flows will only be available after the specification of strategic
programs for the implementation of the strategic measures in Step
Four of the proposed planning process. Nevertheless we suggest that
planners should try to make at least a rough estimate of the magni-
tude of investments needed: they need to know whether the option

chosen can be financed and therefore has a chance of being realized. This seems particularly important for small and medium-sized companies with limited financial means, which are either not in a position to go public to finance their development, or do not wish to do so.

Part V

Developing business strategies

Part Five deals with the development of business strategies. Business strategies specify the resources and offers which are needed for each business so that it can achieve or protect the target market positions set out in the corporate strategy. To this end, the business strategies identify the competitive advantages which have to be built up or maintained. Competitive advantages have to be identified on two levels: for market offers and for resources (success potentials IIA and IIB). In addition, it is necessary to ensure that the different success potentials dovetail in such a way as to produce positive synergies.

In order for a business strategy to function as a long-term framework for the development of a business it has to answer the following questions:

- What customer groups will be served and what types of products and services should be offered to them?
- Which generic business strategy will be followed to do this?
- What competitive advantages will have to be built up on the level of the market offer?
- What resources will be required to maintain or upgrade these competitive advantages?

After the development of corporate strategy, the production of business strategies is the second key task in strategic planning. **Figure V-1** shows how it fits within the overall process.

Part Five is divided into four chapters:

- Chapter 13 introduces the generic business strategies. Generally one of these will be adopted. If this is not done, the business runs the risk of being less effective.
- Next, in Chapter 14, we look at ways of specifying the selected basic generic strategy at the level of the market offer by determining the success potentials IIA.

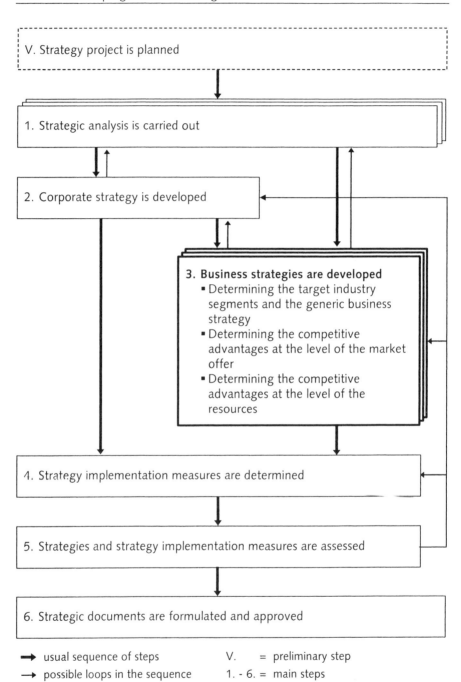

V. Strategy project is planned

1. Strategic analysis is carried out

2. Corporate strategy is developed

3. **Business strategies are developed**
   - Determining the target industry segments and the generic business strategy
   - Determining the competitive advantages at the level of the market offer
   - Determining the competitive advantages at the level of the resources

4. Strategy implementation measures are determined

5. Strategies and strategy implementation measures are assessed

6. Strategic documents are formulated and approved

→ usual sequence of steps   V.   = preliminary step
→ possible loops in the sequence   1. - 6. = main steps

Figure V-1: The development of business strategies as a step in the process of strategic planning

- In Chapter 15 we examine how to specify business strategies at the level of resources by determining the success potentials IIB. Using value chain analysis allows us to move from the target competitive advantages at the level of the offer to identify the resources which need to be built up or maintained.
- In Chapter 16 we present the process for the development of business strategies. This is based on the methods introduced in earlier chapters. The key point in our heuristic process, and the main focus of this chapter, is the specification of a network of success potentials which can produce positive synergies between the various different success potentials at the level of the market offer and at the level of resources.

13 Generic business strategies

13.1 Basic reflections on the generic business strategies

There are many ways in which a business might approach the task of building or maintaining concrete competitive advantages. However, management literature and strategy planning practice recommend a limited number of basic strategy types derived from a classification of possible competitive advantages. These are referred to as generic competitive strategies or generic business strategies. As Figure V-1 suggests, we propose that first a basic decision should be made as to the type of strategy and that this should then be specified by defining competitive advantages.

Usually the selection of the generic strategy for a business to follow is not problematic: in most cases consideration of the competitive situation and available resources leaves little choice. But it is very important that this choice should be made clearly and explicitly: the generic business strategy provides the framework within which the concrete competitive advantages at the level of the offer and at the level of resources are next determined. If no clear decision is taken, there is the danger that the different target competitive advantages will not fit well together and the hoped-for positive synergies between them will not be realized.

In what follows we first give an overview of the generic business strategies and then comment on each one. We next consider the conditions for success and the risks for each of them. The chapter closes with a discussion of transitional strategies and strategy alternation.

13.2 Overview of the generic business strategies

The insight that there are only a limited number of possible strategic behaviors for businesses can be attributed to Porter (1980). According to his analysis, sustainable competitive advantage can only be at-

tained through low costs or through differentiation in the market offer. Porter linked these two basic types of competitive advantage with
the target scope of activity, thus deriving his three basic competitive
strategies:

- cost leadership
- differentiation
- focus

Figure 13-1 presents Porter's proposal.

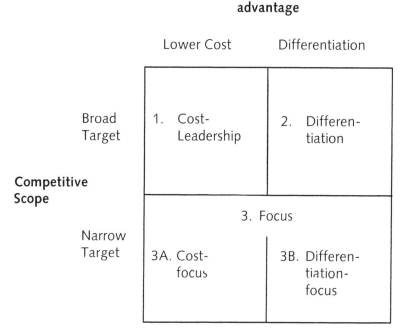

Figure 13-1: Porter's generic competitive strategies
(adapted from Porter, 1985, p. 12)

Building on this analysis, we propose to distinguish the following four
generic business strategies:

- broad scope price strategy
- broad scope differentiation strategy
- niche focus price strategy
- niche focus differentiation strategy

Figure 13-2 shows these four generic business strategies in the same form as Figure 13-1 so that the two approaches can be directly compared.

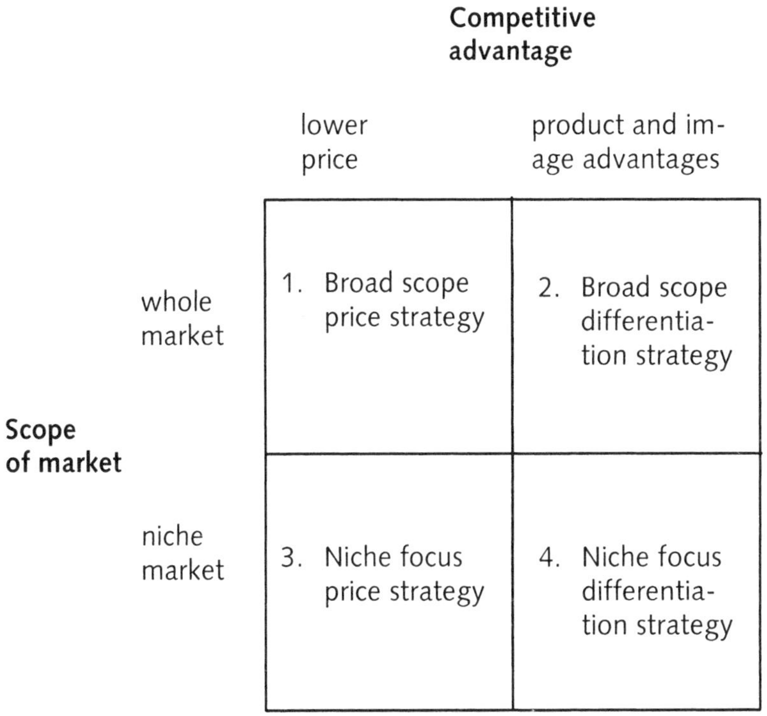

**Competitive
advantage**

	lower price	product and im- age advantages
whole market	1. Broad scope price strategy	2. Broad scope differentia- tion strategy
niche market	3. Niche focus price strategy	4. Niche focus differentia- tion strategy

**Scope
of market**

Figure 13-2: The generic business strategies

These generic business strategies differ from Porter's categories in the following points:

- Rather than generic competitive strategies, we speak of generic business strategies, a term we prefer because the basic strategy chosen not only specifies the competitive behavior at the level of the market offer, but also determines the need for resources.
- Rather than cost leadership, we speak of a price strategy. While a favorable cost position is a precondition for a low price policy, it in no way requires it. Cost advantages can obviously be used in other ways, for example to improve differentiation by developing products or building up a brand image. Cost advantages can also be translated into higher cash flow, which can then be reinvested to

build up another business or distributed to shareholders as dividends.

- We prefer not to combine the two niche strategies under one overall heading because of the differences between the two. These are apparent primarily in the different kinds of resources required for each and in the degree of risk of being forced out of the market by larger competitors.

Inset 13-1 analyses the saw mill industry in Switzerland, showing which generic strategies are used by the companies concerned.

Inset 13-1: Generic business strategies in the saw mill industry in Switzerland

There is intense competition in the Swiss wood processing industry. On the one hand there is a recession in the construction sector which results in low prices for all goods supplied by saw mills. On the other hand, there is increasing pressure from imports. A few years ago the foreign competitors were primarily Scandinavian-based suppliers, but now the competition comes mostly from the former Communist block countries. These companies sell mainly on price, and in some areas offer top quality products at attractive prices. They achieve this by rigorously selecting for the export markets, and selling the rejects in their home markets.

Nevertheless, there are a few Swiss firms following a broad scope price strategy. These firms buy large quantities of low quality timber, of which there is an abundant supply in Switzerland's forest regions. This roundwood is processed in chipper-centers into standard boards. The slabs are shredded into chips. The fact that these mills produce no secondary products eliminates the need for expensive investment in sorting and processing them, while at the same time massively increasing productivity in terms of processed cubic meters of roundwood per employee. These low-price oriented companies also refrain from producing any products to order. Their standard products are sold in large batches to dealers and other large customers like pallet manufacturers.

Equally, there are only a few companies following a broad scope differentiation strategy. Like those following a broad scope price strategy, these are firms with very large production capacities. As well as having equipment which permits them to process round-wood in large quantities, they also have extensive facilities for sorting and processing boards. They offer a wide range of products and also undertake orders to individual customer specifications. Depending on the product group, the markets usually cover a number of regions and for some products the market is nation-wide. Some of the waste products are sold over the border in neighboring countries. The wide product range and the heterogeneity of the customer base make for relatively high sales costs.

The majority of firms in the Swiss wood - processing industry fall into the category of small businesses, some of them very small indeed, following niche focus differentiation strategies. These operations usually have only one main saw, usually a band saw, although sometimes the company may have a gang saw. These companies can be divided into two types:

- A relatively large number of these companies occupy a regional niche. They are situated on the edge of forest areas, buy their wood from local landowners and sell their finished products almost exclusively in the same region. They have a wide product range and products are normally only made to order. The high degree of flexibility, together with good customer relations, allows for above-average pricing.
- There are also small sawmills specializing in processing the highest quality timber: These companies buy wood from all over Switzerland, from France, from Germany and from Austria. The premium wood is cut into boards which are sold to veneer manufacturers or exclusive cabinet-makers.

There are also a large number of medium-sized companies, often without a clear generic strategy. The strategy followed is often a watered-down version of the broad scope differentiation strategy. It is not surprising that it is principally companies in this group, stuck in the middle, who have been falling victim to industry restructuring.

13.3   The broad scope price strategy

Where a company follows an aggressive price strategy, this means that it seeks to distinguish itself from competitors mainly in terms of price and conditions. This rather one-dimensional approach means that products will be easily substitutable and leads to the risk that customers will switch suppliers as soon as a more attractive price offer becomes available. For this reason, a price strategy should only be followed if sustainable cost advantages can be secured.

A company's cost position depends essentially on two factors (Porter, 1985, p. 97):
- the structure of the value chain
- the cost drivers in the different activities in the value chain.

Cost leadership is only possible if, in comparison with competitors, a company's value chain consists of a small number of activities linked together in a straightforward manner. For this reason, cost leaders usually offer only a small number of relatively common product types, often building on a single basic module.

The term 'cost drivers' indicates variables which have a considerable influence on the costs of a value-creating activity. Typically there are very few cost drivers for each activity, often only a single factor. Typical examples of cost drivers are the number of different product types and batch sizes. For almost all industries the most significant cost driver is production volume. The production volume, measured in pieces, tons, hectoliters, person-miles, accommodation nights or consultant hours normally has a less than proportional influence on the total costs. A company seeking to follow a price strategy is thus forced to go for high volume.

But high volume is not enough in itself to achieve and maintain cost advantages. As experience shows, it is necessary to motivate people to constantly seek opportunities for additional cost reductions in order to protect competitive cost advantages against erosion. Normally this means that the company has to develop a cost-oriented business culture.

The fact that the success of a broad scope price strategy is determined not only by the relative cost position of the company, but also by market conditions is often overlooked. More specifically, in order to be a success, the price strategy should only be applied in markets with a large number of price sensitive customers which produces significant price elasticity in demand. Market oriented price strategies are thus typically found in markets where large numbers of customers are satisfied by products of a standard quality.

13.4   The broad scope differentiation strategy

In the differentiation strategy, the market offer stands out from its competitors not through price and conditions but through its uniqueness. There is a wide range of advantages which can be used to achieve this. For example, differentiation can be achieved through a quality advantage, especially through innovative product features, or an attractive image created through marketing efforts. It is clear that there are very many different ways in which competitors following a differentiation strategy can seek to distinguish their products from those of their rivals in the market. Unlike the price strategy, which has been characterized as one-dimensional, differentiation is usually based on a combination of variables. The construction of a multi-dimensional differentiation may be a long process, but this kind of competitive advantage is more easily defended against competitors.

What is required for a successful differentiation strategy is that customers should perceive the offer as clearly distinct from that of competing products and services. There are basically two approaches to achieving this: either the product or service is recognized as superior in quality or innovation, or the company succeeds in building a distinct company or product image through clever use of marketing communication tools. If the differentiation is based on clearly - recognized advantages in the products and services, we speak of a USP (= unique selling proposition). If the individuality of the firm or its products is essentially dependent on marketing communication efforts we refer to a UAP (= unique advertising proposition). We should add that, despite the term, a UAP need not necessarily be based on advertising efforts, but can also be built on the use of other marketing communication elements. In markets for capital goods, for example, a UAP may be realized more through personal sales contacts and relationship marketing than through advertising.

In practice often mixed strategies are followed, typically combining small product differences with marketing communication efforts.

13.5   The niche focus strategies

13.5.1 A niche as a specific form of industry segment

Our discussion of price and differentiation strategies aimed at the market as a whole in the previous two sections applies equally to niches. What follows here, therefore, is a discussion of what a niche is (13.5.1), how it can be identified (13.5.2) and what the criteria are for selecting a niche market (13.5.3).

An industry market is rarely a homogenous whole. Usually it can be divided into submarkets or product groups and into customer segments. The demand from different customer segments for the various product types will be different in degree. This means that we can construct product-customer units. Porter refers to these as industry segments (1985, p. 231 ff.). There is thus a distinction, both for Porter and in this book, between industry segments and customer segments. A customer segment is a group of customers with relatively uniform needs and demand. An industry segment is a combination of one or more product groups and one or more customer groups.

Companies whose capacities are tailored to follow a strategy aimed at the market as a whole, often do not serve all industry segments with the same intensity:

- Businesses with a broad scope price strategy are obliged to concentrate on product types with low unit costs and to sell these to price-sensitive customers.
- Even large companies following a broad - scope differentiation strategy cannot cover all industry segments. Sales are usually con-

centrated in a number of product-customer units. General Motors, for example, with all of its different automobile brands and ranges, certainly covers a large proportion of the market. Nevertheless it is not hard to find industry segments where it is weak, or has no position at all, and where other suppliers dominate.

A niche oriented business strategy does not mean simply serving fewer industry segments than larger competitors following a whole market strategy. This would not be enough for a small firm to be able to survive in the face of the competition from large rivals. Higher unit costs and a smaller marketing budget create disadvantages compared to larger competitors. This would lead to a strategically unsatisfactory position often referred to as 'stuck in the middle'.

A genuine niche market exists only when there is an industry segment which is clearly set apart from the rest of the market, because the customers (almost) exclusively buy a particular product type. Genuine niches are characterized by special customer needs which create specific requirements for the products and services. Niches are usually occupied by a small number of suppliers. Often the customers have such specific demands that they rarely or never take products from the rest of the market into consideration when making a purchase decision. In the market for automobiles, for example, there is a niche for Italian sports cars. In this niche there are customers who have high requirements in terms of performance, design, equipment and image. When purchasing a new car, they would not consider a Porsche, but probably confine their thinking to a choice between models from Ferrari, Maserati and Lamborghini.

One danger for companies following a niche strategy is that what they are focussing on are false niches. A false niche is an industry segment
- whose product demands are not sufficiently specific,
- whose customers include in their purchase decisions products from suppliers following a broad scope strategy.

An example of an industry segment which is a false niche would be the market for four wheel drive vehicles. The 'know how' required to build such vehicles is now widely available. Four wheel drive vehicles are often compared by customers to products with two wheel drive. And almost every car manufacturing group, serving the whole market, has four wheel drive models in its range. This has not always been the case. At the beginning of the seventies four wheel drive cars constituted a genuine niche. Producing them required special knowledge and the suppliers were specialists like Jeep and Landrover. They were also considerably more expensive to buy, and were slower and less comfortable vehicles to drive than standard vehicles. For these reasons four wheel drive vehicles were purchased almost exclusively by customers who needed an off-road vehicle or were concerned about safety in wintry conditions.

As this example shows, changes in technology and in customer needs can create new niches or destroy existing ones. Thus the disappearance of the served niche is perhaps the greatest risk for suppliers following a niche focus strategy.

Figure 13-3 summarizes our discussion of industry segments and niches in the automobile industry, linking them to broad target and niche focus business strategies.

13.5.2 The identification and assessment of niches with the help of industry segment analysis

The choice of a suitable niche, which must remain stable in the long term, requires precise knowledge of the industry concerned. An industry-segment analysis should be carried out.

For niche suppliers in particular, industry segment analysis forms the basis for the identification and assessment of niche markets and is thus an essential requirement. But we also recommend industry segment analysis for companies following a broad scope market strategy. It is a relatively inexpensive undertaking, as the knowledge required is generally available within the company. The advantage is that industry segment analysis makes it possible for a broad scope market supplier to choose which product-customer units, or industry to focus on.

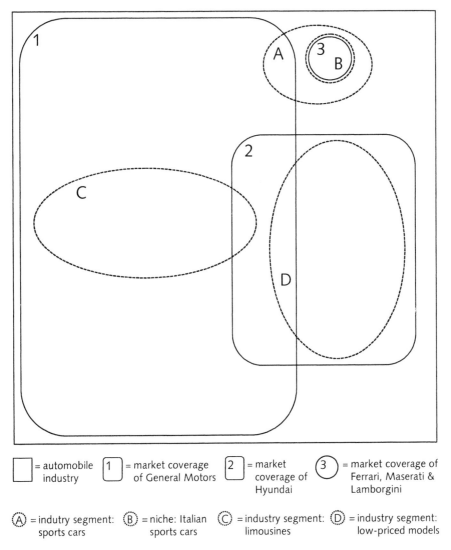

= automobile industry   [1] = market coverage of General Motors   [2] = market coverage of Hyundai   (3) = market coverage of Ferrari, Maserati & Lamborgini

(A) = indutry segment: sports cars   (B) = niche: Italian sports cars   (C) = industry segment: limousines   (D) = industry segment: low-priced models

Figure 13-3: Industry segments and niches in the automobile industry

This is important, for as we have seen, broad scope market suppliers too cannot serve all industry segments with the same intensity, nor should they attempt to do so.

Industry segment analysis consists of three steps:

1. First the customers in the industry must be classified into customer segments, groups with similar needs and product requirements. The different types of products and services available in the market are also divided into categories, known as submarkets. A matrix is drawn up on the basis of these categories and this matrix points to possible industry segments.

2. Next each square in the matrix is considered and a certain number eliminated because they are not significant. To do this it is necessary to calculate market volume and market growth for each box: if the calculation shows low volume plus below average growth, then that square can be eliminated from further consideration. At this stage too, we must consider whether certain squares can be combined into single industry segments, because the resources used for serving these areas are the same. Applying these two considerations will usually mean that the number of industry segments remaining is now much smaller than the total number of squares in the matrix.

3. The third step is to analyze each of the industry segments. For each of them the customer requirements must be identified and the most important suppliers in the market and their market positions must be determined.

Inset 13-2 gives the results of an industry segment analysis for banking services.

This form of analysis quickly reveals what niches are available, together with the specific demands of each of these, and indicates the companies that are currently operating in each niche market and their degree of success. This is the information which forms the basis for choosing a niche.

For niche market suppliers, the choice of a niche is of prime importance for the success of their business strategy. For this reason we devote the next section to describing the requirements which must be met if a niche is to form a solid basis for the achievement of long term success.

Inset 13-2: Industry segment analysis for banking services

In the market for banking services seven customer segments can be identified:

- companies quoted on the stock exchange or with the potential to go public
- individual private customers
- individual private customers who are wealthy
- individual private customers with loans, savings needs etc.
- institutional investors, like pension funds, insurance companies etc.
- small and medium-sized companies
- small businesses and self-employed, like small independent shops, medical practices etc.

The seven customer segments differ in the type of services they need and in terms of the particular requirements they have for each of these services. Taking these two aspects into account, seven relatively broad types of banking services can be identified:

- business loans, mortgages, leasing loans and private loans
- international payments
- managing large institutional portfolios
- managing private investment portfolios
- payments, internet banking and credit cards
- structured financial packages
- traditional savings and bonds and shares investments

Figure 13-4 brings the customer segments and submarkets to-gether in a matrix, no longer in alphabetical order, as above, but grouped to facilitate the formation of industry segments. As the figure shows, the matrix has 49 squares, but only 15 are important in terms of turnover and margin, with three more which are in-cluded because they are important as complementary services. The matrix proposes a grouping into five industry segments, in each of which there will be shared resources:

- A: Retail banking
- B: Private banking
- C: Business banking

- D: Investment banking
- E: Asset management

	Individual private customers	Private customers with loans, savings etc.	Small businesses and self-employed	Wealthy individual customers	Small and medium-sized companies	Quoted companies	Institutional investors
Traditional savings and bonds and shares investments	X	X	X A				
Mortgages, business loans, leasing and private loans		X	X				
Payments, internet banking and credit cards	X	X	X	(x) B	X C		
Private investment portfolios				X	(x)	X D	
International payments					(x)	X	
Structured financial packages					X	X	
Investment portfolios of institutional investors						X	X E

x = important in terms of turnover and margin
(x) = important service feature for a customer segment
☐ = industry segment

A: Retail banking
B: Private banking
C: Business banking
D: Investment banking
E: Asset management

Figure 13-4: Industry segments for banking services

13.5.3 Requirements for niches

Following Porter (1985, p. 256 f.), if an industry segment is to be attractive for a niche strategy it must have a relatively low competitive intensity. Competitive intensity can be determined relatively simply by applying the Five Forces model to the industry segment concerned. If the industry segment is found to have a clearly lower competitive intensity than the industry as a whole, then the first condition is satisfied.

A second requirement for a niche is a sufficient size combined with above average growth (Porter, 1985, p. 256 f.). This must be seen relatively in terms of the company concerned. The larger the company (if it is a company operating in a single industry) or the business (if it is one business in a company operating in a number of different industries), the larger the industry segment must be in order to justify a niche strategy. In order that investments can be repaid, whether in a niche differentiation strategy or a niche price strategy, the niche market must have a higher rate of growth than the industry as a whole.

A third important condition, which is not made explicit in Porter's analysis, is that the industry segment must represent a true niche. A company following a niche strategy in a submarket which is not a genuine niche market with its own specific customer demands will find itself in direct competition with broad - scope market suppliers who can take advantage of economies of scale and who have much larger marketing budgets. In particular, fatal consequences can ensue when a niche price strategy is applied in a submarket which is not a true niche.

A fourth and final condition is that the targeted niche should fit with the strengths of the company. The resource situation (success potentials IIB), in particular, must be appropriate for the fulfilment of the specific requirements of the niche (Porter, 1985, p. 257). This is the case if the available resources are already suitable for meeting customer needs in the niche and building competitive advantages over other firms acting in the niche. More risky are cases where the resources required for serving a niche market successfully need to be newly developed, whether partly or wholly.

13.6   Success conditions and risks of the generic business strategies

13.6.1 Success conditions of the generic business strategies

Figure 13-5 gives the success conditions for the four generic business strategies.

As the figure shows, the choice of a broad scope business strategy requires a certain minimum size. In many industries most of the suppliers do not fulfill this first requirement. They are thus obliged to look for an industry segment with demands which are as specific as possible and which they can meet with their resources. The success conditions for a price strategy, whether in the whole market or a niche market, are also clear. In addition to a cost-conscious culture, a company must have the ability to develop, produce and market standard quality products in an uncomplicated cost-efficient manner.

With these clearly defined success conditions for three of the four generic business strategies, for most companies the choice of which strategy to follow is straightforward and almost obvious.

In any given industry we can assume that:

- one only, or a very small number of companies, will follow a broad - scope price strategy
- a few companies will follow a broad differentiation strategy
- very few or no companies at all will follow a niche focused price strategy
- many suppliers will be obliged to choose a niche focused differentiation strategy
- a number of companies will follow no clear business strategy and find themselves stuck in the middle.

13.6.2 Risks of the generic business strategies

Each of the four generic business strategies has its own specific risks. Following Porter (1985, p. 22) these can be summarized as follows:

- For price strategies, whether in the total market or in a niche, there are two main dangers. The first is that the basis for cost advantage may disappear. This can happen, for example, when new technologies are introduced into an industry. The second important risk is that the quality difference in products and services compared to suppliers following a differentiation strategy becomes too great. This can lead to a decline in the number of buyers who remain price-oriented.
- For differentiation strategies, whether in the whole market or in a niche, the main danger is also that the basis for the strategy may disappear. Either the differentiation feature can lose importance for the buyer, or more and more competitors may start to offer the same or similar product or image features as those which were intended as the basis for differentiation. The second important risk is in too large a price difference, compared with the low price suppliers. In this situation, an increasing number of buyers may decide to do without the advantages of the differentiated product or service and content themselves with a standard product instead. Finally there is the specific danger for broad - scope differentiation strategies that increasingly different industry segments come to be occupied by niche suppliers, leading to a reduction in volume for the offers aimed at the total market.
- Finally there are specific risks for niche suppliers. A key danger is that technological developments or market developments may erode the niche or cause it to disappear completely. A second danger is the opposite tendency. If rival niche suppliers are able to develop even more specific products for some of the buyers in the niche, the existing niche may subdivide. For companies whose size and structure are geared to serving the whole existing niche, this may lead to very painful losses in turnover.

According to Porter a company should make a clear decision for one of the four generic business strategies. If this is not done, Porter argues, the resulting "stuck in the middle position" will not allow the company to develop important and sustainable competitive advantages and thus leads to failure in the long run.

Based on these ideas, two types of 'stuck in the middle' strategic positions can be distinguished:

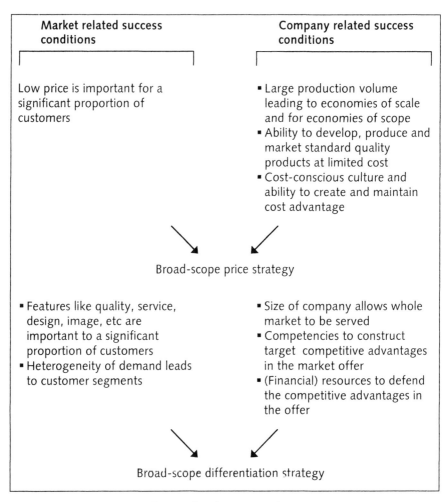

Figure 13-5: Success conditions for the generic business strategies

- The first and most often discussed stuck in the middle business strategy consists of a situation, where a company provides a market offer which is less expensive than the offers of competitors with high quality differentiation strategies, but gives better than the standard quality offered by competitors with aggressive pricing. In polarized markets, these stuck in the middle offer will be too expensive to be attractive for price conscious customers, while the low margin will not allow the company to compete on equal terms with competitors investing in quality, service or image and serving

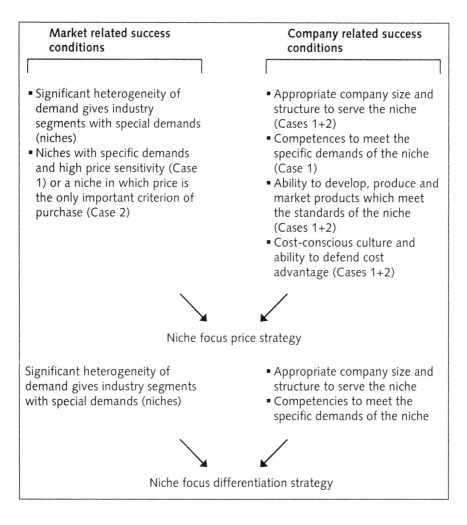

Market related success conditions	Company related success conditions
• Significant heterogeneity of demand gives industry segments with special demands (niches) • Niches with specific demands and high price sensitivity (Case 1) or a niche in which price is the only important criterion of purchase (Case 2)	• Appropriate company size and structure to serve the niche (Cases 1+2) • Competences to meet the specific demands of the niche (Case 1) • Ability to develop, produce and market products which meet the standards of the niche (Cases 1+2) • Cost-conscious culture and ability to defend cost advantage (Cases 1+2)

Niche focus price strategy

| Significant heterogeneity of demand gives industry segments with special demands (niches) | • Appropriate company size and structure to serve the niche
• Competencies to meet the specific demands of the niche |

Niche focus differentiation strategy

the customers in the high quality segments. The dangers of this type of stuck in the middle position are aggravated by the fact that in most markets different strategic resources and corporate cultures are needed to be competitive in the fields of quality on the one hand and price on the other. Stuck in the middle positions are often not the result of a conscious strategic choice but of individual decisions leading to an emerged strategy. Price leaders, for example, are from the danger that over time additional services, new products with enhanced quality and extra features will transform the original price strategy into a stuck in the middle one.

- The second type of stuck in the middle position occurs when a company is too small to compete with the big players serving the whole market and too large to focus on a niche (see **Figure 13-6**). This leads to market offer which are not specific enough to allow for competitive advantages over companies with a clear niche focus. Paradoxically it is often niche suppliers who get into this position. Their success in the niche market leads them to extend their business activities and often they leave their niche without even realizing that they are doing it. Some of their products are now in the whole market where they must compete with large competitors following a broad scope differentiation or price strategy without having the strength to do this effectively.

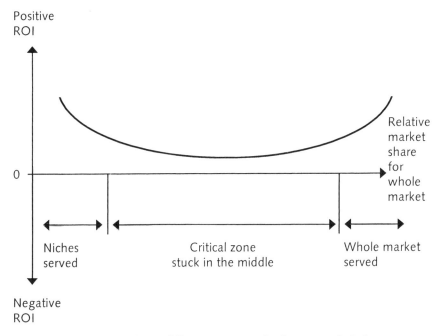

Figure 13-6: Stuck in the middle situation and relative market share
(adapted from Porter, 1980, p. 43)

Both experience and empirical studies show that, in reality, business units can be successful in spite of their stuck in the middle position, for instance, where most companies competing in the market have no clear commitment to either quality or price. It can also happen that the structure of a particular market or of the competitive forces allows or even demands some form of mixed strategy. Strategic options which can be recommended in these circumstances are discussed in the next section.

13.7   Transitional strategies and strategy alternation

13.7.1 Basic reflections on transitional strategies and strategy alternation

So far our discussion has assumed the following:

1. There are only four generic business strategies.
2. The more clearly a company follows one of these four generic business strategies, the more successful it will be.
3. The selected generic business strategy can only be successful if it is adopted and implemented for the long term.

In most cases these three rules must be followed, but there are exceptional situations in which it can be useful to:

- follow a different type of strategy,
- combine two generic business strategies,
- alternate between two generic business strategies

Section 13.7 looks at these special cases, beginning by examining the combination of generic business strategies and additional strategic possibilities in section 13.7.2. The use of a combination strategy or a different variant can only be useful in the short term and for this reason we refer to these as 'transitional' strategies. Finally, section 13.7.3 explains strategy alternation: periodic strategic change.

13.7.2 Transitional strategies

In certain circumstances it is possible, and advantageous, to follow a hybrid strategy, in which the company is both price leader and also differentiates. Porter (1985, p. 17 ff.) gives three situations in which this is feasible:

- All important competitors are stuck in the middle.
- Volume is the key cost driver and high volume rapidly brings down unit costs. The cost of differentiation is relatively small in comparison.
- The company is able to introduce an important innovation which combines quality and cost-advantages.

In practice, none of these three situations is likely to last for a very long time. In the first case, all that is required to end it, is for one of the competitors to change to a clear price or differentiation strategy. In the second situation, technological developments can reduce the importance of volume as cost driver and increase the importance for total costs of features like design. The consequence will be that it is no longer possible for the company to be both the price leader and to continue to differentiate itself from the competitors. As for the third situation, the innovation will eventually become available to rival suppliers. A company following a hybrid strategy is therefore obliged to plan and prepare to switch later to a clear price or differentiation strategy.

Two further transitional strategies are the market development strategy and the submarket development strategy. These may be used during the introduction phase and the first half of the growth phase of the market life cycle (see Inset 11-2) and will be replaced later on by one of the four generic competitive business strategies. **Inset 13-3** discusses these two options. Market and submarket development strategies are of relatively slight importance in North America and Western Europe, as there are few markets and submarkets which are in the introduction or early growth phase. In Africa, Asia, Eastern Europe and South America the situation is different. The large potential for new demand in these regions should produce many expanding markets over the coming years.

Inset 13-3: Market and submarket development strategies
(Kühn, 1997, p. 35 ff.)

We speak of market development strategies when the measures taken are primarily intended to build up a new market or increase the growth of the market volume. This normally requires changes in habits and norms of use and consumption. Market development strategies dominate the first phases of the development of a new market and thus represent temporary transitional strategies, which will be replaced after some years, depending on market developments, by competitive strategies. Submarket strategies are also transitional strategies. They are used in market situations in which new product types are displacing existing ones. **Figure 13-7** compares market and submarket development strategies with the four generic competitive strategies introduced in section 17.2.

A company following a market or submarket development strategy should determine from the outset whether it will switch later to a price or a differentiation strategy. This is important, above all, for price setting. If the company's later strategy is based on price, then low initial prices will allow rapid market penetration and the building of market share, while at the same time erecting entry barriers for potential competitors. Companies which plan to move on from the market or submarket development strategy to introduce a differentiation strategy will tend to skimming pricing. The realized contribution margin can be reinvested in the differentiation of products and services.

An example of market development strategies can be found in the early suppliers of video machines in the early seventies. Television advertising showed how these machines were used, focusing primarily on the benefits of the products, rather than promoting particular brands or models. An example of the submarket development strategy can be found in the market for electricity meters. The electromechanical appliances installed by the electricity companies to record electricity consumption of domestic clients are being replaced by electronic devices. The suppliers of these electronic meters have been following a submarket development strategy, in

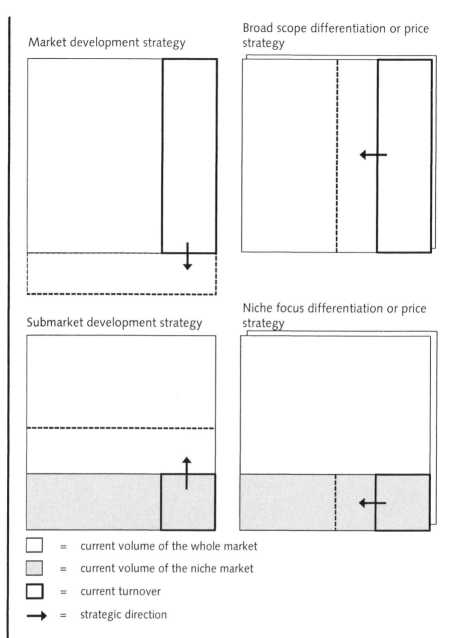

Market development strategy

Broad scope differentiation or price strategy

Submarket development strategy

Niche focus differentiation or price strategy

☐ = current volume of the whole market
▨ = current volume of the niche market
☐ = current turnover
→ = strategic direction

Figure 13-7: Market development strategy, submarket development strategy and generic competitive business strategies (adapted from Kühn, 1997, p. 37)

which they emphasize the general performance advantages ofelectronic products in order to force the tried and tested but older appliances off the market and grow the market for electronic meters. As soon as this market has reached the critical size, at which the displacement of the older devices has developed its own momentum, the companies will switch to competitive strategies.

13.7.3 Strategy alternation

Generally it makes sense to maintain the selected generic business strategy. Change always means a new beginning and the loss of existing strategic investments. However, for companies which dominate their industry, it can be effective to alternate systematically between a broad - scope price strategy and a broad - scope differentiation strategy. This approach was first discussed by Gilbert & Strebel (1987, p. 28 ff.), who gave it the name of 'outpacing'. We will briefly outline and justify this approach.

The development of an industry is often characterized by an alternation between periods of standardization and periods of rejuvenation (Gilbert & Strebel, 1987, p. 29 ff.):
- Important innovations, introduced by the market leader, are eventually taken up and copied by competitors. What were originally special features in an Innovative product become accepted as standard. Suppliers who cannot provide these features may go out of business. Those suppliers who can offer these features will engage in a bitter price war, because price is now the most important difference between products.
- Sooner or later one of the suppliers is able to create a new innovation and this introduces a new period of rejuvenation in the industry. The competition in the industry now shifts again from price to performance. This phase ends when the most important competitors have managed to copy the innovation and a new, improved, standard is installed.

Figure 13-8 shows this process.

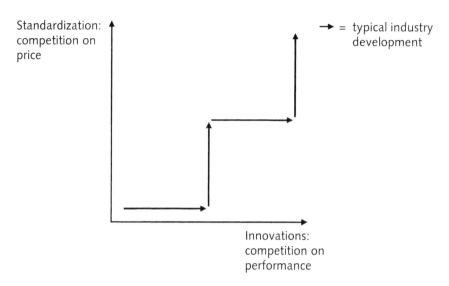

Figure 13-8: Industry development

This cyclical development pattern leads Gilbert & Strebel (1987, p. 31 ff.) to an interesting conclusion as regards strategic behavior. Companies seeking to dominate an industry must be able to alternate between a price strategy and a differentiation strategy. They refer to this as an outpacing strategy: if used successfully the leader always remains ahead of the rest of the field. As soon as competitors catch up on the innovation, the leader, with low unit costs, makes a rapid switch to a price strategy. Once competitors have improved their cost structure and can offer similarly low prices, the leader introduces a new innovation which breaks the industry standards. This introduces a new phase, in which competition is once more based on product performance.

Gilbert & Strebel (1987, p. 28) illustrate their idea with the case of diaper manufacturers. Until the mid-sixties cloth nappies were used. In 1976 Procter and Gamble introduced Pampers, disposable paper diapers. When competitors brought similar products onto the market, Procter and Gamble lowered their prices and their rivals were not able to compete, because of their unfavorable cost structure. In 1983, Kimberly, a competitor, developed a superior form of disposable diapers. Although these were sold at a 25% premium, it took only two years for Procter and Gamble's market share to fall from 60% to

50%. But in 1985 the market leader launched their own version of the Kimberly product at a lower price and succeeded in re-establishing price-based competition in the industry.

14 Specifying business strategies at the level of the market offer

14.1 Basic reflections on specifying business strategies at the level of the market offer

It is important to be clear about the difference between the generic strategy for a business and the concrete strategy that is required for strategic management. The chosen generic business strategy determines the overall strategic direction of a business, but in order to be successful in competition, a business requires a detailed and specific understanding of its target competitive advantages, both at the level of the offer (success potentials II A) and at the level of resources (success potentials II B). This is especially important for drawing up the implementation programs which are required (see Chapter 17) to ensure that the planned strategy is effectively implemented.

Chapter 14 is concerned with the specification of the chosen generic business strategy in terms of the market offer. There are four sections: Section 14.2 looks at how to specify a price strategy. The next section considers how to specify a differentiation strategy, where the problem is to position one's own offer in the market so that it is effectively differentiated from those of the competitors. Section 14.4 discusses strategic success factors and strengths and weaknesses analysis for the specification of the target competitive advantages for the offer. The chapter closes with reflections on how to assess different options for competitive advantages in the offer.

14.2 Specifying the market offer for a price strategy

14.2.1 Three areas of specification

The principal competitive advantage of an aggressive low price strategy is obvious: the lower price in comparison with rival suppliers. But in order to compete successfully we require specific understanding on the following points:

- Specification of products and services
- Depth and range of product mix
- Pricing

We now look at each of these three points in turn.

14.2.2 Specifying the products and services

In every industry there are standards. An offer which fails to meet these will not even be considered in customer buying decisions. In addition to these standards, there are always aspects which serve to distinguish between products and services fulfilling the basic standards. It is according to these dimensions that customers make their final purchase decisions.

For a company following a price strategy, the market offer must fulfill the required industry standards, but must do no more than this. If products do not reach the standards then they will not be considered in buying decisions. But if the offer goes beyond the basic standards and meets increased requirements, then most probably additional costs will be involved, and this will make it difficult or even impossible to realize a price strategy.

Figure 14-1 compares the passenger service package provided by an airline following a differentiation strategy with that of a competitor with a price strategy, where customer services have been trimmed to a minimum (Meyer & Blümelhuber, 1998, p. 396 ff.).

One means of limiting products and services to the requirements of the industry standards is what is known as 'unbundling'. Products and services are analyzed into their component parts and then the standard elements are reassembled into basic products and services.

Services provided by airlines with
a differentiation strategy
(e.g. Virgin, Atlantic Airways)

Services provided by airlines with
a price strategy
(e.g. Southwest Airlines)

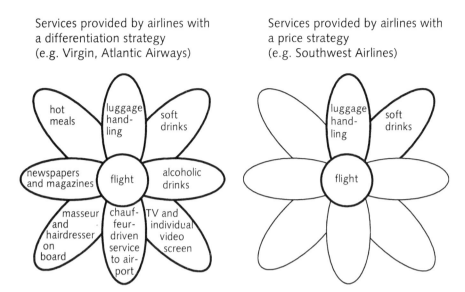

Figure 14-1: Traditional and trimmed down service package for airlines
(adapted from Meyer and Blümelhuber, 1998, p. 397)

14.2.3 Specifying the mix of products and services

Price leadership is often only possible with severely limited product
lines. This means that the strategy must clearly specify both the
breadth of the product mix, in terms of the number of different product and service categories, and the depth of the range of product
versions in each category.

It is not possible to make any generalizations about how broad the
product mix should be for companies following a price strategy. The
differences between industries are considerable and so any global
recipe would be too undifferentiated to serve as a satisfactory recommendation. However, as **Inset 14-1** shows, the reduction in product range undertaken to facilitate a price strategy can be extremely
drastic.

Inset 14-1: The drastic trimming of product range at a Swiss retailer switching to a price strategy
(Müller & Hauser, 1997, p. 7)

At the beginning of the eighties, Denner, a discounter for food and near food products, was in a double 'stuck in the middle' position. In terms of relative market share, it was significantly behind its two main mass market rivals, Migros and Coop. But with a smaller product range together with prices which were only a little lower, it was also stuck in the middle as regards differentiation and price leadership.

In 1994 Denner switched to an aggressive "hard discount" price strategy. Advertising emphasized the much lower prices compared to Migros and Coop. But in order to be perceived as a globally and significantly cheaper place to shop than its two main competitors, Denner had to lower its prices to consumers for all its products by 10% to 20%.

To achieve this price reduction the company was obliged to reduce its product range from 3850 to less than 1000 items. With this Draconian measure
- Transport and warehousing costs were reduced
- Unit sales for each item increased, which improved the company's bargaining position with its suppliers.

This second effect was crucial for the success of the "hard discount" price strategy because in a retail chain material costs account for almost 80% of total costs.

Whether or not this change to a clear price strategy will be successful will depend on the following:
- How great the drop in turnover will be as a result of the reduction in the product range
- Whether this can be compensated for by increases in gross profit margins

Unfortunately Denner does not publish detailed information about its financial situation, so it is not possible to determine the total effect of the change from a stuck in the middle position to a clear cut price strategy. But, in spite of considerable losses in turn-over, the company remains on the same strategic track and this seems to indicate that the Denner management has reasons to trust in the success of its "hard discount" strategy.

14.2.4 Specifying the pricing

The specification of price and conditions starts with a specification of the average percentage price difference as compared to suppliers with a differentiation strategy. As price is the only feature by which the products or services must appear at an advantage, the difference must be a significant one for the potential customers. What this means in terms of percentage difference depends on the price sensitivity for demand in the industry? The greater the price sensitivity, the smaller the price differential required for the success of a price strategy. The required price difference is slight in steel wholesaling, for example, but for perfumes at the retail level, the differential is relatively high.

Once a general idea has been formed as to the price compared with suppliers with differentiation strategies, guidelines must be drawn up for the price system. This means not only that a pricing policy for each product or service has to be set, but also involves the question of discounting rates, and the billing of additional services. The price system should respect the following principles:

- To keep costs down, companies following a price strategy must reward customers who purchase large numbers of units of a single product. Small orders, especially if they are made up of a number of different items, should be penalized with higher prices. Customers who undertake to place regular orders so that demand remains constant over time, should be rewarded with particularly favorable conditions.
- Any form of additional service makes the value creation process more complicated and increases costs. For this reason, it would be

an error to bill the costs of such services in terms of variable costs. Additional services typically require additional investments and increase the load on management. The fixed costs involved should also be rolled over onto the customer. Customers should therefore be discouraged from ordering them by prohibitively high prices.

14.3   Specifying the market offer for a differentiation strategy

14.3.1 The importance of a clear view of the served industry segment(s) and of the main competitors

In a differentiation strategy, uniqueness is the target. Specifying the competitive advantages at the level of the offer means the determination of the sources of uniqueness. This is only possible, if there is a clear understanding of two important premises.

Before the set of competitive advantages for the offer can be specified, there must first be a clear understanding of what the primary served industry segment or segments are. Niche suppliers must concentrate on an industry segment with special requirements, a niche. Companies serving the whole market will choose a number of target segments, rarely the totality of the market.

Usually the choice of industry segment or segments is made together with the decision about the generic business strategy. It is unlikely that a generic business strategy will be chosen without at least an approximate idea of the market segments in which it is to be realized.

Secondly there must be a clear view of the main competitors. In the context of the strategic analysis, a strength and weaknesses analysis was carried out. In this analysis, the company under review was compared with its main competitors. It should therefore already be clear, who the main competitors are.

Normally the most important competitors belong to the same strategic group as the company itself. But there are important exceptions. The main competitor of a local savings and loans bank can be the post office or the subsidiary of a business bank in the same town. On the other hand there can be only a limited competition with the savings and loans bank of the neighbouring district. As **Figure 14-2** shows, in this case the direct competitors belong to other strategic groups.

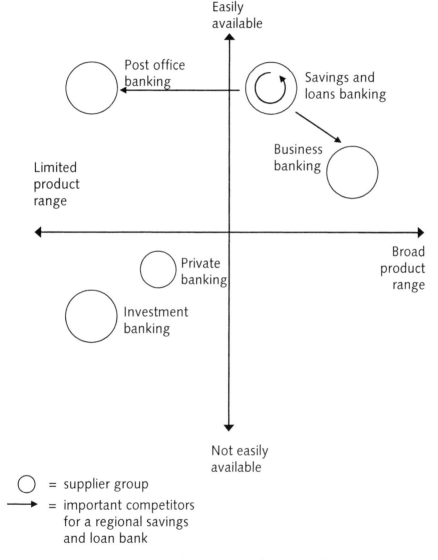

= supplier group

= important competitors
for a regional savings
and loan bank

Figure 14-2: The competitors of a savings and loans bank

14.3.2 Strategic positioning of the market offer

With the strategic positioning of the market offer, the company occupies a specific position in the industry market. This determines the differences in the market offer in comparison with the main competitors and identifies the target customer segment(s).

Once the target market segment or segments and the most important competitors have been identified, the process of strategic positioning can begin. The key questions to answer are the following: What is the position that we wish to occupy in the future? How can we achieve this position?

In a broad scope market differentiation strategy it is possible to occupy more than one market position. If a company has a number of brands, more often than not it will even be necessary to occupy different positions. The Swatch group, for example, has a number of brands, occupying various different positions. For niche suppliers, on the other hand, the offer usually occupies only a single position.

It is always a challenging task to find forms of differentiation from one's competitors, but it is especially critical in markets that are mature or saturated.

There are two basic approaches to the creation of effective differentiation from competitors (Kühn, 1997, p. 38):

- Through attributes of the product or service such as quality of the core product or service, product or service design and features of additional services (delivery service, after sales service etc)
- Through communication: like advertising, promotions, PR, sponsoring etc. and through the quality of personal contacts with customers

A significant product or service difference can be defined as (Kühn, 1997, p. 38):

- an objective attribute of the offer which is unique (principally an attribute of the core product or service, but also possibly an attribute concerning additional products and services), and

- which the buyer perceives as an advantage and which thus leads him to favorable decisions.

A communication difference can be defined as (Kühn, 1997, p. 38):

- an attribute of the offer, produced or strengthened by communication (advertising, PR, personal relations with customers), and
- which the buyer considers subjectively to be an advantage and which thus leads him to favorable buyer decisions.

As **Figure 14-3** shows, genuine product or service differences and communication differences are ideals which are not too often encountered in practice, where moderate or small differences predominate.

In practice, as **Figure 14-4** suggests, the differences in product or service and in communication go hand in hand. Often innovative companies can count on an offer difference when they start to market a new type of product. But this difference will dwindle as competitors catch up. If they are not successful in building up corresponding communication differences to create a permanent advantage in their image, then loss of market share is inevitable, with even the possibility of disappearing from the market altogether. Whether it is possible to maintain a competitive advantage without a significant product or service difference, simply through communication differences, depends on the type of product or service, and especially on the importance of technology. With technical products, whether consumer goods or capital goods, it is necessary to continuously support the maintenance of a positive image with customer-oriented product or service differences (Kühn, 1997, p. 38 ff.).

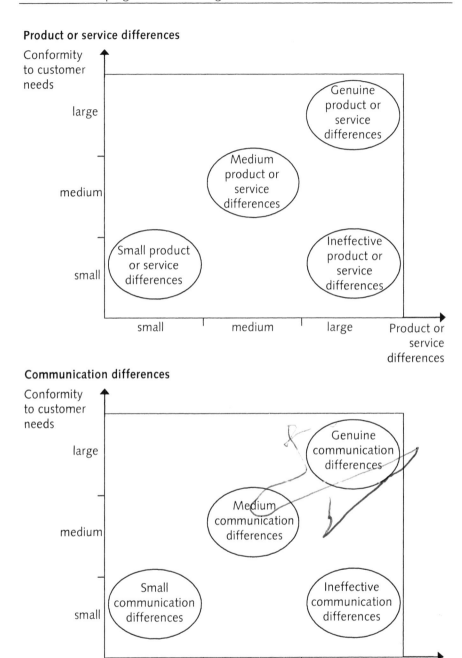

Figure 14-3: Product, service and communication differences
(Kühn, 1997, p. 39)

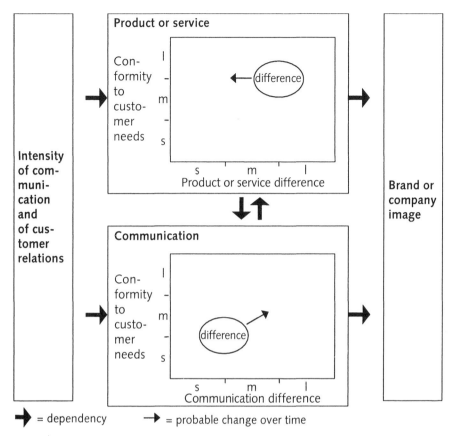

Figure 14-4: Multidimensional positioning of the market offer
(adapted from Kühn, 1997, p. 40)

14.3.3 Ideas for the strategic positioning of the market offer

In most industries, there are a large number of ways to build up competitive advantages in the offers. This is especially true for segmented markets: in these markets product or service differences and communication differences can be constructed not just on the level of the whole market, but also for individual customer groups.

There are three basic areas of differentiation in the offer:
- Unique attributes of products or services

- Unique attributes of the company and its resources (such as site, corporate culture, quality of technological resources, people, know how etc) as evidence of the ability to offer specific products or services
- Claimed satisfaction of customer needs (such as physical or intellectual pleasure, social success, identification with peer groups or with a specific life-style, risk reduction etc)

Each of these three areas contains many concrete possibilities for defining product or service differences and communication differences. For example, as **Figure 14-5** shows, product quality comprises a number of different possible attributes, each of which can serve alone or in combination with other as a basis for the positioning of the market offer.

- Performance
- Features
- Reliability
- Ease of use
- Conformity to norms and standards
- Durability
- Serviceability
- Aesthetics
- Safety
- Perceived Quality

Figure 14-5: Possible attributes of product quality
(adapted from Garvin, 1987, p. 101 ff.)

Competitive advantages in the offer (success potentials II A) can be targeted either at the end-user or, if products are not sold directly, at the retailers who then are the immediate customers. Producers of branded goods use positioning to try to create consumer demand for their products and services. The expectation is that the customer at the kiosk will ask for, say Marlboro cigarettes, or in a specialist retailer, will ask to see, say an Omega watch. But positioning can also be targeted at retailers. In this case, the aim is to motivate retailers to actively sell these products to consumers, often by using a private label owned by the retailers. **Inset 14-2** describes the strategic positioning of a chocolate producer, targeted primarily at retailers.

**Inset 14-2: The strategic positioning of the offer of two
businesses of a chocolate manufacturer**
(Lanner, 1999 b)

Edelweiss is a Swiss chocolate producer employing 90 people and
with a turnover of approximately $25 mil. Its share of the total
Swiss market for chocolate is about 3%. In comparison, competitors such as Nestle, Lindt & Sprüngli, Kraft-Jacobs-Suchard and
Chocolat Frey, a subsidiary of a large retail chain, all have a market
share between 13% and 18%, which makes Edelweiss one of the
medium-sized suppliers.

Up to now Edelweiss has marketed three types of product: chocolate bars, pralines and seasonal products (such as chocolate Easter
rabbits and Christmas tree decorations made from chocolate).

The range of chocolate bars is broad and they are sold at low
prices. In addition to traditional types such as milk, hazelnut, al-
mond and dark chocolate, there are bars in an extensive range of
soft fillings including honey, caramel, coconut, coffee and pepper-
mint. Edelweiss distributes its chocolate bars primarily through two
large retailers, A and B. In 1998 two thirds of the sales from chocolate bars came through these two retail chains. Total sales of
chocolate bars are declining and with strong competition from foreign imports the margin is extremely modest. Furthermore, for the
production of chocolate bars, setting up the outdated machines at
the main plant for the different flavors and sizes is difficult and
time-consuming.

As far as the pralines are concerned, the range shows a good deal
of creativity in both products and packaging, and here attractive
margins are possible. In addition to conventional gift packs, the
range includes a number of souvenir articles:
- The gift packs are traditional in design and well-established in
  the market, available in a range of sizes and shapes.
- The souvenir range emphasizes variety in packaging types and

sizes. The pralines are packaged in a variety of boxes, tins and pouches carrying pictures of Switzerland. But there are also more unusual products such as miniature rucksacks or milk churns filled with pralines. The souvenir products are sold primarily in locations where there is contact with tourists: at well-known sights, beauty spots, in railway stations, motorway service stations, airports, and so on.

- There is great demand for one particular type of praline, the prune liqueurs. These are damsons steeped in cognac and coated with dark chocolate. They are available in a variety of packs and sizes and also as souvenir articles.

With the seasonal products too, Edelweiss has shown flexibility in meeting individual customer demands, and creativity in developing products and packaging. The most important buyers are the large retail chains and the independent retailers.

Figure 14-6 gives the structure of company sales and the trends for the future.

Customer segments / Product groups	Speciali-zed retailers	Independent general retailer	Independent retailers at tourist sights	Kiosks, shops in motorway service stations, railway stations and airports	Large retail chains
Chocolate bars					
• traditional	–	0.5 ↘	–	1.0 ↘	4.0 ↓
• filled	–	1.0 ↘	–	0.5 ↘	1.0 ↓
Pralines					
• traditional	–	–	–	2.0 ↑	1.5 ↗
• souvenir packs	–	0.5 ↗	1.5 ↑	5.0 ↑	–
• prune liqueurs	–	–	–	2.0 ↑	0.5 ↗
Seasonal products	–	1.5 ↑	–	–	2.5 ↗
numbers = sales in mil. $			↗ = trend in sales and margin		

Figure 14-6: Sales for Edelweiss

The difficulties experienced with chocolate bars have persuaded the management to abandon this product group, which until now has contributed a large proportion of turnover.

- The crucial sales to the mass retailer A are now at risk, as a Polish producer has put in a bid with which Edelweiss cannot compete.
- The filled chocolate bars have long been a cause of trouble and the problems are getting worse. Retailers and consumers have been complaining that fillings dry out and become hard. Despite their best efforts, the company has not been able to solve this problem.
- The machinery used for producing the chocolate bars is nearing the end of its life. But it would require much larger output to justify an investment in new machinery.

As it is now concentrating on the remaining businesses pralines and seasonal products Edelweiss has to rethink its positioning for these businesses. A clear understanding of the competitive advantages in its offer should lead to an improved concentration of effort and a clearer communication with the retailers. The hope is that part of the turnover lost as a result of giving up the production of chocolate bars can be compensated for by additional sales in the two remaining areas.

In the future, the company plans to adopt a clearer niche differentiation strategy for both businesses.

The strategic positioning for both businesses is primarily focused on retailers. For gifts and souvenirs, the independent points of sale at beauty spots and tourist sights and the kiosks and shops at motorway service stations, railway stations and airports will be the most important outlets, while the most important customers for seasonal articles will be the large retailers and independent general retailers.

Edelweiss products, if they are sold under the company's name, should be known to the end-consumer as giving good value for money. In addition, the souvenir and seasonal articles should be perceived as amusing and innovative. The prune liqueurs will be promoted more heavily as an exclusive specialty produced up to now only by Edelweiss.

Only limited financial resources will be allocated to communicating the relatively minor competitive advantages focused on the end-consumers. The company's modest budget will be concentrated to effectively promote the prune liqueurs, with advertising and information at point of sale. One possibility to be investigated with regard to the marketing is to install special holders next to the prune liqueurs at the point of sale, with information leaflets about the products and how they are made.

The main emphasis, however, will be for both businesses on positioning the offer from the point of view of the retailers. In order to achieve a differentiation from larger producers like Nestle and Lindt & Sprüngli the company will offer the following:

- Edelweiss is ready to produce traditional pralines, souvenir articles and seasonal products to be sold under the retailers' brands, provided certain minimum quantities are respected. Retailers can also get exclusive seasonal articles and a number of exclusive souvenir products.
- Edelweiss offers favorable terms under which it will accept the return of seasonal product that remains unsold.
- Conditions of purchase offer relatively large price reductions depending on quantity and number of deliveries. This should make Edelweiss an attractive partner for retail chains and larger independents such as shops at tourist sights.

These differences will be communicated through personal contacts, with Edelweiss using its CEO, the Head of Marketing or the regional heads of sales, according to the importance of the potential customer.

14.4   The identification of success factors and the analysis of strengths and weaknesses as a basis for specifying the market offer

Now that we have seen how companies determine the success potentials in the offers when pursuing price or differentiation strategies, we return briefly to fundamentals. During strategic analysis (Chapter 8), a great deal of important information was collected and structured, both for the corporation as a whole and for the individual businesses and the industries they operate in. The data for the individual businesses and the industries they operate in can now be valuable for specifying the competitive advantages in the offer.

When discussing strategic analysis, we recommended that for each business a market system analysis should be carried out and success factors identified. We also recommended a strengths and weaknesses analysis of each business. The market system analysis serves to provide a useful overview of the industry, while the other two give a good basis for the specification of success potentials for the business on the level of the offer. We have described these methods above in Part Three. What will concern us here is their importance for determining competitive advantages in the offer.

Identifying the industry specific success factors means determining the dimensions in which it is possible for a company to build competitive advantages. If an attempt is made to build a competitive advantage outside these areas, then there is the risk that the advantage being constructed is not in fact a genuine competitive advantage since it does not correspond to existing customer needs. For electricity companies, for example, a margin of error of 10 watts is satisfactory when measuring electricity consumption. For these customers, the advantage supposedly provided by electronic meters which are accurate to 0,1 watt is only an imaginary one. At the same time these machines are not accurate enough to compete successfully in the niche market for electricity consumption measurement in physics laboratories.

Strengths and weaknesses analysis reveals the success potentials on three levels: market position, market offer and resources, and it does this by comparing the company's position to that of its chief competitors. What we are interested in here is the strengths and weaknesses of the offer. These reveal the areas in which the company currently enjoys competitive advantages, together with the areas in which the company is at a disadvantage compared to its direct competitors. As it is rarely possible to outperform one's competitors in every single respect, the strengths and weaknesses analysis must serve to determine the priority areas where measures must be taken during the planning period to improve one's own success potentials at the level of the offer. Here the company may have to opt for one of two different approaches. One option may be to build on the company's strengths, while attempting to stabilize the position in areas of weakness. The other approach takes the opposite path: existing competitive advantages must be maintained and areas of disadvantage reduced.

Inset 14-3 presents a scheme which can be used to specify future competitive advantages in the offer, based on the identification of success factors and on strengths and weaknesses analysis.

Inset 14-3: Determining competitive advantages in the offer on the basis of the identification of success factors and of strengths and weaknesses analysis

In every industry, there are only a few specific parameters important for success. We refer to them as industry specific success factors. At any given time, the existing concrete use of these success factors by a competitor in the industry constitutes its success potentials. Strengths and weaknesses analysis should take account only of competitive dimensions relevant to success, and should thus be based on identified success factors. The identified strengths and weaknesses represent the current success potentials and form the basis for determining the target success potentials and the measures to reach them.

We can communicate this idea more simply by expressing it in diagram form. Each pole on the diagram represents a known success factor for the market offer. After carrying out a strengths and weaknesses analysis, we can use the diagram to map the current position for each competitor in the market. The diagram will then show the current success potentials. Next the company determines its target positions for the end of the planning period and these are added to the diagram. The target positions represent the desired improvements and form the basis for the design of implementation programs. We now provide an illustration of this with the case of Do-it-yourself, a company well established in the most important European countries.

Do-it-yourself is a producer of electric power tools for domestic use: drills, jigsaws, sanders etc. In the power tool industry the following six dimensions constitute the most important success factors:

- Safety of tools
- Reliability
- Versatility
- Average trade price
- Distribution coverage
- Market share

Do-it-yourself is the quality leader with good success potentials in the areas of safety, reliability and versatility. It is well established among specialist retailers, but with its relatively high prices, it is not present in the larger stores and hypermarkets. For this reason its market share is less than that of its strongest competitor Cheap Tools, whose strategy is based on cheap factory prices and which supplies the large department stores and hypermarket chains. **Figure 14-7** presents the current success factors for each of the two companies.

The diagram also shows that Do-it-yourself intends to lower its factory prices during the planning period and to extend its distribution and market share. These target improvements in the success potentials will form the basis for the drawing up of implementation programs. The increased use of basic modules in production and other rationalization measures will help to lower costs. The second important area of implementation concerns contacts with department stores and hypermarket chains. The success of the strategy depends on the company succeeding in getting its products into at least one of the important department stores or hypermarket chains. It may perhaps become necessary to develop an exclusive product category for this purpose. The company may even have to agree to its products being sold under the retailers' own brand. The risk for Do-it-yourself of sliding into a stuck in the middle position was evaluated as "existent, but slight". The management is confident that the company can maintain its competitive advantages in the attributes of safety, reliability and versatility by continuing to invest in product development and in brand advertising.

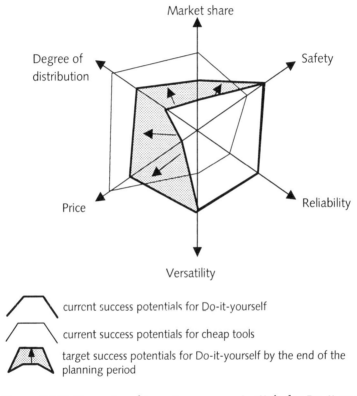

Figure 14-7: Current and target success potentials for Do-it-yourself

14.5   Assessing options for competitive advantages in the market offer

Once one or more options have been produced for future competitive advantages in the offer, the options must be assessed. The assessment must show whether a good solution is available or whether the search for viable options should be continued.

In the majority of cases, the question that must be answered in this assessment is the following: Can the target market position for the business, as set out in the corporate strategy, be achieved and maintained on the basis of the proposed competitive advantages? The competitive advantages for the offer should be assessed by looking first at the market's needs and then at the competitive strength, using the criteria proposed in Chapter Three.

In looking at the market's needs, the question to be answered is whether the proposed competitive advantages are in fact genuine ones, in so far as they correspond to industry-specific success factors. If it is found that there are no industry-specific success factors underlying the proposed success potentials then there must be a strong suspicion that these success potentials are only imaginary ones. In this case a new competitive option will have to be found. When assessing the relevance of proposed competitive advantages to needs it is important to be sure that:

- The competitive advantage is aimed at one or more target customer segments and not at the market as a whole.
- The assessment is based on possible future developments and not just the current situation.

In looking at the competition, the aim is to compare the company's offer with those of the direct competitors and to uncover strengths and weaknesses. Once more, it is the industry-specific success factors which should be used as the criteria for evaluating the offers. Strengths and weaknesses analysis is the most suitable method. However, unlike the market-based analysis, this analysis of the competition should be seen as provisional only at this stage, because it is only the later assessment of resources which can finally determine whether the target competitive advantages can in fact be constructed or defended against competition.

15 Specifying business strategies at the level of resources

15.1 Basic reflections on specifying business strategies at the level of resources

In the previous chapter we showed how a selected generic business strategy can be specified in terms of the offer (success potentials II A). Chapter 15 now continues with the specification of the generic business strategy in terms of resources (success potentials II B).

In comparison with the specification of the generic business strategy at the level of the offer, in this chapter we face a major difficulty: Whereas for determining competitive advantages in the offer there are a number of different methodological tools, such as for instance the identification of the market-specific success factors, industry segment analysis, and strengths and weaknesses analysis, for resources such tools are missing. Resource-based research has concentrated on clarifying the resource concept, examining the strategic relevance of firm resources and identifying the characteristics of valuable resources. There is a general lack of methods dealing with the analysis and shaping of resources. Black & Boal (1994, p. 131 ff.), with their approach to identifying rare and sustainable resource advantages, are a notable exception.

To fill this gap, we provide our own method for determining competitive advantages in resources. The method builds on Barney's discussion of the characteristics of valuable resources (1991, p. 99 ff.), Black & Boal's method for assessing the rarity and sustainability of resources (1994, p. 131 ff.) and Porter's value chain (Porter 1985, p. 33 ff.). Here, Porter's method will serve to link competitive advantages at the level of the offer with competitive advantages at the level of resources, and is thus used in a different context from that originally suggested by its author.

Chapter 15 is divided into three sections. Section 15.2 discusses what is meant by the term 'resource' and looks at different types of resources. The following section, 15.3, examines what is required for

resources to be considered valuable and therefore to represent competitive advantages. The final section, 15.4, presents a method for
determining what the resources are, which need to be built up and/or
maintained.

15.2   Understanding resources

When speaking of a company's resources, we must bear in mind the
following fundamental characteristics:

- In the resource-based view of strategy the term resources is used in
  a very wide sense. It not only includes material assets, financial assets and human resources, but also competencies, skills and other
  "soft" success potentials at level II B. In addition to this, specific aspects of the market position, such as strong customer relations or a
  positive customer image - success potentials at level I - are also
  considered as resources. This wide interpretation takes into account
  the fact that, for example, an existing brand image can be used to
  facilitate the introduction of new products or that strong customer
  relations can be the basis for successful cross-selling efforts.
- A company's market offer, success potentials at the level IIA,
  should however not be included in the resources. But competitive
  advantages in products, services and communication are the consequence of corresponding resource advantages on which they
  rely.
- Resources are hard and soft attributes of the company which management can control or at least influence (Barney, 1991, p. 1).

Based on these essential characteristics we can define a company's
resources as:

- tangible and intangible assets, individual and organizational competencies, and specific elements of market positions
- which are under the control of the company
- and which form the basis of competitive advantages in the offer.

Having defined what is meant by the term, it is helpful to introduce a
classification of the various types of resources. **Figure 15-1** shows
resources classified into five main categories, with a number of ex-

amples illustrating the great variety of phenomena involved. We have not, however, attempted to provide an exhaustive list, as this is neither possible nor useful.

Physical resources
- plant and equipment, logistics centers, geographical locations, real estate, computer hardware, communications networks
- financial resources such as liquid assets and credit facilities

Internal non-material resources
- structures, systems and processes such as planning and controlling systems, human resources management systems, organizational structure, production processes, information systems and processes etc.
- information and legal rights such as data, documents, brands, patents, licenses, contracts etc.

External non-material resources
- recognition and image of company and product brands, quality and size of customer base
- company reputation with suppliers, banks, potential employees and other stake holders

Individual human resources
- knowledge and skills of managers and employees
- motivation of managers and employees

Collective human resources
- features of corporate culture such as basic attitudes and values enacted in the company or specific parts of it
- primary competencies like quality procurement competencies, marketing competencies and competencies for serving export markets
- metacompetencies such as the ability to innovate, to cooperate, to implement change

---

Figure 15-1: Classification of resources
(Kühn & Grünig, 2000, p. 144)

15.3   Valuable resources

A resource may be considered valuable if it makes an essential contribution to sustained competitive advantage. According to Barney (1991, p. 105 ff.), such resources must be:

- rare
- able to create customer value
- imperfectly imitable
- imperfectly substitutable

We will now review each of these four characteristics. Our discussion is based on Kühn & Grünig (2000, p. 150 ff.).

Resources which can be acquired easily or built up quickly can hardly help to provide unique products or services, because any competing firm can establish the same resources and use them to launch similar offers. Competitive advantages in the offer must therefore be based on rare resources.

Rarity is a relative idea here. Resources can be:

- generally available in an industry
- available to a small number of competitors in an industry
- available to a single competitor only, and therefore unique

Consider, for example, the availability of machines to produce absolutely flat steel girders or, the expertise required to devise and implement marketing promotions. Both of these fall into the middle category. Not every company in the industry can afford the very expensive machines required to mill the flat surfaces of large girders accurately enough; not every producer of consumer goods has the experience and creativity to carry out an excellent promotion campaign. But these resources will be available to more than one company in the industry concerned.

The rarity of a resource is determined by

- whether the resource can be bought in factor markets
- whether the resource needs to be closely integrated into the company

A resource that is easy to purchase and that does not require special integration into the company can be regarded as generally available:

an example would be a heavy goods vehicle. Generally available resources, when used in a normal way, cannot be the basis for a sustainable competitive advantage.

If a resource is available only from specialist suppliers, with perhaps long wait times, and if special measures are needed to integrate the new resource into the company, then the resource belongs in the second category of resources available only to a small number of industry competitors. In our two examples, buying, installing and putting into service a specialized milling machine on the one hand, and the recruitment, selection and introduction of a promotions specialist on the other, will each require time, expertise and considerable financial outlay.

Unique resources are closely integrated into the resource system of the company concerned. The Coca Cola brand, for example, can only theoretically be purchased. From a practical point of view, it is only possible to get the brand together with the company behind it.

A rare resource is not by itself a sufficient condition for the creation of competitive advantage in the offer. The resource must also be able to create customer value. This requirement is more difficult to assess because it is not a question of the resource itself, but of the products and services which are created by the resource. To carry out this assessment a method is required which can link customer needs, the offer and the resources. Here, value chain analysis (see Inset 15-2) will be used to make this link.

It is interesting to note that this requirement for creating customer value means that the so-called resource-based view (see Inset 12-2) also needs to include a market-focus: it requires an assessment of how far the offers produced with the help of resources actually conform to customer needs. Because of this a number of researchers have concluded that the future development of strategic planning depends on achieving a synthesis of the resource-based view and the market-based view (see for example Mahoney & Pandian, 1992, p. 371 ff.).

Rare resources which create customer value allow a company to achieve competitive advantage in the offer. But the resource advantages must also be sustainable. The advantages in the offer can only be defended in the long term, if the resources which underlie them are imperfectly imitable and substitutable by competing companies.

Imperfect imitability of resources depends on the following interrelated factors:

- A resource is the result of a historical process. The market image of Lindt & Sprüngli, for example, was not created overnight, but is the product of decades of investment.
- Where resources are the result of the interplay of many factors, some of them soft factors, imitation becomes very difficult. Think, for example, of the producers of airplanes, rockets and satellites. The companies concerned comprise a large number of specialist scientists and complex networks of facilities. The processes such an organization has developed, and its cultural features, mean that the organization as a whole has a much greater value than the sum of its individual parts.
- Although it seems paradoxical, the bundles of resources which are best protected against imitation are those where even the company concerned does not understand how they work together to create value. Of course, in such situations, it is also difficult for the company to undertake measures to maintain its resource advantages.
- Resources are also well protected against imitation when to attempt this brings considerable risk. A customer service network, for example, is only strategically valuable, if it has achieved a certain level of intensity. If a company is seeking to imitate this type of resource, it will have to make very large investments before beginning to profit from the resource, thus incurring a much increased risk.

To produce sustained competitive advantage a resource must not only be protected against imitation, but must also be imperfectly substitutable. In technologically - driven industries imperfectly imitable resources are often substituted by new technologies and lose all value. For example, the transition from mechanical to electronic watches meant that the expertise required to produce mechanical watches cheaply was substituted. An interesting case of substitution concerns the Smart Car, which is distributed through department stores and hypermarkets, rather than using a traditional network of authorized dealers. In this way expensive and difficult resource imitation is avoided.

The dividing line between imperfect imitability and imperfect substitutability is fuzzy. If a company judges that a competitor has a very powerful management team and therefore decides to engage a top international executive as its new CEO, this could be classed as either imitation or substitution. It deals with the same type of resource, but the new manager of the competitor will probably manage differently and use different tools, so it could also be seen as substitution. Which way one decides to classify such a case is probably only of academic interest; in practice what is important is to be mindful of both sources of danger to resource advantages.

15.4   Determining which resources to build or maintain

15.4.1 Overview of the process

Investment in the construction and care of resources must concentrate on resources which:

- create customer value
- can resist imitation and substitution

It is wise to concentrate financial power on resources which fulfill these conditions and are therefore capable of producing sustained competitive advantage.

Black & Boal (1994, p. 131 ff.) propose a method for the identification of those resources, within a wider network of company resources, which contribute most essentially to the creation of sustainable competitive advantage. **Inset 15-1** summarizes the proposition.

The suggestions of Black & Boal are useful because:

- they do not merely list criteria, but describe a process for the identification of valuable resources
- resources are not examined in isolation, but appraised in terms of the position they occupy in the resource-system of a company

Unfortunately they do not take explicit account the aspect of creating customer value when identifying key resources. Black & Boal's process allows the identification of rare and sustainable resources only. Because of this limitation, Black & Boal's method has not been directly adopted here, but forms only one element of our suggested process.

The resources which need to be constructed or maintained can be identified in a three-step process, as follows:

1. Identifying the resources creating customer value
2. Determining which of the resources creating customer value are rare
3. Assessing sustainability of the resources creating customer value and found to be rare

We now look at each of these three steps in identifying the resources which need to be built or maintained.

Inset 15-1: Black & Boal's method for identifying rare and sustainable resources
(Black & Boal, 1994, p. 131 ff)

Black & Boal's approach is based on a classification of resources into four categories according to two criteria (1994, p. 133 f.):

- Whether or not they can be procured: tradable or non-tradable
- Whether or not they can be acquired quickly: asset-flow or asset-stock

As **Figure 15-2** indicates, these two parameters produce four possible combinations, or types of resource.

In addition to this 'four types' scheme, Black & Boal propose a series of six questions to which the answer is either yes or no. The answers to these questions determine whether resources are rare and/or sustainable (1994, p. 142):

① Is the resource part of a complex system?
② Can it be substituted?
③ Can it be compensated for by a different tradable resource?
④ Can it be compensated for by a different non-tradable resource?

Procurement / Time to procure or construct	Tradable resources	Non-tradable resources
Rapidly procured or constructed resources	Tradable asset flow	Non-tradable asset flow
Resources can only slowly be procured or constructed	Tradable asset stock	Non-tradable asset stock

Figure 15-2: Black & Boal's four types of resources

⑤ Does the resource strengthen the effect of another resource within the system?
⑥ Does the resource reduce the effect of another resource within the system?

In order to determine whether resources are rare and sustainable, these six questions are applied in turn to each of the four types of resources. **Figure 15-3** shows how the answers are linked in four flow charts. On the right of the charts there are 22 cases, labelled from **a** to **v**, in which resources are judged to be either valuable or very valuable in terms of the criteria of rarity and sustainability (Black & Boal, 1994, p. 142 ff.). As experience would suggest, the largest number of cases where resources are rated valuable or very valuable fall into the category of non tradable asset stock (9 out of 22). But as Black & Boal's approach demonstrates, both valuable and very valuable resources can be found in the other three categories too. This is because of the value of a resource as an integrated part of a resource system.

Tradable asset flow

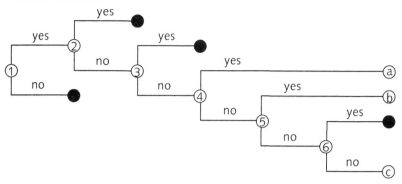

Tradable asset stock

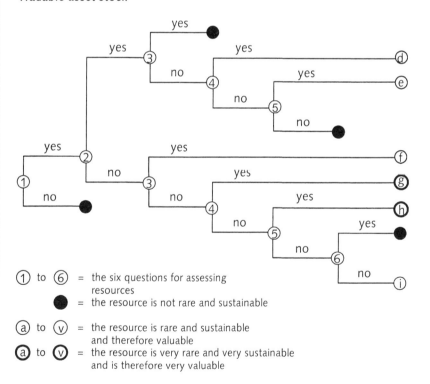

① to ⑥ = the six questions for assessing
resources
● = the resource is not rare and sustainable

ⓐ to ⓥ = the resource is rare and sustainable
and therefore valuable
ⓐ to **ⓥ** = the resource is very rare and very sustainable
and is therefore very valuable

Figure 15-3: The identification of rare and sustainable resources
(adapted from Black & Boal, 1994, p. 142 ff.)

Non-tradable asset flow

Non-tradable asset stock

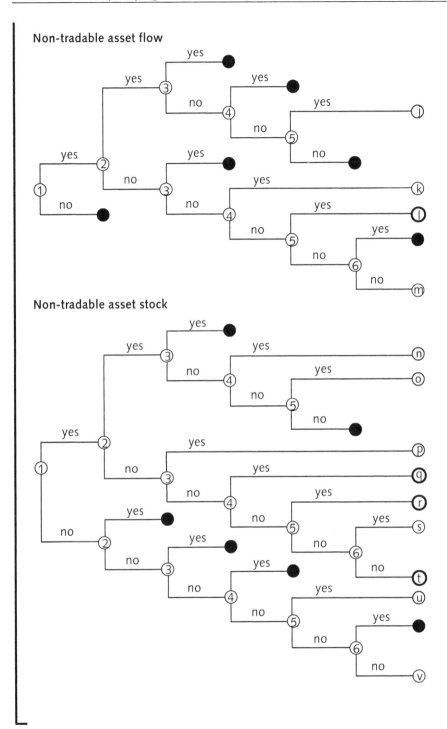

15.4.2 Identifying the resources creating customer value

The first step in the process of determining which resources to build or maintain is the identification of those resources within the overall resource system which play a key role in creating customer value. As customer value is created in the offer, this is where we have to begin. The methodological approach which allows us to link competitive advantages in the offer to the resources underlying is Porter's value chain analysis (1985, p. 33 ff.). It is introduced in **Inset 15-2**.

The choice of value chain analysis for this purpose is based on the following considerations:

- Each of the activities in the value chain brings a contribution to the company's offer, which can be described in both qualitative and quantitative terms. Inextricably linked with each activity, there are various resources, ranging from employees, facilities and capital, to licenses and access to information systems, not forgetting specialist knowledge and necessary cultural features such as customer focus. Provided that an activity is described clearly enough, it is relatively easy to identify the resources linked to it. If this is not possible, then the activity must be subdivided into more precise and detailed activities.
- The value chain and the activities it comprises thus link together the offer and the resources. This means that the value chain can be used to link success potentials at each of the two levels, the level of the offer and the level of resources.

Inset 15-2: Porter's value chain analysis
(Porter, 1985, p. 33 ff.)

1.   Value system, value chain and value activity

The activities of a focused company or of a business field of a diversified company form a whole. Such a set of activities is called a value chain. Value chains are not free standing but should be seen as part of a wider value creation process or value system (Porter, 1985, p. 59 ff.). **Figure 15-4** presents two examples of value systems, for a leather goods wholesaler, and for a drinks company with three business fields: beer production, production of mineral

Value system for a leather goods wholesaler

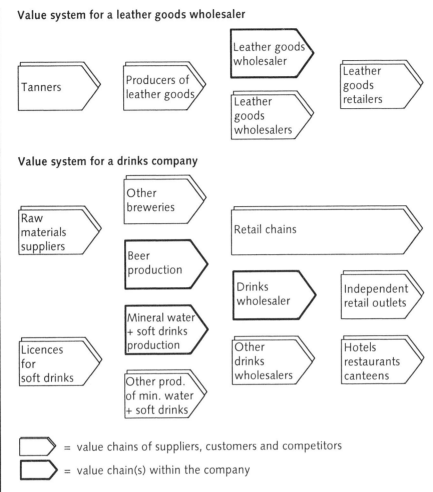

Value system for a drinks company

= value chains of suppliers, customers and competitors

= value chain(s) within the company

Figure 15-4: Two examples of value systems

water and soft drinks, and drinks wholesaling.

A great variety of different activities can appear in a focused company's or business field's value chain. For example, the activities required to produce beer, on the one hand, and to operate a leather goods wholesale business, on the other, are obviously very different. But even if we limit the field to breweries, we will hardly find two where the value chains are identical. Porter's analysis cuts across the variety which can be found in different value chains and recognizes nine major types of activity, grouped into five primary activities, which contribute directly to outputs, and four support activities, which sustain the primary activities by procuring and organizing the necessary resources (Porter, 1985, p. 36 ff.). **Figure 15-5** gives the value chain model with the nine types of activity.

Firm infrastructure					
Human resources management					Margin
Technology development					
Procurement					
Inbound logistics	Operations	Outbound logistics	Marketing & sales	Service	

Figure 15-5: Porter's value chain with nine categories of activity
(Porter, 1985, p.37)

Porter's nine categories provide a comprehensive overview of the activities of a focused company. Practical experience in using the value chain suggests, however, that for certain industries it can be effective to develop somewhat different categories. This is particularly useful when employing value chain analysis to examine activities in service industries. If preference is given to an adapted scheme, then it is important that this is also used when analyzing competitors. This is because significant differences in competitors' value chains will stand out more clearly if a single system is used for analysis.

Within a company, or a business field, the value chain is made up of a large number of different linked activities. Porter calls these value activities (1985, p. 39). The number of these activities, their type, and the way they are linked, are of crucial importance for product or service differences and for communication differences and for costs for the company or business field concerned. The value activities determine the competitive advantages in the offer, and thus are of immense strategic importance.

To achieve a clear understanding of the situation it is important to focus separately on activities which:

- have different interrelations with activities inside or outside the value chain and/or
- a great potential for differentiation and/or
- high or increasing costs (Porter, 1985, p. 45).

In addition, the activities have to be classified into the correct categories. Often this is straightforward enough: the production of goods, for example, would be classified under operations. But there are cases where judgment is required: the processing of orders, for example, can be seen as part of marketing and sales or as part of outbound logistics (Porter, 1985, p. 45 ff.). If it is mainly a technical problem, then it might better be placed within logistics, but if the activity seems to play an important role for customer contact, then it should be seen as falling within marketing and sales.

2. Value chain analysis as a tool for identifying competitive advantages in the offer

Porter's value chain analysis serves to identify existing or target competitive advantages in the offer. The analysis can be used in four different ways, giving four approaches to the identification of competitive advantages.

The first, simple use of value chain analysis consists in identifying the different primary or support activities which make an important contribution to low costs or to uniqueness (Porter, 1985, p. 38 f.).

A second approach to identifying competitive advantages consists in examining new possibilities for linking value activities within the value chain. If a company controls the links, it can

- identify alternative processes and select the optimal solution. For example, a company can fulfill customer demands for precision either by full quality control of the finished products or through low tolerances in production standards.
- reduce costs: for instance the cost of holding stock can be re-

duced by improved coordination in logistics activities
- reduce order processing time to supply customers more quickly

Companies who wish to introduce a price strategy will need to redesign the links between activities, so that the number of interfaces and the need for coordination are minimized (Porter, 1985, p. 48 ff.).

A third approach to competitive advantages is to be found in the connections between the company's own value chain and those of the suppliers and traders. Porter's idea is not that cost saving should be achieved at the expense of the suppliers or traders: both sides can gain here because it is normally not a zero-sum game. As an illustration of this, consider a confectioner who decides to accept liquid chocolate from his supplier, rather than solid bars. The confectioner now saves on the melting process, while the supplier cuts out the pouring and solidifying stages required to produce solid chocolate bars (Porter, 1985, p. 50 ff.).

The fourth and final approach consists in coordinating the company's value chain with that of the end user, which may be a company or a domestic household, depending on the product or service concerned. Where the end- user is a company, the value chains may be coordinated directly, as in the case of suppliers and traders. In the case of domestic consumers as end users, it is a matter of understanding the customer's value chain and adapting products and services accordingly. It is very important, for example, for a producer of equipment for climbing and alpine touring to know the kinds of terrain and climatic conditions in which the products will be used. The better the products are adapted to the real needs and possibilities, including perhaps extremely dangerous or difficult situations, the greater will be their commercial success.

Figure 15-6 shows how to identify resources which create customer value by working backwards. The procedure assumes that key competitive advantages in the offer (success potentials II A) have been provisionally specified (They can only be definitively fixed once the resource-based analysis has shown that it is feasible, and financially possible, to construct or maintain them over the long term.). We begin at A, on the right of the diagram, by recalling the competitive advantages in the offer. Next a list of value activities is produced and those activities are identified which are essential for the target competitive advantages in the offer. Since the offer depends directly on primary activities, it is best to begin by looking at these. This is B1 on the diagram. After that the necessary support activities (= B2) can be identified and evaluated in terms of their contribution to the competitive advantages in the offer. The final step is to look at the resources which are necessary for these value creating activities to take place (= C1 and C2). It is not necessary to produce a comprehensive detailed list with buildings, plant, information, knowledge and so on. It is more helpful to have a clear and concrete understanding of those specific resource elements which are needed to produce the target competitive advantages in the offer. Where the required resource strengths are already present, measures taken during the strategy implementation phase will aim to make sure that they are properly maintained. Budgets will be required, for example, for the maintenance or renewal of equipment and for development and recruitment of staff. If the resources are insufficient, programs will be required to build the required resource strengths.

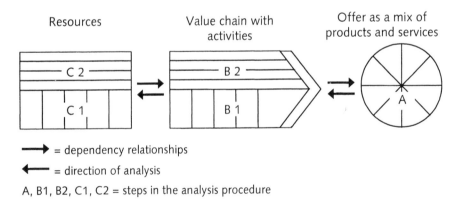

⟶ = dependency relationships

⟵ = direction of analysis

A, B1, B2, C1, C2 = steps in the analysis procedure

Figure 15-6: Identifying resources which create customer value using the value chain model

15.4.3 Determining which of the resources creating customer value are rare

The value chain has helped to identify the resources in the resource system which are the basis for the competitive advantages in the offer. But these resources creating customer value will vary greatly in their degree of rarity. The set of resources behind the competitive advantages of the offer will at the same time include:

- some which are generally available in an industry
- some available to a small number of competitors in an industry
- some unique because linked to the company

So now the second step in identifying resources to be maintained or built up requires us to determine which resources belong in the categories of those owned by only a few companies, or only by a single company. By eliminating the others, a shortlist of resources is produced. These both create customer value and are also rare. It is important to make this selection because resources which are not rare are either already owned by competitors too, or can be quickly procured. So while resources which are not rare can contribute to an advantageous offer, they cannot be the basis of a sustainable competitive advantage. A supplier of meat and fish specialties to hotels and restaurants, for example, may seek differentiation through a good delivery service. The vehicles needed for this are certainly an element in the underlying resource system, but they cannot provide a basis for a delivery service which creates a competitive advantage. Resources which could achieve this might be:

- software for processing orders that outperforms competitors,
- a large storage capacity,
- a twenty-four hour ordering service and/or
- employees who are customer-focused and willing to process urgent orders at short notice and outside normal working hours.

15.4.4 Assessing sustainability of the resources creating customer value and found to be rare

As a result of the process described above, we now have a list of resources which fulfil the two conditions of creating customer value and of rarity, and which might constitute competitive advantages at the level of resources. The third step in our process involves assessing the sustainability of these resource advantages. This is important, because a company should invest primarily in competitive advantages which can resist imitation and substitution. It is only resources which are sustainable that can create long-term competitive advantages in the offer.

Based on Barney (1991, p. 105 ff.) and Black & Boal (1994, p. 140 ff.), there are four ways in which competitors might proceed and which therefore must be investigated:

- Examine the availability of equivalent resources and the length of time required to procure them and to integrate them into the resource system.
- Examine whether equivalent resources can be built up and how long it would take to do so.
- Examine whether the resources could be substituted and how long it would take to procure the substitute resources and to integrate them.
- Examine whether substitute resources can be built up and how long this would require.

If any of these options seems feasible in a practical time period, then the resource advantage cannot be sustained. If none of these options seems possible even over a long period, then the competitive advantage is sustainable.

16   The business strategy development process

16.1   Overview of the process of developing a business strategy

Step Three in the process of strategic planning is the definition, in parallel, of the various business strategies, based on the target market positions for each business determined in the previous step. In Step Two the approximate investment budgets for each business were also determined, and these budgets now represent the most important limiting conditions for the development of the business strategies. Chapter 12 emphasized that target market positions and planned investment budgets must be seen as provisional in character, as one possible outcome of the process of developing business strategies may be that the financial means available is shown to be insufficient for meeting the targets. If this happens, the corporate strategy has to be revised.

The various business strategies are normally developed simultaneously in parallel working groups. Where different business fields are involved, there is little need for dovetailing between them, but with business unit strategies, where the offers focus on the same market and/or where the same resources are used, very close coordination is required. There are two measures to guarantee this:

- A useful coordination tool is the corporate strategy: this can either be for the company as a whole, where the company is active in a single market, or for the business field to which the units belong, in a more diversified company. In addition to specifying target market positions and investment priorities, a corporate strategy, used for the coordination of different business units, should prescribe the generic strategy to be followed and the most important target competitive advantages.
- Regular coordination meetings must take place between the different groups working on the development of the various business unit strategies.

Developing a business strategy is a complex task, made more difficult by the need to produce and compare different options, in order to guarantee quality. The task is therefore best broken down into subtasks, as shown in **Figure 16-1**. Loops in the process will often be required, and the most important of these is shown in the diagram with a thin arrow.

This chapter is organized as follows: Section 16.2 deals with the first subtask, assessing the current business strategy, and the following section considers how to identify and assess options for the future generic business strategy and the target industry segments. These two sections draw on the methods introduced in Chapters 13 to 15, and are therefore relatively short. Section 16.4 takes a longer look at identifying and assessing options for competitive advantages, showing how networks of success potentials can be constructed and assessed. The chapter ends with the case of a watch manufacturer developing a business strategy.

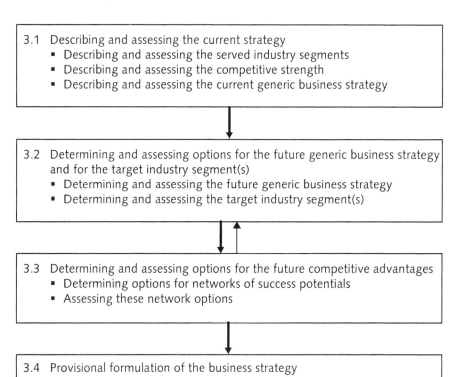

3.1 Describing and assessing the current strategy
- Describing and assessing the served industry segments
- Describing and assessing the competitive strength
- Describing and assessing the current generic business strategy

3.2 Determining and assessing options for the future generic business strategy and for the target industry segment(s)
- Determining and assessing the future generic business strategy
- Determining and assessing the target industry segment(s)

3.3 Determining and assessing options for the future competitive advantages
- Determining options for networks of success potentials
- Assessing these network options

3.4 Provisional formulation of the business strategy

→ usual sequence of steps
→ possible loop in the sequence

Figure 16-1: The process of developing a business strategy

16.2   Describing and assessing the current business strategy

The first step in developing the future strategy for a business is to assess the current strategy. Following the model introduced in Chapter Three, this means assessing both the market/industry and the company's competitive strength.

The assessment of market and industry begins with an industry segment analysis of the served industry market. The five forces model and, if appropriate, the strategic groups model can afterwards be used to assess the industry. In some cases these models will already have been used as part of the planning of corporate strategy. If this is the case, it is sufficient merely to restate the results, but if the assessment has not yet been carried out, it must now be done.

The assessment of competitive strength should be based on the results of the identification of success factors and the strengths and weaknesses analysis, both carried out as part of strategic analysis. There are three stages:

- Assessment begins with the competitive advantages in the offer. These have to be described as specifically as possible and then evaluated. The information presented in Chapter 14 can provide a basis for this work.
- Next the resources are considered and competitive advantages and disadvantages identified, using the approach described in Chapter 15, especially Section 15.4.
- Finally the current strategy is assessed in terms of the generic business strategies. The principal question to answer is whether the current competitive advantages are sufficient for the successful realization of the generic competitive strategy pursued. If not, the question becomes one of whether there are realistic means of developing the required competitive advantages at the level of the offer and at the level of resources. If the answer is again a negative one, then changes must be foreseen in terms of the selected generic competitive strategy and/or the choice of the industry segment(s) served.

Figure 16-2 provides an overview of this step, 3.1.

Assessment of market and industry aspects	Assessment of competitive strength
• Industry segment analysis • Five Forces model • Where necessary: model of Strategic Groups	• Description of the current competitive advantages and disadvantages at the level of the offer • Description of the current competitive advantages and disadvantages at the level of resources • Assessing the current business strategy based on the generic business strategy pursued

Figure 16-2: Assessing the current business strategy in step 3.1

16.3   Determining and assessing options for the future generic business strategy and the target industry segment(s)

In view of what we know about the success conditions for each of the generic business strategies, it is frequently the case that there is no choice regarding the future generic business strategy. It is often dictated by the previous history of the business and its existing resource situation.

With generic business strategies, genuine options exist only in the following cases:

- If up to now the current generic business strategy has not been fully and systematically implemented, there may be a degree of freedom in the resource situation to allow for a change of strategic direction. But there is always an important risk of failure involved in such cases, and such strategic change should only be considered in situations where the majority of the competitors have also not been following either a clear price or a clear differentiation strategy.
- A second case concerns new entry into an industry where the competitive position is built up from new within the company (The situation is not the same in the case of an acquisition, where the

new owners usually continue with the current generic business strategy of the acquired company).
- A third case is the switch from a market development strategy (see Inset 13-3) to a competitive strategy.

There is also frequently little room for manoeuvre in the choice of industry segment or segments to serve. The resource situation and investments that have been made in building a market position often make major change extremely difficult and risky. Sometimes, however, the results of analyzing the customer segments and submarkets force a change in direction. A company with broad - scope differentiation strategy may readjust its priorities in terms of the segments served, give up a segment, for instance, or attempt to serve a new segment. A niche supplier may redefine its niche somewhat. But in both these cases the core customer groups will largely remain the same.

16.4   Determining and assessing options for the future competitive advantages

16.4.1 The reason for identifying and assessing options

Unlike the choice of generic business strategy and of industry segment(s) to serve, where there is often little room for manoeuvre, in the case of competitive advantages there is usually plenty of genuine choice available, especially with differentiation strategies. This opportunity should be exploited: although a great deal of time and money may be needed to devise and compare a range of options, this is the only way to guarantee that a good solution will finally be found.

The next section looks at how an option for competitive advantage can be developed and represented in the form of a network of success potentials. Then we show where in practical terms the options can be found. Finally we present a number of criteria for assessing options.

16.4.2 The network of success potentials as an approach to developing options for competitive advantages

An option for competitive advantages in a business can be thought of as a network of different success potentials, both in the offer (IIA) and in resources (IIB). A success potential network must:

- be directed towards achieving the target market positions specified in the corporate strategy
- respect the limits imposed by the investment budgets in the corporate strategy
- implement the chosen generic business strategy in the chosen industry segment or segments, in line with the decisions made in Step 3.2
- exploit clear synergy effects

Figure 16-3 presents the success potential network and shows what is meant by an option for competitive advantages of a business.

Most of the arrows in the diagram point upwards. Influence either occurs within a category of success potentials or has its effect on the category immediately above it in the hierarchy. Success potentials in resources are thus usually the basis for other resource success potentials or for competitive advantages in the offer. Success potentials at the level of the offer normally strengthen other competitive advantages in the offer or form the basis of attractive market positions. An exception is the direct influence of resource advantages on the market position (Arrow a). A luxuriously appointed jeweler's shop in a top location, for example, greatly contributes to the image and thus to the market position of the jeweler concerned. A second exception concerns the influence of market position on competitive advantages in the offer (Arrow b). This can be interpreted as follows: stable features of market position are to be considered as resources and, just like level IIB resources, they can be the basis for competitive advantages in the offer. To illustrate this, consider how high market share makes it possible for a food manufacturer to be represented in hypermarket chains with a comprehensive product range rather than isolated products. This in turn represents a clear competitive advantage in the offer, compared with rival companies with only single products in the important retail chains.

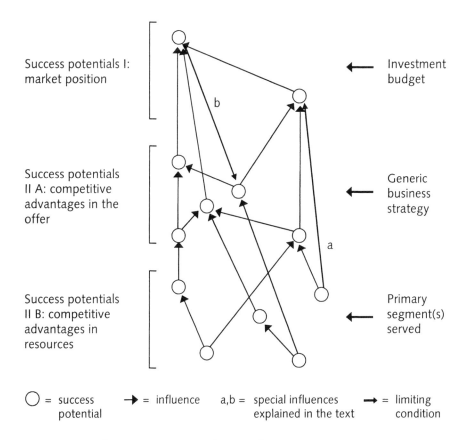

Success potentials I:
market position

Success potentials
II A: competitive
advantages in the
offer

Success potentials
II B: competitive
advantages in
resources

Investment
budget

Generic
business
strategy

Primary
segment(s)
served

b

a

○ = success
       potential
→ = influence
a,b = special influences
        explained in the text
➔ = limiting
       condition

Figure 16-3: The success potential network

The identification of success potentials is usually carried out by working in the opposing direction to that of the influences just examined.
Starting from the target market positions defined in the corporate
strategy, first the competitive advantages in the offer are specified
and only then are the competitive advantages in resources considered. This is the normal procedure, known as the outside-in approach.
The opposite approach, known as inside-out, is used less frequently.
Inset 16-1 compares the two methods.

Inset 16-1: Outside-in and inside-out approaches to developing and assessing success potentials
(Kühn & Grünig, 2000, p. 168 ff.)

In order to identify the success potentials on levels I, II A and II B there are basically two approaches, known as outside-in and inside-out.

The outside-in approach is derived from the market-based view (see Inset 10-1). It begins by determining target market positions, derives the competitive advantages in the offer from these and finally determines the resources required. The outside-in approach is generally used when it is necessary to examine the existing competitive advantages in the offer and in resources and to see how they can be improved so as to safeguard or build up existing market positions. As this is usually what strategy projects focus on, it is considered here to be the normal approach.

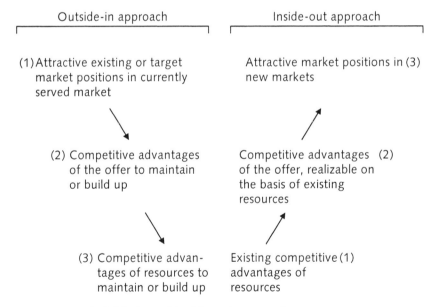

Outside-in approach	Inside-out approach
(1) Attractive existing or target market positions in currently served market	Attractive market positions in (3) new markets
(2) Competitive advantages of the offer to maintain or build up	Competitive advantages (2) of the offer, realizable on the basis of existing resources
(3) Competitive advantages of resources to maintain or build up	Existing competitive (1) advantages of resources

Figure 16-4: Outside-in and inside-out approach
(adapted from Kühn & Grünig, 2000, p. 170)

The inside-out method derives from the resource based-view (see Inset 12-2). It begins by detailing resource strengths and then proceeds to look for possible competitive advantages in the offer. These are then assessed in terms of their fit with resource strengths. The final step is to determine the market positions which could be achieved with these competitive advantages. The inside-out approach is preferred when it is a question of identifying markets which could be successfully served with existing resources. This arises when companies are looking to diversify. As strategy projects are much more frequently concerned with existing market positions than with diversification, it is considered here as the exception.

Figure 16-4 presents the two approaches side by side.

Inset 16-2 discusses the success potential networks for a leading Swiss manufacturer of luxury watches and for an international consulting firm.

Inset 16-2: Success potential networks for a luxury watch manufacturer and for an international consulting firm

The manufacturer is based in the watch region in Switzerland. The company makes the mechanisms for the watches itself. Over the years the company has bought up a number of component suppliers in vertical integration moves so that the company now also produces a considerable proportion of the components required. The watches produced all belong in the luxury class, and the firm is market leader in this highest price category.

In qualitative terms, the target market position is as follows: the company wishes to produce watches which will be bought as prestige products of lasting value. In quantitative terms, the company wishes to hold on to its position as the leader in luxury watches.

Figure 16-5 gives the success potential network for this watch manufacturer. Resource advantages and product features are systematically employed to create the desired image. This creates

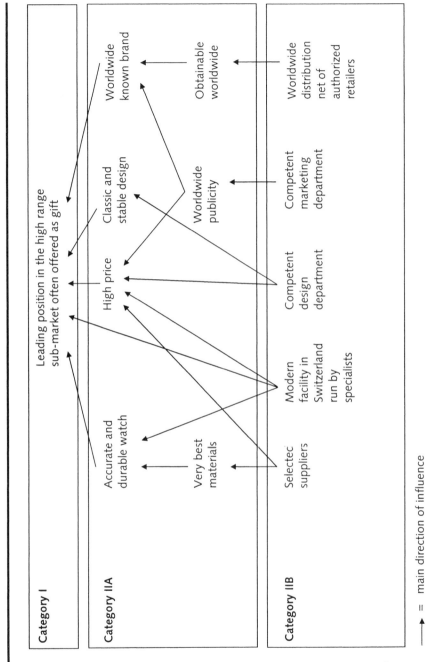

Figure 16-5: Success potential network of a luxury watch manufacturer

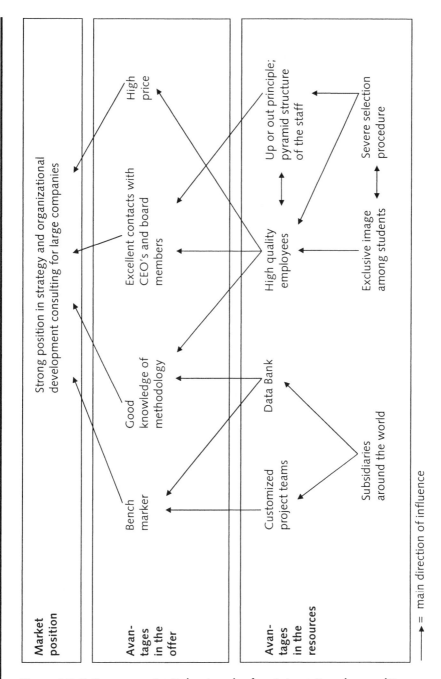

Figure 16-6: Success potential network of an international consulting firm

positive synergies: the whole success potential system is clearly of more value than the sum of its individual parts. The image aspect of the offer and the quality elements in resources are relatively well protected against imitation and substitution, so this system should be sustainable and allow the company to maintain its market leadership.

The consulting company has a worldwide network of branches which all work with the same problem solving methods. It is the market leader for strategy and organizational management consulting among large international corporations. **Figure 16-6** gives the network of success potentials on which this position is based. There are two important sub-systems:

The company is able to succeed in engaging highly competent consulting staff. But the up-or-out principle means that costs are kept low. As a by-product of this policy, there is a wide network of former employees and this helps to bring in consulting contracts for the firm.

The company makes optimal use of its accumulated knowledge. There is a central data bank with information on markets around the world and it is able to put together customized project teams using specialists from its various overseas branches.

16.4.3 Basic options for competitive advantages

It is in terms of competitive advantages, both in the offer and in resources, that the generic business strategy must be specified. Depending on whether this is a price strategy or a differentiation strategy, the options will be different.

The specification of a price strategy at the level of the offer is explained in section 14.2 above. As far as product features and product range are concerned, in general, it is the minimum standard that must be reached. The area, in which competitive advantages are sought, is the price system. But in different industries there may be different approaches to this: a manufacturer of lifts who is following a price strategy may, for instance, either offer new lifts at lower prices than competitors, or seek to gain advantage through cheaper service and maintenance contracts. A manufacturer of inexpensive trucks, too, can either target larger and more price-sensitive customers by offering attractive discounts for fleets of vehicles or, alternatively, decide to offer better terms to customers who are willing to do without any special features. These are solutions for specific industries, but there is also a more general choice for companies between two basic alternatives: either to use advertising to gain a low-price image among end-buyers or to offer good conditions to wholesalers. This second option means that it will be the wholesalers who determine the extent to which the company's low prices are passed on to the end buyers.

With a differentiation strategy too, a company must decide whether to try to cement relations with the end buyers or to look to partner-ship with the wholesalers. If the marketing mix looks primarily at the wholesaler, it is not enough to hope to be seen as a fair and flexible partner. Just as when targeting the end buyers, there must be a clear view of the target competitive advantages.

Another way of understanding basic options for differentiation is in terms of where to put the main emphasis. We saw earlier that differentiation is usually based on a number of different elements. However, this does not change the fact that a company can decide to put its main effort into product/service features or into communication messages or into a high intensity of communication and customer relations.

Figure 16-7 summarizes the basic options for competitive advantages.

Experience has shown that once an option from Figure 16-7 has been determined, a number of concrete possibilities remain for its realization. It should not be imagined that for successful implementation it is enough merely to select one of these basic options: the business strategy needs to specify the competitive advantages in detail, for instance, in the form of a network of success potentials.

Companies following a price strategy	
Target the end-buyer with low retail prices	Target the wholesalers with good conditions

Companies following a differentiation strategy		
	Target the end-buyer	Target the wholesalers
Emphasis on product or service		
Emphasis on communication message		
Emphasis on a high intensity of communication and customer relations		

Figure 16-7: Basic options for competitive advantages

16.4.4 Criteria for assessing options for competitive advantages

Assessing options for competitive advantages in a business strategy is a challenging task, generally more difficult than assessing options for corporate strategy. There are two main causes of difficulty:

- For corporate strategy, the assessment of market positions uses quantitative measures, like market share and market growth. But success potentials in the offer and in resources can often only be characterized in qualitative terms. This is true for important variables, like image and competencies.
- The success potentials of a corporate strategy are always aspects of industry attractiveness and competitive strength. But the success potentials of a business strategy lie on completely different levels, ranging, for example, from corporate culture, to the knowledge required to carry out promotions campaigns and the capacity of storage installations, perhaps measured by the number of possible movements in a 24-hour period.

Because this assessment is such a tricky task, only relatively abstract general criteria can be suggested here. We suggest that each option, in the form of a network of competitive advantages, is assessed in two stages: first check that the option respects important facts and limiting conditions, second decide whether the option is suitable for achieving the target market position(s) specified in the corporate strategy.

To check that the option fits with important facts and conditions the following questions can be used:

- Are the target competitive advantages in the offer based on industry-specific success factors?
- Is the selected generic business strategy readily apparent from the network of success potentials?
- Is the success potential network geared towards the primary target market segment or segments?
- Is it realistic to try to build or maintain the target system of competitive advantages with the budget specified by the corporate strategy?

If these questions can all be answered in the positive, then an option has been found which is basically feasible and its quality can be judged in the next step. If there are negative replies to some of the questions, or if a clear answer cannot be given, then the option requires revision. But where the second, third, or fourth question produces a negative response, there remains the possibility of modifying the framework of limiting conditions. This means looping back and reiterating earlier steps in the process, such as step 3.2, which involves selecting the future generic business strategy and the primary industry segment or segments to be served, or even step 2, the development of corporate strategy.

After checking for conformity with important facts and conditions, the option must be assessed in terms of its ability to achieve target market positions. The following criteria should be used:

- Can the target relative market share be achieved?
- What is the extent of positive synergies in the network of success potentials?
- How do we assess the competitive advantages, the strengths of the option?

- Are the competitive advantages sustainable?
- How do we assess the competitive disadvantages, the weaknesses of the option?
- To what extent can these disadvantages or weaknesses be compensated for?

As these criteria demonstrate, it is not the individual competitive advantage, but the system as a whole that is assessed here. The individual success potentials were already assessed earlier when the network was created.

There will usually be two or three options to assess. It is best to examine them by comparing them with the status quo.

16.5   Developing the business strategy of a watch manufacturer

To conclude, the method of developing a business strategy presented in this chapter is illustrated with a practical example. **Inset 16-3** presents the development of a business strategy for a watch manufacturer.

Inset 16-3: Developing the business strategy of a watch manufacturer for China
(Bauch, 1999)

1.   Lotus

Lotus was established in 1919 in the Swiss watch-making town of Grenchen. The company is still owned by the same family today and currently employs some 60 people in production, marketing and administration.

Lotus produces watches for the middle and upper price-segments, which sell at ex factory prices between $60.– and $400.–. These prices correspond to retail prices of approximately $180.– to $1,200.–. Lotus watches are almost all hand-assembled at their facility in Grenchen, and have mechanical automatic movement. This is unusual: most watches in this price category have quartz movements. The few competitors offering mechanical watches at comparable prices all buy the movements as finished products. Lotus has preferred its more expensive alternative in order to be able to influence quality throughout the manufacturing process.

The mechanism consists of around 120 tiny parts, all of which are purchased from Swiss manufacturers. The cases, straps, and faces for the watches, however, are obtained from various international suppliers. In all, raw materials account for over 50% of total costs, despite an increasing budget for advertising.

In most countries the watches are distributed through agents, who also provide marketing support to the retailers. It is only in the important market of China that the situation is different. Until recently the watches were sold to a single Government authority which then distributed the products. To support the retailers, Lotus set up a number of 'information offices'. Since China switched to a more open economic policy, there are now a number of state and private wholesalers, but these do not assume the same functions as an agent. This is the reason why Lotus has maintained its information offices to support the marketing efforts of the retailers.

After-sales service is organized locally through selected retailers. Agents, or in China the information offices, take care of training and are responsible for supplying parts.

Figure 16-8 presents an overview of the geographical markets and product groups. The percentages refer to the total volume of sales in units, while the arrows indicate Lotus management predictions of future trends.

If we focus on the important market of China, the typical customers for the various product ranges can be characterized as follows:
- The Long Life range sells mainly to older customers amongst the rural population. Longevity and quality of the product are important selling features.

	Long Life price $ 220.– 60%	Emperor price $ 500.– 15%	Prince price $ 340.– 2%	Youth price $ 410.– 12%	Active price $ 310.– 5%	Classic price $ 375.– 6%
China 50%	30% →	9% ↗	0.5% ↘	6% ↗	2.5% ↑	2.5% →
Southeast Asia* 20%	15% ↘	3% ↗	—	1% ↗	1% ↑	—
India and Pakistan 10%	8% →	1% ↗	—	0.5% ↗	0.5% ↗	—
Middle East** 10%	6.5% →	1% ↗	—	1% ↗	0.5% ↗	0.5% →
USA 5%	—	—	1% ↘	3.5% →	3.5% →	—
Russia and Ukraine 5%	1% →	—	1% ↘	—	—	3% →

price = average retail price in $
% = percentage of total units
→ = sales trend
* = Thailand, Malaysia, Indonesia, Vietnam, Singapore
** = Saudi Arabia, U. A. E., Bahrain, Qatar, Kuwait

Figure 16-8: Lotus product groups and markets

- Customers of a higher social class, who are looking for a prestige watch of traditional design, are the target of the Emperor range. The watch is regarded as an item of jewelry and is often bought as a gift. The Prince models were launched as a cheaper alternative targeted at the same customer profile, but their success has been modest.
- The younger, urban customers prefer watches from the Youth and Active ranges. Here the modern design is a crucial feature

and advertising is targeted specifically at the young. Sales have grown well for these ranges and the future continues to look very promising.

- The Classic product group does not seem to fit into any specific customer segment and sales have stagnated at a low level for some years.

Assessment of the current corporate strategy reveals success potentials but also negative aspects:

- Lotus is well established in the Far East, especially in China. Its relatively strong position in the medium price segment is based on products and advertising adapted to Asian customers, a well organized and extensive distribution network, and good understanding of Asian cultures. Moderate success has been obtained in India, Pakistan and the Middle East, while results in USA, Russia and the Ukraine have been poor.
- Four product lines are clearly positioned and show stable or growing turnover. However, two product groups seem to be failing, either because they are not closely enough matched to needs in their customer segment or because they have not targeted a sufficiently specific segment.

In the future, Lotus will try to concentrate its activities more, both geographically and in terms of product groups. America, Russia and the Ukraine will be abandoned, and there will be no further investment in India, Pakistan and the Middle East, where the aim is simply to hold the current positions. Efforts will be concentrated on the Far East. With regard to products, the Prince and Classic ranges will be discontinued. Although the Long Life watches will continue to be available, they will not be actively promoted.

2. The development of a business strategy for China

With the concentration on the corporate level, the importance of China will increase. This is the reason for the development of a business strategy for China

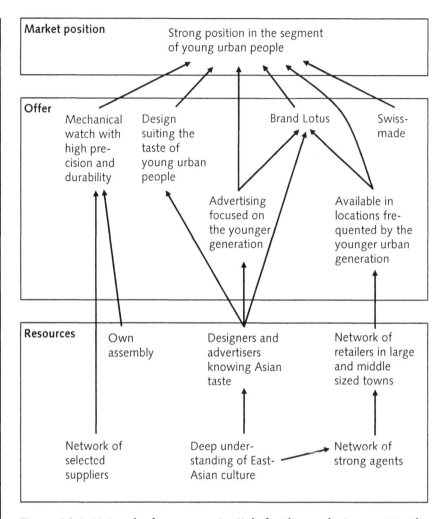

Figure 16-9: Network of success potentials for the product group Youth and Active

The current market position in China is strong and it is the objective not to lose market shares. Both now and in the future a whole market differentiation strategy will be pursued. Three industry segments will be served:

- In the future too, long life products will be sold to the rural population
- An important industry segment is the emperor models for customers of a higher social class.

- Finally the young urban customers will be served with watches from the Youth and Active range.

Figure 16-9 shows the target success potentials for the two product lines which are important to the future of the company: Youth and Active. A similar network exists for the Emperor range. The two networks of success potentials are closely linked, especially as far as resources are concerned. This is necessary in so far as these product groups only represent business units linked in terms of both markets and resources.

This strategy requires a large number of implementation measures:
- The retail network of dealers will need to be adapted. Shops will have to be acquired in locations frequented by the younger generation. Shops in rural areas will need to be examined and closed down if their results are poor.
- New advertising targeted at younger urban customers has to be developed for Youth and Active. The style and media used will be very different from that of the advertising for the Emperor range.
- The product lines for Youth and Active will be extended, while the Long Life range will be gradually pared down.

The final strategy must be discussed in detail with the heads of the various agents and information offices, who will then be asked to develop and present business plans for their regions with quantitative targets and investment budgets.

Part VI

Defining the implementation measures and assessing and approving the strategies

In Parts IV and V we described in detail the two key steps in the process of strategic planning: the development of corporate strategy (Step Two) and the development of business strategies (Step Three). Our process of strategic planning has three further steps which prepare for implementation and subject the strategy to a final review. These final three steps form the content of Part VI of our book. **Figure VI-1** presents the three steps dealt with here in Part VI and gives the subtasks for each in key words.

There are three chapters in Part VI, one for each of the final three steps in the strategic planning process.

- Chapter 17 deals with Step Four: the definition of implementation measures.
- Chapter 18 looks at the final overall review of the new strategies and of the realization measures, which is Step Five.
- Chapter 19 concludes with the final step in our process: the definitive formulation and approval of strategic documents. These documents contain the strategic thinking and the decisions taken and will function as a management tool for implementation.

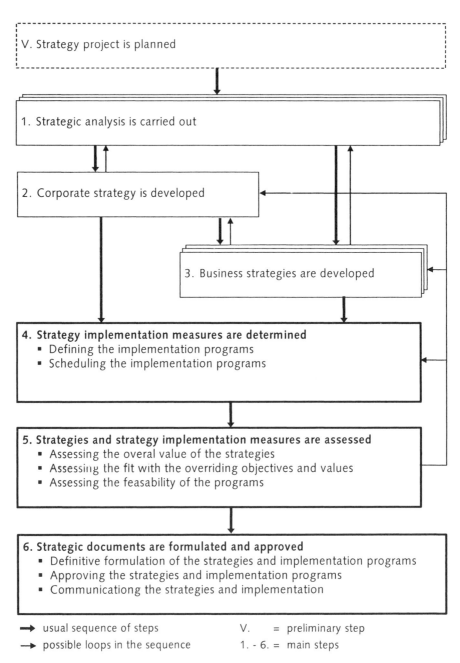

Figure VI-1: The definition of implementation measures and the final review and approval of strategies as steps in the process of strategic planning

17 Defining the implementation measures

17.1 Basic reflections on implementing strategies

Until the mid-eighties, management specialists focused primarily on strategic planning, but when it became clear that firms were still failing despite thorough strategic analysis and detailed strategies the field widened and now both researchers and practitioners have become much more interested in the area of strategy implementation.

In strategy implementation we can distinguish between
- realization needs which arise directly from the strategies, and
- indirectly derived measures needed for adjustment and support.
- Examples of directly derived strategy realization measures are: the sale of an unprofitable business as a consequence of a new corporate strategy; the introduction of direct delivery to large end-customers according to new business strategy requirements.

The range of measures for adjustment and support runs from training courses to improve understanding of the new strategies to adjustments to organizational structure to accommodate newly-defined business fields.

In addition to this first distinction, it is also useful to distinguish between measures related to material requirements and those related to personnel. In order to successfully implement a strategy a large number of measures may be required, such as the development of new products, the purchase of distribution channels or the introduction of a new reporting system adjusted to the new strategy. At the same time the company must ensure that employees are willing and able to implement the strategies. To secure this commitment, information should be made available, properly adjusted to the requirements of the employee's positions in the company. Some managers have been known to keep their strategies secret, which makes it virtually impossible for employees to contribute to successful implementation. But successful implementation usually requires much more elaborate measures than the mere provision of information. For example, rewards systems often need to be adjusted and training programs may also be necessary. Often personnel changes will even be required, with existing staff being let go and/or new employees recruited.

A third distinction can be made between implementation through strategic programs and the simple incorporation of the new strategy into day-to-day management, which means that the new strategy requirements are intended to be observed and taken into account in short and long-term operational planning and in individual decision-making (Kühn & Grünig, 2000, p. 63 f). Approaching strategy implementation by leaving strategy implementation to day-to-day business has proved to be in many cases an inadequate approach. The reasons for this are as follows:

- In the daily corporate round the danger exists that the burning problems of the moment will occupy the greater part of management time. The result of this is that more long-term matters, like strategy implementation, are pushed to the back of the queue, making it probable that consideration of measures to implement strategy is repeatedly deferred. Balanced scorecards help to diminish this danger but cannot remove it totally.
- Strategy implementation is particularly at risk if management performance is judged by demonstration of short-term success and if the rewards system reinforces this effect.
- The third point is that implementation in this way, through the usual management processes, is particularly vulnerable to all kinds of hidden resistance. As strategy implementation is planned and realised at the same time as other matters, it is less easy to check if it is being done properly, and this leaves the opponents of the strategy good opportunities to delay strategy implementation or to implement the strategy only half-heartedly.

There are thus a number of good arguments in favor of adopting specific strategic programs to implement planned strategies. These programs will be carried out outside the normal daily management process and will therefore be less vulnerable to the dangers identified above.

Figure 17-1 gives an overview of the three criteria and the resulting types of implementation measures that we have discussed.

Criteria to distinguish implementation types	Resulting implementation types	
Link to the strategies	Direct implementation	Indirect adjustment and support
Content of the implementation measures	Implementation at the material level	Implementation at the personnel level
Form of the implementation	Implementation by program	Implementation through the normal management process

Figure 17-1: Types of strategy implementation

17.2   Types of strategic program

Section 17.1 showed that effective strategy implementation requires the definition of strategic programs, to guarantee that the necessary time, resources and, above all, mental focus are brought to bear on the question of implementation. As the range of possible measures for implementation is extremely wide, it is important to have an overview and to categorize the various types of programs. Our classification is based on our discussion above of the different types of implementation measures:

- Programs focussing on direct implementation measures are distinguished from those which primarily focus on indirect measures of adaptation or support.
- Programs addressing realization at the material level are distinguished from those addressing realization at the level of personnel.

As **Figure 17-2** shows, this approach identifies five different types of program, located within three of the four squares in the matrix:

- Direct implementation at the material level takes place through programs to realize the corporate strategy and through various programs to realize the various business strategies.
- Indirect adjustment and support at the material level is also carried

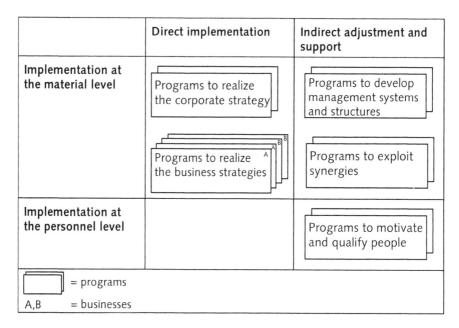

	Direct implementation	Indirect adjustment and support
Implementation at the material level	Programs to realize the corporate strategy	Programs to develop management systems and structures
	Programs to realize the business strategies	Programs to exploit synergies
Implementation at the personnel level		Programs to motivate and qualify people

☐ = programs

A,B   = businesses

Figure 17-2: Overview of the different types of strategic program

out in two ways: programs to develop management systems and structures and programs to exploit synergies.

• Adjustment and support is also required at the personnel level and this gives us the category of personnel-related implementation programs.

But as Figure 17-2 indicates, there are no direct implementation programs to be taken into account at the personnel level. If implementation measures can be derived directly from the strategies then these should be realised at the level of individual decision-making rather than through programs.

We now briefly describe each of the five types of program.

The objective of corporate strategy is to define future businesses and fix their objectives. The content of corporate strategy implementation programs can be derived from these two functions. The programs are designed either to take the company from its current portfolio of businesses to the target situation, or to create the conditions required for the achievement of the specific objectives. Typical programs for corporate strategy implementation focus on the search for new businesses, mergers or acquisitions, the liquidation of unprofitable areas of activity or the obtaining of required financial resources.

In line with our characterization of business strategies, the business strategy implementation programs focus on the safeguarding or the construction of success potentials at the level of the market offer and/or at the level of resources. Because there is such a range of targetable product and communication differences as well as a wide area of possible key resources and core competencies, there is a great range of possible programs.

Strategies often require the adjustment or development of management systems and structures. Programs are required to implement these indirect measures, otherwise the impact of the direct implementation measures can be adversely affected. For example, a company seeking to improve its performance by targeting specific attractive customer segments can only achieve the desired result if its cost accounting is adapted to the new target customer groups. In general, the realization of business strategies is simpler if the businesses are not simply virtual entities but correspond to real areas of responsibility. Adjustment to the company organization is often required according to Chandler's recommendation that "structure follows strategy" (Chandler 1962, p. 14).

A tool for supporting strategy implementation which is used quite often in practice is the balanced scorecard (Kaplan & Norton, 1996) described in **Inset 17-1**. Accordingly the program to define the balanced scorecards is an often needed and important program of the third category.

Inset 17-1: The Balanced Scorecard
(Brogini & Freudiger, 1999)

1. The four perspectives of the balanced scorecard

The origins of the balanced scorecard go back to a research project at the beginning of the nineties carried out by Kaplan & Norton (1992, p. 123 ff.). The aim of the project was to develop a tool which would display, quantify and communicate all the factors which are important to a company's success. Kaplan & Norton claim that for successful strategy implementation indicators from four different perspectives are required. As well as key financial figures, the balanced scorecard also integrates indicators representing customers, internal processes and learning capabilities within a system which provides a compact view of company activity (see **Figure 17-3**).

The first perspective fixes the financial targets towards which all the other indicators are working. At the same time it ultimately makes plain the economic consequences of company activities by showing how well the expectations of equity holders are being met in terms of growth in profits, improvements in productivity or return on investment.

The second perspective is intended to represent customer estimations of the firm. In this way it shows what value must be created in order to positively influence the performance figures. The indicators here include values for customer satisfaction, market share, image and customer loyalty.

The third perspective is that of internal processes and includes indicators of those processes with which the company plans to have an impact on the market. The indicators here focus on the activities which have the biggest influence on customer satisfaction and the achievement of corporate objectives.

In the fourth perspective, learning and growth, the indicators measure the conditions for maintaining and developing knowledge

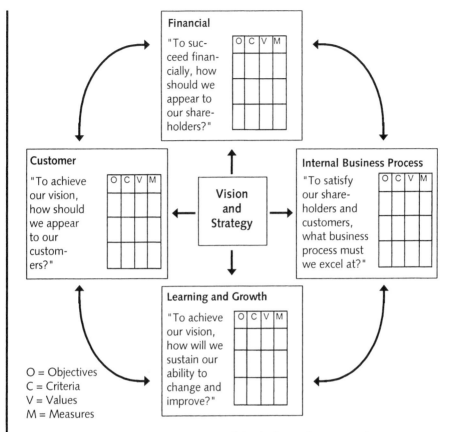

Figure 17-3: The four perspectives of the balanced scorecard
(adapted from Kaplan & Norton,1996, p. 9)

in relation to customer needs and efficient internal processes. This perspective shows what capabilities and knowledge must be built up in order that the objectives in both customer and process perspectives can be achieved.

Thus the balanced scorecard can be described as a management tool which combines both financial and non-financial indicators. The name suggests a balance not only between the four perspectives, but also between early warning indicators and results, and between hard and soft success factors.

2. The balanced scorecard as a tool for strategy-oriented leadership

Kaplan & Norton's balanced scorecard links strategies and the performance management of different operational units. The balanced scorecard translates strategies into concrete goals and actions by organizational units. With the four perspectives the balanced scorecard gives a precise and well-balanced view of the strategies, in which each indicator can be seen as a building block in implementing them.

The balanced scorecard helps the management to concentrate on controlling those areas which have the greatest impact for the achievement of strategic objectives. Balanced scorecards link strategies to the goals of departments, teams or individuals and make it therefore possible for employees at all levels to see how they can contribute to the realization of the strategic objectives.

3. The process of constructing a balanced scorecard

A balanced scorecard is constructed in essentially the same as more traditional management information systems. There are three steps: in the first step, the information required by management in order to implement the planned strategics has to be identified and structured. In the second step, gaps in the data and information are analyzed and then the future information system is designed. In the third and final step, the balanced scorecard is created and the computerized information system to handle it is designed (Brogini & Freudiger, 1999).

Often, almost as a by-product, strategic analysis uncovers unused synergies: a new cash management system for all businesses might, for instance, save a great deal in unnecessary interest payments or produce a surplus that can be invested; a differentiation strategy based on quality may have been neglecting cost efficiency and there is a potential for cost savings which is not incompatible with the quality focus. Other areas where potential synergies can be found include finance structure, recruitment and brand policies. What this fourth category of programs has in common is that they apply horizontally, across business or departmental boundaries. They often turn up astonishing opportunities for improvements which have been overlooked during the planning of business strategies, because of the parallel procedure used in that stage of planning.

The final category of programs that is required will aim to motivate and qualify people and so create favorable conditions for the implementation of strategies at the level of personnel. **Figure 17-4** presents four subtypes of programs to motivate and develop people.

As the figure indicates, they can be classified in two ways:

- either according to their purpose: programs to improve motivation or programs to build knowledge and competencies,
- or alternatively following Herzberg's theory of motivation: programs which create positive conditions for success in strategy

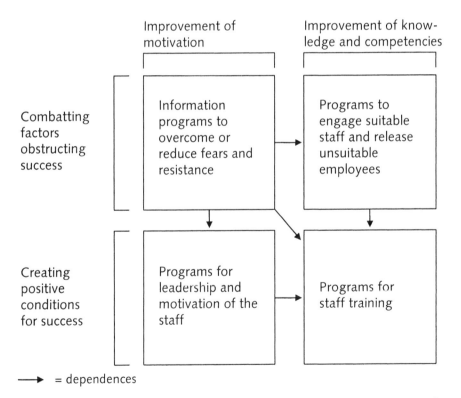

Figure 17-4: The implementation programs to motivate and develop people

implementation and programs which combat factors obstructing success.

This gives the following four subcategories of implementation programs to motivate and qualify people:
- Information programs to overcome or reduce fears and resistance
- Programs to engage suitable staff and release insuitable employees
- Programs for staff training
- Programs for leadership and motivation of the staff in line with the new strategies

17.3   The process of defining the implementation measures

17.3.1 Overview of the process of defining the implementation measures

The definition of the implementation measures forms Step Four of the process of strategic planning. As **Figure 17-5** shows, we recommend dividing this step into six subtasks. The next section now explains these subtasks and shows how to carry them out.

17.3.2 The steps in defining the implementation measures

The definition of the implementation programs begins with determining the programs for the direct realization of the corporate strategy and the business strategies. Two points are important here:
- Activities that have strong interdependencies, and therefore absolutely require coordination, must be dealt with in the same program.
- Programs should be limited so that clear responsibilities can be allocated.

Sometimes these two aspects can be in conflict. For example, according to the first principle, it can be sensible to put the development and

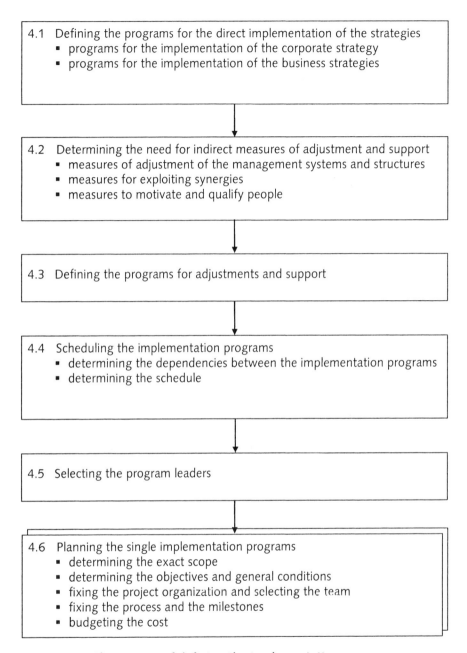

4.1 Defining the programs for the direct implementation of the strategies
   - programs for the implementation of the corporate strategy
   - programs for the implementation of the business strategies

4.2 Determining the need for indirect measures of adjustment and support
   - measures of adjustment of the management systems and structures
   - measures for exploiting synergies
   - measures to motivate and qualify people

4.3 Defining the programs for adjustments and support

4.4 Scheduling the implementation programs
   - determining the dependencies between the implementation programs
   - determining the schedule

4.5 Selecting the program leaders

4.6 Planning the single implementation programs
   - determining the exact scope
   - determining the objectives and general conditions
   - fixing the project organization and selecting the team
   - fixing the process and the milestones
   - budgeting the cost

Figure 17-5: The process of defining the implementation measures

launch of a product into a single program. But research and development on the one hand, and marketing and sales on the other, are generally functions which are located in different organizational units within a company: in a common program this could mean conflicts of responsibility.

After defining programs for direct implementation of strategies, subtask 4.2 is the identification of the need for adaptation and support. As we have seen, measures may be needed in the following areas:

- management systems and structures
- the exploitation of synergies
- motivation and qualification of human resources

In order to identify the need for action, for each of these three areas the following questions need to be addressed:

- What adaptations are urgently required for the implementation of strategies or for the programs defined in subtask 4.1?
- What changes, in connection with the implementation of corporate and business strategies, while not being absolutely required, are nevertheless desirable?
- What opportunities are there to improve productivity and/or reduce costs, which will contribute indirectly to strategy realization?

While the answer to the first of these questions produces measures which are urgently required, with the other two, it is options for action which are revealed. Whether or not to proceed with these options will depend on available human and financial resources. The corresponding decision should be taken as part of Step Five, the global evaluation of strategies and strategic programs.

Subtask 4.3 involves grouping together in the form of programs the various measures for adaptation and support. For criteria which can be used in this step, see the discussion above, under subtask 4.1.

When all implementation programs are defined, we pass on to the next subtask, 4.4. This task poses considerable intellectual challenge as it requires:

- the identification of interdependencies between programs, and
- the production of a schedule for carrying out the programs

Dependencies between the programs can arise because of material, financial or personnel reasons. A material dependency exists, for example, when the increased production capacity as target of a program is the precondition for a market launch program. An example of a financial dependency would be a link between the divestment of one existing business and the carrying out of an acquisitions program to strengthen a remaining company business. Finally human resource related implementation programs can be preconditions for the success of programs at the material level. An example of this would be the wide-ranging program Swisscom carried out from 1995 - 96 in order to improve its employees' abilities in English so that the company could enter into strategic alliances, move into new markets and strengthen its existing operations outside Switzerland.

In drawing up the schedule for the programs, consideration must not only be given to the interdependencies, but also to what is feasible on the level of human resources and finance. There is no sense in starting so many programs at the same time that there is soon not enough impetus left to bring them all to fruition.

Figure 17-6 gives a grid used for scheduling strategy implementation programs in a company producing and distributing electricity. The matrix provides more than the mere timetable: it also affords an overview of the costs incurred.

For practical reasons, it is a good idea to select the program leaders (subtask 4.5) before planning implementation programs in detail. This allows the involvement of the program leaders in the detailed planning of their programs; they may even be invited to take complete charge of it.

An ideal program leader has the following characteristics:

- he/she has the necessary technical knowledge,
- occupies a position in the company hierarchy which allows him/her to push the program forward against opposition,
- can make the necessary time available for the program.

In practice it is always difficult to appoint program leaders who fulfill all three requirements. But this difficulty should not be allowed to stand in the way of clear decision-making. What is of overriding importance here, is that for every program a senior manager should always be given responsibility for detailed planning and execution.

half year — Programs and cost categories		Jan to June year 1	July to Dec year 1	Jan to June year 2	July to Dec year 2	Jan to June year 3	July to Dec year 3	Jan to June year 4	July to Dec year 4	Jan to June year 5	July to Dec year 5	Total
Pro-	a	20	20	–	–							40
gram	b	30	30	40	40							140
A	c	50	50	40	40							180
Pro-	a			110	100	90	80	70				450
gram	b			60	60	60	60	60				300
B	c			170	160	150	140	130				750
Pro-	a						70	70	70			210
gram	b						10	10	10			30
C	c						80	80	80			240
Pro-	a						–	–	–	–	–	–
gram	b						30	50	50	50	50	230
D	c						30	50	50	50	50	230
Pro-	a	50	50	50	50	700	700	700	700	700	700	4400
gram	b	50	50	50	50	90	90	90	90	90	90	740
E	c	100	100	100	100	790	790	790	790	790	790	5140
Total	a	70	70	160	150	790	850	840	770	700	700	5100
	b	80	80	150	150	150	190	210	150	140	140	1440
	c	150	150	310	300	940	1040	1050	920	840	840	6540

a   = external cost in $ 1000
b   = internal cost in $ 1000
c   = total cost in $ 1000
☐   = program length

Figure 17-6: Schedule for the strategy implementation programs in a company producing and distributing electricity

Subtask 4.6 is the planning of each program. For each program the following is required:

- the focus of the program must be clearly stated,
- specific objectives and constraining conditions must be listed,
- the program team and organization must be specified,
- the schedule for the program, with milestones, must be determined,
- a budget must be drawn up.

As you can see in Figure 17-6, we recommend budgeting for the costs of internal staff time as well as for external costs; employees involved in comprehensive and challenging programs will not be able to perform at 100% in their usual functions at the same time as working on the programs. The company will incur costs indirectly as a result of their involvement in program teams, in the form of a loss in profits or an increase in other staff costs. For this reason it is useful to include internal services in the budget.

18 Final assessment of strategies and strategy implementation measures

18.1 The need for a final assessment

As we have seen, strategic planning is a complex process, the outcome of which typically comprises a considerable number of strategies. In this situation, a final overview of the whole is essential, not only because coordination between the various planning outcomes is often lost, but also in view of the fact that evaluation of the elements of the future strategies takes place step by step. These assessments remain provisional until the final assessment shows that overall a solution has been reached which is practical, coherent and worthwhile (Kühn & Grünig, 2000, p. 181 f.).

18.2 The assessment criteria

18.2.1 Overview of the assessment criteria

Our suggestion is to use four different sets of criteria for the final assessment of strategies and strategic programs, as shown in **Figure 18-1** (Kühn & Grünig, 2000, p. 184).

In what follows the four types of criterion and the various individual criteria are explained, and we discuss how to apply them in practice.

18.2.2 Assessment of the total value of the strategies

The suggested process for strategic planning factorizes the complex problem of analysis and design into a number of manageable subtasks. These can either be tackled one after the other, as in the case of corporate strategy and business strategies, or in parallel, as in the case of the various different business strategies. The whole package of different strategic plans should be subjected to a final overall

Sets of criteria	Criteria
Overall value of strategies	▪ Overall value of success potentials ▪ Returns from assets not belonging to the core business ▪ Risks
Degree of fit with values which constrain the pursuit of profit	▪ e.g. fit with ethical values ▪ e.g. fit with workforce-related social values ▪ e.g. fit with ecological values
Coherence of strategies and strategic programs	▪ Coherence between the different strategic targets ▪ Coherence between investment priorities and strategic targets
Feasibility of successful implementation of the programs	▪ Feasibility at the level of personnel ▪ Feasibility at the level of finance ▪ Likelihood of internal acceptance ▪ Likelihood of external acceptance

Figure 18-1: Criteria for final overall assessment of strategies and strategic programs
(adapted from Kühn & Grünig, 2000, p. 184)

assessment.

The overall value of the strategies is assessed on the basis of three criteria which will now be explained.

The first and most relevant criterion is the overall value of the success potentials. As **Figure 18-2** shows, the success potentials represent a complex network linking the different types of success potentials for all the various businesses. In addition to the interdependencies we have already examined between the different success potentials for each business, this network will show interdependencies between the success potentials of the different businesses. How important these are will depend on how far the different businesses are linked in markets and resources. The figure presents a case in which three different

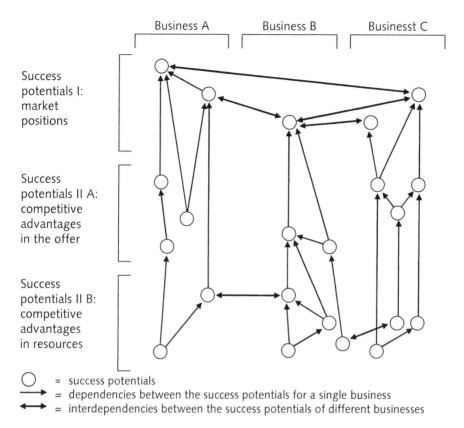

Business A   Business B   Businesst C

Success
potentials I:
market
positions

Success
potentials II A:
competitive
advantages
in the offer

Success
potentials II B:
competitive
advantages
in resources

○   = success potentials
──►   = dependencies between the success potentials for a single business
◄──► = interdependencies between the success potentials of different businesses

Figure 18-2: Success potentials as a two-dimensional network

business units are tightly bound by intensive market and substantial resource interdependencies.

Strategic options differ in terms of the total amount of investment tied up in the businesses. In order to take such differences into account when examining the overall value of a strategic option, the returns from assets outside the core business must be considered. Strategic options which require relatively little capital can sometimes make up for their smaller success potential with returns on assets outside the core business.

The third criterion concerns the risks attached to the strategies (Hofer & Schendel, 1978, p. 194). As with the assessment of the overall value of the success potentials, a detailed analysis is not required: what is necessary is to identify possible developments or events which could undermine the strategies and make it necessary to start planning anew.

From a practical point of view the simplest procedure is to express the total value of a strategic option using an ordinal scale indicating its relative value in comparison with the current realized strategy. **Inset 18-1** presents values for two strategic options for a wood processing company.

> **Inset 18-1: Assessing the overall value of two strategic options for a wood company**
>
> Wood S.A. is a European company with more than 200 employees and relatively widely diversified activities:
> - A large proportion of the company's turnover comes from sawing softwood. With one older and one modern facility, altogether the company processes some 55,000 cubic meters of roundwood a year. Products cover the whole range.
> - 'Wood constructions' is a business field which produces bridges and noise protection barriers made of wood. In order that capacity should be used in the colder months of the year, traditional carpentry work is also carried out. The assets used include a hall for producing components and tools and other appliances for building sites.
> - 'Salt impregnation' is an activity which supports the other businesses by impregnating their products. In addition work is accepted from building firms and carpenters who need wood impregnated. The business also sells garden items such as posts, half logs and palisades. Salt impregnation is carried out in two facilities, a pressure plant and a vacuum pressure plant.
>
> Wood S.A. has two reasons for wishing to reconsider its corporate strategy:
> - Over-capacity in the softwood sawing business, pressure from imports and a slump in the construction industry have together brought about a severe fall in profitability over a number of

years.
- The introduction of tougher regulations on the environment means that the company's local permit for the salt impregnation activity will not be renewed after it expires in three years' time.

Within the company management, which must now develop options for the new corporate strategy to deal with the situation we have described, there is agreement that the 'wood constructions' business field should continue with its current niche strategy. For the other two businesses the situation is less clear-cut. In fact, after studying the situation in detail, there seem to be two options. These are summarized below in **Figure 18-3**:

- Abandon softwood processing entirely and relocate the entire salt impregnation operation.
- Close the old softwood mill together with the vacuum pressure plant and relocate the pressure plant (Dellmann & Grünig, 1999, p. 47).

Figure 18-4 shows how these two options were assessed. The assessment uses an ordinal scale indicating the relative improvement or worsening in comparison with the current realized strategy. We

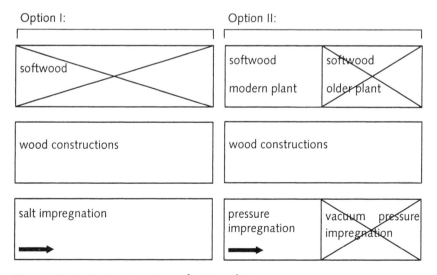

Figure 18-3: Strategic options for Wood S.A.
(Dellmann & Grünig, 1999, p. 47)

	Option I	Option II
Bargaining power of customers	+ 3	+ 1
Real market growth	+ 2	0
Relative market share	+ 2	- 2
Competitive advantages in the offer	+ 2	+ 1
Competitive advantages in resources	+ 3	+ 1
Average value for success potentials for softwood sawing	+ 2.4	+ 0.2
Bargaining power of customers	0	0
Real market growth	0	0
Relative market share	0	0
Competitive advantages in the offer	0	0
Competitive advantages in resources	0	0
Average value for success potentials for wood constructions	0.0	0.0
Bargaining power of customers	0	0
Real market growth	0	0
Relative market share	0	- 2
Competitive advantages in the offer	0	- 2
Competitive advantages in resources	+ 3	+ 1.5
Average value for success potentials for salt impregnation	+ 0.6	- 0.5
Risks	+ 1.0	+ 0.5
Returns from assets not belonging to the core business	+ 2.0	0.0
Average value for all success potentials	+ 1.2	- 0.04
+ 3 = Very much better than status quo + 2 = Much better than status quo + 1 = Better than status quo 0 = No change over status quo - 1 = Worse than status quo - 2 = Much worse than status quo		

Figure 18-4: Assessing two strategic options for Wood S.A.

should also note that:

- Option I presents the problem of how to calculate the value of the divested softwood activity. The solution adopted was to compare the current situation of the business with a low-risk capital market investment.
- In Option II the partial closure of both the softwood sawing and the impregnation activities leads to a loss in relative market share. In salt impregnation, the range of products and services is also reduced, leading to negative effects on competitive advantages in the offer.
- Wood constructions remain unchanged in both of the two options. For this reason the value zero is applied for all criteria. But this low value should not lead one to conclude mistakenly that the business is weak. In fact, in absolute terms, this business has the greatest competitive strength.

This analytic assessment of the two options clearly shows that the first is to be preferred. The general lesson to learn from this case is that it usually makes strategic sense for small and medium-sized companies to concentrate on a small number of strong businesses.

18.2.3 Assessment with the remaining sets of criteria

Up to now our assessment of strategies has been oriented almost exclusively towards success potentials and the long - term opportunities they offer for profit. This is true both for the assessment of options for corporate strategy and business strategies in Parts 4 and 5 and also for the final examination of the total value of the strategies in the previous subsection. Steinmann & Schreyögg (1990, p. 210 f.) justifiably demand that strategies should fit a company's existing value system. In particular it is important to assess the fit of strategies with company policies concerning ethical, social and ecological issues.

If there are contradictions between statements in strategies and programs, this not only has a negative effect on implementation at the material level, but also often damages motivation amongst those responsible for it. For these reasons it is important to check the documents for consistency before they are formally approved (see for example Steinmann & Schreyögg, 1990, p. 209 ff.).The first point to check is whether the target success potentials are consistent and dovetail together. The target market positions, for example, given in the corporate strategy and in the business strategies should correspond. Check too whether the target competitive advantages in resources will be able to create the customer value which is targeted at the level of the offer. Also verify that the investment priorities correspond with the success potentials to be maintained or constructed.

The final step is to assess the likelihood of successful implementation of the programs:

- To do this, on the one hand compare the staff and finance requirements with available resources. **Inset 18-2** shows the assessment of the financial feasibility of strategic programs in a retail group. The inset shows a situation which is often experienced in practice. It is the case where the implementation of programs takes the company to their financial limits. If the strategies and programs are approved and implemented as proposed, for many years the company will be left with very little room for strategic maneuver. To choose such a strategy is perhaps not the best solution. The highly volatile environment means that is useful to maintain a financial reserve to allow the company to seize any opportunities that may present themselves.
- It is important to look at internal and external resistance in order to assess the feasibility of implementing the strategies, as either form of resistance can cause strategies to fail. A large Swiss drinks company decided to reduce fixed costs by closing one of its large breweries, but demonstrations and an organized boycott of the company's products forced the company to go back on its decision. The failed attempt to close the production facility not only induced financial loss but also did considerable damage to the company's image.

Inset 18-2: Checking strategic programs for financial feasibility in a retail group

Inset 11-4 described the portfolio analysis and planning for the Baer group a Swiss regional retail company. After management approved the target portfolio, the corporate strategy and the business strategies were developed. On the basis of these strategies a number of strategic programs were defined:

- Abandoning food retailing and leasing the space that this frees to a specialist delicatessen retailer
- Expanding textiles with more branded goods and more intensive advertising
- Developing a marketing concept to maintain the current strong position in the growing markets for sports goods and for home electronics
- Opening two new body shops
- Management buy out of the advertising agency Kreativ
- Total refurbishment of the department store

In implementing these new strategies the Baer group management will generally hold to the principle of self-financing. But intermediate financing based on medium term loans will be permitted.

Financial feasibility is assessed by calculating capital flow:

- The first step, shown in **Figure 18-5**, is to estimate turnover for the department store, the body shops and the advertising agency on the basis of predictions for market growth, of the target market share and of the strategic decisions taken.
- The turnover figures are used to estimate cash-flow, including from the store's property holdings. This account will not only include income from space rented by third parties, but also include amounts for rents from the different business units of the department store, calculated at market rates.
- Finally the figure for free cash flow is calculated, taking into account the investments and divestments required for the programs and any dividend payments.

	Current year	Year 1	Year 2	Year 3	Year 4	Year 5
Textiles	70	73	76	79	82	85
Cosmetics and toiletries	10	10.2	10.4	10.6	10.8	11
Food	20	10	–	–	–	–
Household goods	40	40.8	41.6	42.4	43.3	44.2
Sports goods	25	27	29.1	31.5	34	36.7
Home electronics	20	22	24.2	26.6	29.3	32.2
Other	7	7.1	7.3	7.4	7.6	7.7
Total turnover for department store	192	190.1	188.6	197.5	207	216.8
Body shops	3.3	4.2	5.1	5.5	5.9	6.4
Advertising agency	2.4	1.2	–	–	–	–
Total turnover for Baer group	197.7	195.5	193.7	203	212.9	223.2
Figures given are in millions of Swiss francs adjusted for inflation						

Figure 18-5: Baer Group turnover plan

Figure 18-6 presents the results for the cash flow and free cash flow calculations. The table shows that in Years Two and Three finance will be required. The total refurbishment of the department store will exceed the group's ability to finance itself. Until the required loans have been paid off, the free cash-flows of several years must be used. The approval of these strategies and programs means that, for a number of years to come, the group will have very little room for strategic maneuver. This means that the company would not be able to take advantage of an opportunity, such as its move into natural cosmetics a few years before, unless, of course it is ready to abandon the principle of self-financing.

	Current year	Year 1	Year 2	Year 3	Year 4	Year 5
Cash flow department store	9.52	9.40	10.26	10.84	11.45	12.09
Cash-flow body shops	0.24	0.33	0.40	0.44	0.47	0.51
Cash-flow advertising agency	0.12	0.06	–	–	–	–
Cash-flow property	2.00	1.80	1.80	2.60	2.60	2.60
Cash-flow Baer group	11.88	11.59	12.46	13.88	14.52	15.20
Group management costs	- 2.40	- 2.40	- 2.40	- 2.40	- 2.40	- 2.40
Dividend payments	- 5.00	- 5.00	- 5.00	- 5.00	- 5.00	- 5.00
Maintenance and renewal	- 4.00	- 3.00	- 2.00	- 4.00	- 4.00	- 4.00
Revenue of divestment of food	–	1.00	–	–	–	–
Expansion of textiles	–	- 0.80	- 0.80	- 0.80	- 0.80	- 0.80
Holding sports goods	–	- 0.30	- 0.30	- 0.30	- 0.30	- 0.30
Holding home electronics	–	- 0.50	- 0.50	- 0.50	- 0.50	- 0.50
Opening new body shops	–	- 0.60	- 0.60	–	–	–
Management buy out of advertising agency	–	0.24	–	–	–	–
Refurbishment of store	–	–	- 5.00	- 10.00	–	–
Free cash-flow before financement	0.48	0.23	- 4.14	- 9.12	1.52	2.20
Figures given are in millions of Swiss francs adjusted for inflation						

Figure 18-6: Cash flow and free cash flow plan for the Baer Group

As strategy implementation extends over a longer period in the future, assessing the question of financial feasibility is often difficult. The starting point for assessing financial feasibility is the budget for the implementation programs produced in step 4.6, which gives at least an approximate indication of the implementation costs. The question now is whether the finance is available. A number of different sources can be considered. These differ in their reliability and this must be taken into account:

- The company may have a basic reserve of liquid assets which the owner or board will wish to be invested, and which can therefore be used for strategy implementation.
- Companies with an established reputation and image often have considerable potential for raising money by issuing shares or bonds. This is a relatively secure method of finance. However, it can happen that a group of shareholders, for example members of a family linked to the company, has retained a majority stake in the company and that they will then block this possibility.
- With implementation programs usually taking a number of years, free cash flow from existing businesses (businesses whose continuation is not put in question by the strategies) can form a third source of funds but usually strategies cannot be implemented without using such free cash-flow, and basic portfolio thinking sees cash cows as providing finance for programs for stars or question marks. Caution requires that free cash flows from existing businesses should not account for more than, say, two-thirds of what is required.
- Much less reliable is finance based on income from the sale or other disposal of businesses which will not figure in the future strategy. As it is difficult to predict when such sales will take place and how much they will bring in, one should be careful about including funds from this source in the overall financial picture. An alternative approach, practiced by some European companies, is to launch a program only after funds have become available through sales of unwanted businesses.
- On no account should the free cash flow from businesses which are being newly constructed be used to finance strategies. No reliable forecast can be made of the income likely to become available from such a new business.

Our admittedly rather conservative conclusion is thus that the implementation of strategies and the launching of the required programs should only be undertaken if sufficient finance is available of the first three types. A number of supplementary programs can, however, be planned and started once divestments (=fourth type of finance) or new businesses (=fifth type of finance) have brought in the necessary funds.

18.3   Process of final assessment of strategies and strategy implementation measures

18.3.1 Overview of the process of final assessment of strategies and strategy implementation measures

The final assessment of strategies and strategy implementation measures is Step Five in the overall process of strategic planning. **Figure 18-7** divides this step into four subtasks, each of which will be described below.

18.3.2 The steps of final assessment of strategies and strategy implementation measures

The way that the complex process of analysis and planning is structured often means that some members of a decision-making group are not sufficiently familiar with all of the strategic targets. It is thus important to restate the strategies and programs before proceeding to the final assessment. This is Step 5.1. In particular, it is important that the decision-making body is in no doubt about the cases, if any, where it is required to make a choice between different options. During the development of strategies, different alternatives will usually have been discussed for a number of the subproblems. Often, following the heuristic principle of factorization (see Inset 5-1), only one of these alternatives has been pursued. The final assessment process now provides another opportunity to compare the original options. What Step 5 is all about is looking at the strategies one last time with a critical distance before they are approved and implementation begins. So it does no harm at all if alternatives are recalled and the group reflects again on the reasons why one particular alternative was rejected and another pursued.

5.1 Restatement of the strategic targets and possibly of strategic options
- Restatement of the strategies and strategic programs for assessment
- Restatement of possible strategic options

5.2 Decisions on methods to use
- Choice and weighting of assessment criteria
- Choice of process for final assessment and possibly of methods

---

5.3 Assessment of strategic targets and possibly of strategic options
- Where necessary: collection of missing information
- Assessment of strategic targets
- Where necessary: comparison of strategic options

5.4 Decision on strategic targets and eventually of strategic options
- Where necessary: choice of option
- Decision regarding strategic targets

Figure 18-7: The process of final assessment of strategies and strategy implementation measures

Once the subject of the evaluation process has been brought clearly into focus, step 5.2 involves determining the criteria and the procedure to be used in the final assessment.

The list in Figure 18-1 can be used as the basis for choosing which criteria to use and how to weight them.

In addition it is important that the assessment process is specified in terms of the order in which the various sets of criteria are applied. There are two possibilities:

- one can either begin by assessing how far the strategic targets are coherent and in conformity with the overriding values, and then calculate their value,
- or one can tackle the problem the other way around.

Step 5.2 also raises the question of whether to use a specific assessment tool. If a group decision is being made and there are at least two options, then Saaty's (1980) analytical hierarchical process is an interesting possibility (See **Inset 18-3** for a brief introduction to this method).

Step 5.3 is the actual assessment of strategies and strategic programs. In order to gain an added value over the partial assessments made earlier in Steps Two and Three, it is vital that the group should at no point shift from their overall focus. What this means is that only the most important strategic targets and options should be assessed using a small number of criteria. Too great differentiation in the final assessment can lead rapidly to a situation in which Step Five no longer achieves its objectives.

Clear decisions must be taken at the end of the final assessment with reference to the production of the strategic documents and the implementation of strategies and programs. This is Step 5.4. As these decisions are extremely important, they should be taken in a formal manner and appropriately documented.

Inset 18-3: The analytical hierarchical process
(Dellmann & Grünig, 1999, p 31 ff.)

The analytical hierarchical process (AHP) was developed by Saaty in the late sixties and early seventies (see for example Saaty, 1980). AHP is a method of assessment which allows the structuring of complex decision scenarios in a systematic way and to assess the possible courses of action. AHP has proved its value repeatedly in business administration, politics, and many other areas (Dellmann & Grünig, 1999, p. 34).

The essential features of the method are captured in its name:
- 'Analytic' means that the object of the decision is broken down into criteria. Both quantitative and qualitative criteria can be used to compare the available options and the criteria can be weighted. The overall assessment of the possibilities is found by linear algebra.
- 'Hierarchy' refers to the manner in which the criteria, relevant environmental factors and the alternatives are treated. AHP al-

ways uses a number of different hierarchical levels and attributes the different elements of the problem to them.
- 'Process' indicates that the solution to complex decision making problems is achieved through a systematic sequence of steps.

The AHP technique consists of five steps, which are described briefly below (Dellmann & Grünig, 1999, p. 35 ff.).

Step 1 is setting up the evaluation model. This requires the definition of relevant parameters, including the final goal, the criteria, relevant environmental factors and the alternatives, of which there must be at least two.

Step 2 requires the establishment of a hierarchical structure for the problem. The final assessment goal is set at the top of the hierarchy and the alternatives are at the bottom. The intermediate levels represent the main or subordinate criteria, together with environmental factors, if any. With the exception of the highest level, each level must have at least two elements or factors. The elements on each level are linked to the elements on the level above.

Figure 18-8 gives an example of a hierarchy of this kind.

Step 3 consists of the setting of priorities. Priority means the relative importance or strength of influence of a factor in relation to a factor that is placed above it in the hierarchy:
- If possible, the priorities are expressed in terms of ratios.
- With quantitative data which do not represent ratios (e.g. temperature) and with qualitative data (e.g. attractiveness), the priorities are established by comparison, in pairs. For each pair of factors, the relative preferences in relation to the hierarchically superior factors are established and entered into a matrix. The basis for these preferences is the Saaty scale, which appears below in **Figure 18-9**. The scale goes from 1 to 9 as shown in the figure. But it includes also the reciprocals from 1 to 1/9 which are not explained in the figure.
- Next the paired comparisons must be checked for consistency. If there is inconsistency, the procedure must be repeated.

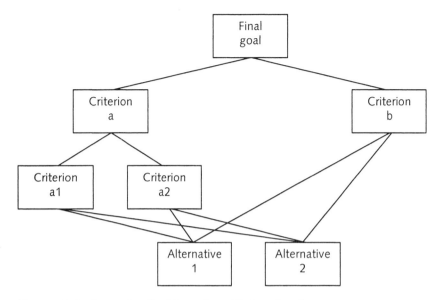

Figure 18-8: Example of a hierarchy with four levels

- Finally, the ordinal numerical values are normalized, so that the sum of all values equals one. This makes it possible to link the data from the different scales in step four.

In Step 4, the overall priorities of the possibilities are calculated. This is done by continually multiplying and adding the priorities from the top to the bottom level. These overall priorities give a figure for the relative desirability of the possibilities.

The final Step 5 is sensitivity analysis. This measures the stability of the result, revealing how strongly variation in the strength of influence for individual factors influences the final result.

The AHP method can be a valuable tool for choice of a strategic option:
- Through the shared process of modeling the decision problem, a collective view is established, both of the different relevant factors and of their dependencies.
- As the weighting for criteria and the assessment of the alternatives is carried out systematically in a number of steps, differ-

ences in assessment will be revealed. Where these are not resolved through discussion, average values can be used.
- Inconsistencies in evaluations of individuals or groups can be revealed by the method and rejected.

Value	Definition	Comment
1	equally important	the two factors are of equal importance for fulfilling a hierarchically superior criterion.
3	slightly more important	one factor is slightly preferred than the other.
5	significantly more important	one factor is strongly preferred to the other.
7	very significantly more important	one factor is very strongly preferred to the other.
9	maximally more important	the supremacy of one factor is absolute.

Figure 18-9: The Saaty scale
(adapted from Saaty, 1995, p.73)

19 Formulating and approving the strategic documents

19.1 Overview of the process of formulating and approving the strategic documents

Step Five is the final step in fixing the content of the new strategies, but for practical reasons it would be wrong to conclude the process with the final assessment of strategies and implementation programs. For successful implementation of the strategies and programs, the decisions taken and the underlying thinking must be carefully summarized in comprehensible and well presented documents. Such strategic management documents are also the basis of strategic control.

Formulating and approving the strategic documents is Step Six in the process of strategic planning. As **Figure 19-1** shows, it is divided here into five steps, and these are explained in the following section.

19.2 Steps in formulating and approving the strategic documents

Before starting on the formulation of the documents, the first step is to produce a list of the required documents with a specification of what should be in each one. This is substep 6.1, which generally has a very beneficial effect on the quality of the documents produced afterwards and also makes the production more efficient. So it is a step which offers excellent value.

As to which documents will be required, this depends largely on the heterogeneity of products and services, on the number of different industries and on the number of geographical markets for the company or strategic business in question. Based on the considerations presented earlier in Chapter Four, we can identify three levels of complexity, as follows:

- Complexity is low where a single product group is marketed in one industry market and region.
- Complexity is at the medium level in cases where a number of

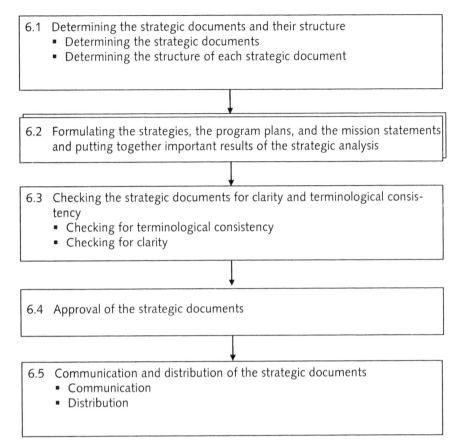

Figure 19-1: Process of formulating and approving strategic documents

different product groups are sold in a single industry market and regional market, or where a single product group is marketed in a number of different regions.

- A high level of complexity is reached in situations where more than one product group is offered in a number of industry markets and/or regions.

Figure 19-2 shows the documents required in the three different cases, together with their purposes. As the diagram shows, a mission statement is included among the strategic documents along with the various strategies and program plans. The mission statement serves to communicate the most important strategic goals and measures to employees, customers, suppliers and other stakeholders. The analysis

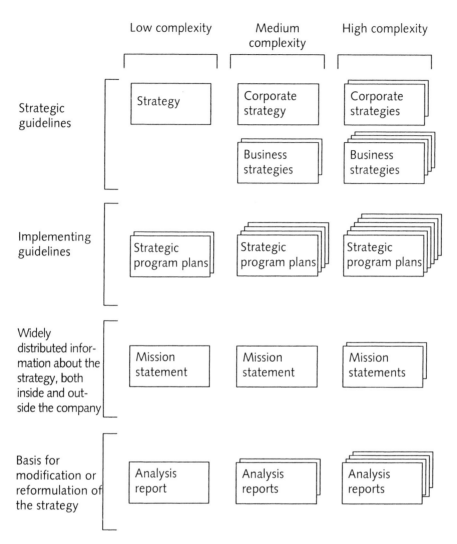

Figure 19-2: Required strategic documents and their purposes

reports produced during Step 1 should be preserved and should form part of the strategic documents. They are of importance for any subsequent modification or re-examination of strategies in the future and also allow managers not involved in the strategy project to understand the decisions better.

Once the set of documents required has been determined, the structure of these should be defined. To allow easy comparison, documents of a similar type should be structured in the same way. **Figure 19-3** presents suggestions for the structure of each type of strategic document.

Corporate strategy	Business strategy	Program plan
1. Introduction 2. Summary of results of analysis 3. Mission or core business 4. Businesses 5. Objectives of each business 6. Key resources at the corporate level 7. Investment priorities 8. Overview of implementation programs 9. Distribution of document	1. Introduction 2. Summary of results of analysis 3. Generic business strategy and industry segment(s) served 4. Competitive advantages in the offer and in resources 5. Overview of implementation programs 6. Distribution of document	1. Introduction 2. Objectives and general conditions 3. Eventually: consultant and his tasks 4. Program organization 5. Process and milestones 6. Program budget 7. Distribution of document

Mission statement	Analysis report
1. Introduction 2. Objectives and values 3. Businesses and target market positions 4. Stakeholder relationships	1. Introduction 2. Procedure and methods used 3. Global environmental analysis 4. Industry analysis 5. Company analysis 6. Threats and opportunities 7. Distribution of document

Figure 19-3: Structure of strategic documents

In Step 6.2 the strategic documents are formulated on the basis of the results of the strategy development process and following the structure determined in Step 6.1.

Next, Step 6.3 requires that the documents should be checked for consistency of terminology and for clarity. Producing a glossary is a good means of ensuring terminological consistency. Terms used in apparently contradictory senses and two terms for the same phenomenon will be rapidly identified. As far as clarity is concerned, different categories of document must meet different requirements. Analysis reports need only be structured according to a given table of contents. They do not need to be worked on intensively and made user-friendly. But the strategies and the program plans are central tools in strategy implementation and these must be carefully worded and clear for managers at all levels. It is the mission statement which demands the greatest care in language, as it must be clearly understood by all company employees and by third parties. It is particularly important to check for possible misunderstandings of the text.

Once the strategies and program plans are available in an effective and uniform presentation they can be submitted to the appropriate body or bodies for approval (Step 6.4). Often it is the board who must approve the strategies and the program plans, but sometimes the board merely approves the corporate strategy and the management then deals with the approval of the business strategies and the program plans.

As clearly formulated documents are being submitted, the body concerned can do more than simply accept the document or send it back for reworking. It is possible for strategies to be approved with specific changes documented in the official minutes. This makes it possible to carry out the corrections and distribute the document without having to resubmit it for approval.

Step 6.5 is communication and distribution of the documents. This requires that every document should carry a list of those persons who should receive it. This means that people are not forgotten, that everyone receiving the document knows who else has received it and thus with whom the document can be freely discussed, and that no one will be left out, if later changes have to be made to the document.

In practice, it is important that strategic documents are not simply sent out, but are the subject of communication activities and are properly discussed. For the implementation of the strategy it is usually worthwhile to hold a workshop or kick off meeting. This gives the opportunity to talk to employees who will be responsible for implementation or who are otherwise affected by the strategy. The session should allocate enough time for questions and comments from the audience.

It is even possible to set up a detailed strategy implementation program to communicate the strategy. But where this option is not taken, serious preparation must be made for the communication of the new strategy. Considering the enormous importance of communication meetings for the implementation of the strategy, thorough preparation is certainly worthwhile.

Final remarks

The goal of this book has been to provide a process-based approach for the development of strategies. The book began by introducing strategic planning in Part One, and then Part Two presented our strategic planning process, consisting of one preliminary step and six main steps. Parts Three to Six then dealt in detail with the complexities of each of these steps.

It is the authors' hope that the ideas presented here will be of practical use, making it easier for companies to develop strategies. But we remain aware that the process alone cannot guarantee success. There are two other important requirements for the development of strategies which are practical and which can lead to success. First, it is essential that the management should be very well-informed about their customers, their competitors and their own company, otherwise they will not be able to develop effective strategies. Secondly, those running the company must be able to convince their employees that the intended strategies are the right ones and motivate them to implement them. For this, the management must inspire trust and enjoy the confidence of their workforce.

Glossary

Assessment of strategies = systematic evaluation of realized strategies or strategic options using predefined criteria.

Business = group of products and/or services with a specific marketing mix. A business has stronger or weaker market and resource synergies with other businesses. Where these synergies are strong, the business has relatively little autonomy. This case is referred to as a → business unit. If the business has a high degree of autonomy and is like a company within the company, the term → business field is used.

Business field = → a business with relatively weak market and resource synergies with other businesses and which thus represents a kind of company within the company.

Business strategy = → intended strategy for a business. It normally consists of the selected → generic business strategy and the target → competitive advantages at the level of the → offer and at the level of → resources.

Business unit = → business which is closely linked to other businesses either in terms of its market or its resources.

Competency = ability of a company to achieve certain effects or to behave in specific ways. Competencies are one type of → resource.

Competitive advantage = characteristic of a company's → offer or → resources, which is rated positively in comparison with competitors. The strategic value of advantages in the offer is determined by the importance of the corresponding → success factors. The strategic importance of resources depends on their rarity, their ability to create customer value and their sustainability.

Competitive position = position occupied by a company's → offer in a specific market in comparison to the competitors. The strategic value of a market position depends not only on its relative value compared to the positions of the competitors but also on the attractiveness of the market. It is important to distinguish the current and the target market position.

Core competency = strategically valuable → competency.

Corporate strategy = → intended strategy for a company with more than one business. The corporate strategy defines the future businesses, sets long term targets for their → market positions and allocates financial resources to them or at least determines investment priorities. The corporate strategy can also address the question of the → resources which need to be built up or maintained at the corporate level.

Customer group = → customer segment

Customer segment = a group of customers with similar needs and who therefore have similar criteria in making buying decisions. In an → industry market there are usually a number of different customer segments.

Customer segment-submarket-combination = → industry segment

Determining the implementation measures = the fourth step in the → strategic planning process. It consists mainly in the definition of the → strategic programs

Developing business strategies = the third step in the → strategic planning process. This means determining for each business the most important → industry segments and the → generic business strategies. In addition the target → competitive advantages must be defined, both in terms of the → offer, and in terms of → resources.

Developing the corporate strategy = the second step in the → strategic planning process. This means the definition of the → strategic businesses, assessing the current → market positions of the businesses and determining the target market positions and investment priorities for the businesses. Typically a → portfolio method is used to do this.

Differentiation strategy = a → business strategy which attempts to achieve competitive advantages over competitors by → product differences, → communication differences and/or greater intensity of communication and customer care. A differentiation strategy may be pursued within the whole market or within a → niche.

Emergent strategy = → current strategy which is not the result of the implementation of an intended strategy, but simply the product of a large number of individual decisions which are more or less coordinated.

Final assessment of strategies and implementation measures = the fifth step in the → strategic planning process. The strategies and programs are assessed in terms of their effects, their consistency, the probability of successful implementation and their correspondence to existing values.

Formulating and approving the strategic documents = the sixth step in the → strategic planning process. After the completion of the analysis and planning, the final main step is to produce clear management documents. These must then be formally approved and the contents communicated appropriately to the various different levels of employee within the company.

Functional area strategy = term sometimes used for a long term plan setting objectives, measures and priorities for a functional area within a company. This is a type of plan which does not primarily serve to construct or safeguard success potentials. Documents of this type are therefore not strategies in our sense of the word and should be given a different name in order to distinguish them from strategies in the strict sense of the term. We recommend that they be called 'plans' or 'agendas'.

Generic business strategy = a basic type of → business strategy. There are four generic business strategies: broad scope price strategy, broad scope differentiation strategy, niche focus price strategy and niche focus differentiation strategy.

Implementation of strategies = a subsystem within → strategic management. Strategy implementation includes all the measures taken to carry out the strategy. It consists mainly in the design and execution of → strategic programs. But it also includes the need to take account of intended strategies in short and medium term planning and daily decision making.

Implementation program = → strategic program

Industry = A specific part of a company's environment which can be delimited in terms of categories of satisfied customer needs, of the technologies required, of the competing firms and of the served geographical regions. Defining an industry is a matter of judgement. When in doubt the boundaries should be cast widely. Generally a business or a focused company does not serve the whole → industry market, but chooses one or more → industry segments.

Industry market = the competitive arena of an industry.

Industry segment = a customer segment-submarket combination, which is part of an → industry market. An industry segment combines related customer needs and similar products or services. Typically an industry segment is served primarily by a group of companies with similar resources and business strategies, known as a → strategic group.

Intended strategy = a system of long - term guidelines aimed at ensuring the construction and maintenance of success potentials. Intended strategies can be divided into → corporate strategies and → business strategies.

Key resource = strategically valuable → resource.

Market-based view = with the → resource-based view, the second of two central strategic ideas. It can be summarized as follows: when building up or divesting businesses, firms make a commitment for or against certain → industry markets and, within these markets, for or against → industry segments. This gives the company a roughly defined competitive position which is then specified more closely by the development of the → offers. Long term success depends on these offers and on the attractiveness of the chosen → industry markets and → industry segments. This approach is summed up in the → Structure-Conduct-Performance paradigm.

Market offer = a package of measures, with products and services, price, distribution and communication. In marketing this is referred to as the marketing mix.

Mission statement = a document which describes a company's raison d'être and its main areas of activity, together with its overriding goals and values.

Niche = → industry segment with specific demands. Customers belonging to a niche market generally only take account of a small section of the total offers of the → industry market when making their buying decisions. Niche demand is generally satisfied by specialist providers. Firms operating in the whole market generally achieve only modest market shares in niches.

Norm strategy = basic characterization for strategy which can be applied to all businesses which fall within a certain square in a → portfolio matrix. As a standard strategy cannot take account of the specific situation of a particular business, it serves simply to provide an initial indication as to the strategy to be followed in the individual case.

Offer = → market offer

Planned strategy = → intended strategy

Portfolio matrix = graphic representation of current and target positions for a company's businesses, using a two dimensional matrix with a division into a number of areas, for each of which → standard strategies can be proposed.   Portfolios typically represent a key element in a → corporate strategy. We often use the term business portfolio simply to mean the set of all the → businesses in a company.

Portfolio method = A strategic planning method which is often applied when developing a corporate strategy. Portfolio analysis and planning is based on a two-dimensional → portfolio matrix. There are two different methods of portfolio analysis and planning which are frequently used: the Boston Consulting Group's market growth-market share portfolio method, and the General Electrics/McKinsey market attractiveness-business strength portfolio.

Price strategy = → business strategy which attempts to differentiate the company from competing firms by means of low prices. A company may follow a price strategy in the whole → industry market or in a → niche.

Product group = → submarket

Realized strategy = a current strategy which may or may not be based on an → intended strategy. If it is the result of → implementing an intended strategy, the realized strategy will achieve a greater or lesser degree of correspondence to it. The realized strategy can be identified empirically by uncovering the current → market positions and the existing → competitive advantages in → offers and → resources.

Realization of strategies = → implementation of strategies

Resource = Important term of strategic management, underlying the → resource-based view. Resources are understood as including not only physical and capital assets but also soft factors such as competencies, knowledge and culture. The resources which are valuable are those which are both rare and able to create customer value. They must also be difficult to imitate or substitute and therefore sustainable.

Resource-based view = With the → market-based view, one of the two central strategic ideas. It can be summarized as follows: Firms may have available or may build up unique → resources which form the basis for → market offers which meet customer needs and are superior to those of competitors. In the long term, differences in performance among rival firms are thus primarily due to differences in resources. This argument is also referred to as the Resources-Conduct-Performance paradigm.

Standard system of strategic plans = one of a number of standard recommendations for the set of → strategic documents. What types of strategic document are necessary for a company depends on the number of product groups, industry markets and geographical markets. Together these three dimensions determine which standard system must be taken as a point of departure for the development of the appropriate individual → system of strategic plans for a company.

Strategic analysis = The first step in the → strategic planning process. Strategic analysis determines the current position and possible future developments in three area of relevance to the company: the global environment, the industry markets and the company itself. Strategic analysis culminates in a rough diagnosis of threats and opportunities for the company.

Strategic control = subsystem of → strategic management. Strategic control includes all those measures serving to observe the environment and to keep track of the strategy implementation. Its purpose is to allow early discovery of any problems with strategies or with their implementation. It can be divided into strategic scanning, strategic monitoring on the basis of an early warning system and realization checks.

Strategic document = document with strategic content which serves as a management tool to achieve strategic goals and to carry out strategic measures. We distinguish four types of strategic document: → mission statements, → corporate strategies, → business strategies and → strategic programs.

Strategic group = A group within an → industry, normally including both businesses of diversified companies and focused companies, which all have similar resources and follow similar business strategies.

Strategic management = a term which covers all strategic activity. There are three subsystems within strategic management: → strategic planning, → strategy implementation and → strategic control.

Strategic option = a possible future strategy. The option which performs best in the evaluation of all the options is designated as the intended strategy. The continuation of the current strategy is an option that must always be included in this → assessment of strategies.

Strategic planning = subsystem of → strategic management. Within strategic planning first the current situation is analyzed, then strategic options are developed and evaluated, next the future strategy is fixed, and finally implementation measures are drawn up.

Strategic planning process = a recommended procedure which divides the complex problem of developing strategies into a sequence of related steps.

Strategic program = a clearly delimited part of the → implementation of strategics. Objectives, boundary conditions, schedule, organization and budget must all be specified beforehand for each program.

Strategy = where not otherwise indicated this means an → intended strategy.

Strategy project planning = preliminary step in the → strategic planning process. Before analysis and planning can take place the project must be closely defined in terms of its content, objectives and boundary conditions. A decision must be taken as to whether to involve consultants and the project schedule and organization must be fixed. A budget must also be produced.

Submarket = part of a market defined by a specific group of products

or services. Usually the various products and services offered in an →
industry market can be divided into a number of sub-markets on the
basis of the customer needs which are satisfied, quality differences or
technological factors.

Success factor = determining factor for market attractiveness or competitive strength. The exploitation of success factors through the
building of appropriate → success potentials significantly influences
long term success. We distinguish two types of success factor: general
and market-specific success factors.

Success potential = condition for long term success. The construction
and safeguarding of success potentials is at the heart of → strategic
management. There are three levels of success potential: advantageous market positions, advantages in the offer, and resource advantages. The relative importance of specific success potentials is determined by the underlying → success factors.

Sustainable competitive advantage = competitive advantage in the →
market offer or in resources which can be maintained in the long
term. Sustainability depends primarily on inimitability and non-
substitutability of the → resources which are the basis for the → competitive advantage.

System of strategic plans = generally a graphic representation of all
the existing or required strategic documents. It gives a useful overview both during → strategic planning and during the → implementation of the intended → strategies and the planned → implementation
measures.

Index

Bibliography

Aeberhard, K. (1996): Strategische Analyse, Empfehlungen zum Vorgehen und zu sinnvollen Methodenkombinationen, Bern etc., 1996

Ansoff, H.I. (1979): Corporate strategy, Mc Graw Hill, 1979

Ansoff, Declerck & Hayes (1976): From Strategic Planning to Strategic Management, in: Ansoff, H.I., Declerck, R.P., Hayes, R.L., (editors): From Strategic Planning to Strategic Management, London etc., p. 39-78

Barney, J.B. (1991): Firm Resources and Sustained Competitive Advantage, in: Journal of Management, Nr. 1/1991, S. 99-120

Bauch, C. (1999): Case study about the business strategy of a watch manufacturer, teaching document of the Chair of Management, University of Fribourg, Fribourg, 1999

Black, J.A., Boal, K.B. (1994): Strategic Resources: Traits, configurations and Paths to Sustainable Competitive Advantage, in: Strategic Management Journal, 1994, p. 131-148

Brogini, M.; Freudiger, M.P. (1999): Die Balanced Scorecard als Instrument der Strategieumsetzung, Arbeitspapier Nr. 1 der impact, massnahmenorientierte Unternehmensberatung AG, Bern 1999

Chandler, A.D. (1962): Strategy and Structure: Chapters in the History of the Industrial Enterprise, Cambridge, 1962

Clark, P.A. (1972): Action research and organizational change, London etc., 1972

Collis, D.J., Montgomery, C.A. (1997): Corporate Strategy, Resources and the Scope of the Firm, Chicago etc., 1997

Daniel G.B. (1961): Management Information Crisis, in: Harvard Business Review, September-October 1961, p. 11 ff.

Dellmann, K.; Grünig, R. (1999): Die Bewertung von Gesamt-unternehmensstrategien mit Hilfe des Analytischen Netzwerkpro-zesses resp. des Analytischen Hierarchischen Prozesses, in: Grünig, R.; Pasquier, M. (editors): Strategisches Management und Market-ing, Bern etc., 1999, p. 33-56

Feigenbaum E.A. & Feldmann J. (1963): Computer and Thought, New York etc., 1963

Freeman R.E. & Reed D.L., (1987): Stockholders and Stakeholders: A New Perspective on Corporate Governancce, in: California Man-agement Review, Nr. 3/1983, p. 88-106

Gälweiler, A. (1987): Strategische Unternehmensführung, Frankfurt and New York, 1987

Garvin, D.A. (1987): Competing on the eight dimensions of quality, in: Harvard Business Review, November-December1987, p. 101-109

Gilbert, X./Strebel, P. (1987): Strategies to outpace the competition, in: The Journal of Business Strategy, Nr. 1/1987, p. 28-36

Grant, R.M. (2002): Contemporary Strategy Analysis, 4th ed., Massa-chusetts, 2002

Hansen, G.S., Wernerfelt, B. (1989): Determinants of Firm Perform-ance, The Relative Importance of Economic and Organizational Fac-tors, in: Strategic Management Journal, 1989, p. 399-411

Heckner, F. (1994): Strategic analysis of the watch industry, teaching document of the Chair of Management, University of Fribourg, Fri-bourg, 1994

Heckner, F. (1998): Identifikation marktspezifischer Erfolgsfaktoren, Ein heuristisches Verfahren angewendet am Beispiel eines pharmazeutischen Teilmarktes, Bern etc., 1998

Hedley, B. (1977): Strategy and the Business Portfolio, in: Long Range Planning, Nr. 1/1977, p. 9-15

Hill, Ch.W.L., Jones, G.R. (1992): Strategic Management, An Integrated Approach, Boston, 1992

Hofer, Ch.W., Schendel, D. (1978): Strategy Formulation: Analytical Concepts, St. Paul etc., 1978

Homburg, C., Sütterlin, S. (1992): Strategische Gruppen: Ein Survey, in: ZfB, Nr. 6/1992, p. 635-662

Johnson, G., Scholes, K. (2002): Exploring Corporate Strategy, 6th ed., New York etc., 2002

Kaplan, R.S.; Norton, D.P. (1992): The Balanced Scorecard - Measures that Drive Performance, in: Harvard Business Review, January-February 1992, p. 123-145

Kaplan, R.S.; Norton, D.P. (1996): Balanced Sorecard, Harvard, 1996

Kühn, R. (1978): Entscheidungsmethodik und Unternehmenspolitik, Bern and Stuttgart, 1978

Kühn, R. (1997): Marketing: Analyse und Strategie, 3rd ed., Zürich, 1997

Kühn, R., Grünig, R. (2000): Grundlagen der strategischen Planung, 2nd ed., Bern etc., 2000

Lanner, Ch. (1999a): Scenario analysis, teaching document of the Chair of Management, University of Fribourg, Fribourg, 1999

Lanner, Ch. (1999b): Case study about the business strategy of a chocolate producer, teaching document of the Chair of Management, University of Fribourg, Fribourg, 1999

Leidecker J. K., Bruno A. V. (1984): Identifying and Using Critical Success Factors, in: Long Range Planning, Nr. 17/1984, p. 23 ff.

Luehrmann, T. A. (1998): Investment Opportunities as Real Options: Getting Started on the Numbers, in: Harvard Business Review, July-August 1998, p. 51-67

Mahoney, J.T., Pandian, J.R. (1992): The Resource-based View within the Conversation of Strategic Management, in: Strategic Management Journal, 1992, p. 363-380

Meyer, A.; Blümelhuber, Ch. (1998): Wettbewerbsorientierte Strategien im Diestleistungsbereich, in: Bruhn, M.; Meffert, H. (editors): Handbuch Dienstleistungsmanagement, Wiesbaden, 1998, p. 375-404

Miller, A., Dess, G.G. (1996): Strategic Management, 2nd ed., New York etc., 1996

Minsky, M. (1963): Steps Toward Artificial Intelligence, in: Feigenbaum, E. A., Feldman, J., (editors): Computer and thought, New York etc. 1963

Mintzberg, H. (1994): The rise and fall of strategic planning, New York, 1994

Müller, A., Hauser, W. (1997): Schweris langer Schnauf, in: Cash, Nr. 45/1997, p. 7

Newell A., Shaw J. C. & Simon H. A. (1965): Report on a General Problem - Solving Program, in: Luce, R. D., Bush, R. R., Galanter, E., (editors): Readings in Mathematical Psychology, Vol. II, New York etc., 1965, p. 41 ff.

Ohmae, K. (1982): The Mind of the Strategist, New York, 1982

Palich, L., Cardinal, B., Miller, C. (2000): Curvilinearity in the diversification – performance linking: An examination over three decades of research, in: Strategic Management Journal, 2000, p. 155-174

Porter, M.E. (1980): Competitive Strategy, New York etc., 1980

Porter, M.E. (1985): Competitive Advantage, New York etc., 1985

Porter, M.E. (1991): Towards a Dynamic Theory of Strategy, in: Strategic Management Journal, 1991, p. 95-117

Prahalad, C.K., Hamel, G. (1990): The Core Competence of the Corporation, in: Harvard Business Review, May- June 1990, p. 79-91

Prahalad, C.K., Hamel, G. (1994): Strategy as a Field of Study: Why Search for a New Paradigm?, in: Strategic Management Journal, 1994, p. 5-16

Raffée, H., Effenberger, J., Fritz, W. (1994): *Strategieprofile als Faktoren des Unternehmenserfolgs, in: DBW, Nr. 3/1994, p. 383-396*

Reibnitz, U. von (1987): *Szenarien: Optionen für die Zukunft, Hamburg, 1987*

Rühli, E. (1994): *Die Resource-based-View of Strategy, in: Gomez, P., Hahn, D.Müller-Stewens, G., Wunderer, R., (editors): Unternehmerischer Wandel - Konzepte zur organisatorischen Erneuerung, Wiesbaden, 1994, p. 31-57*

Rumelt, R.P. (1987): Theory, Strategy and Entrepreneurship, in: Teece, D.J., (editor) The Competitive Challenge, Cambridge, 1987

Saaty, Th.L. (1980): The Analytic Hierarchy Process, New York etc., 1980

Saaty, Th.L. (1995): Decision making for leaders, Pittsburgh, 1995

Simon, H. A. (1966): The Logic of Heuristic Decision Making, in: Rescher, N. (editor): The Logic of Decision and Action, Pittsburg, 1966, p. 1 - 20

Steinmann, H., Schreyögg, G. (1993): Management, 3rd ed., Wiesbaden, 1993

Stringer E.T. (1996): Action Research, A Handbook for Practitioners, Thousand Oaks, London and New Dehli, 1996

The Boston Consulting Group (1970): Perspectives: The Product Portfolio, Boston, 1970

Thompson, A.A., Strickland, A.J. (1996): Strategic Management, 10th ed., Boston etc, 1996

Ulrich, H. (1978): Unternehmenspolitik, Bern and Stuttgart, 1978